Pueblos Mágicos

Pueblos Mágicos

A Traveler's Guide
to
Mexico's Hidden Treasures

CHUCK BURTON

Bayou City Press
THE WORLD IN PRINT

©2025 Chuck Burton
Maps ©2025 Bayou City Press
All rights reserved.

No part of this book may be reproduced in any written, electronic, recording, or photocopying form without the written permission of the publisher. Requests for permission to print brief quotations for use in reviews and the like should be directed to the publisher.

Although every precaution has been taken to confirm the accuracy of the names, places, and facts in this book, the author and publisher assume no responsibility for any errors. No liability is assumed for any damages that may result from the use of information in this title.

Books may be purchased by contacting the publisher directly at Bayou City Press, LLC, 10303 Scofield Ln, Houston, TX 7096 or by emailing Publishing@BayouCityPress.com.

Editing by Luke B. Walker and Julie Gianelloni Connor
Cover design by CoverKitchen | Maps by Daniele De Vecchi

978-1-951331-12-2 (paperback) |978-1-951331-13-9 (ebook)
Library of Congress Control Number: 2025945895

Publisher's Cataloging-in-Publication
(Provided by Cassidy Cataloguing Services, Inc.)
Names: Burton, Chuck, author.
Title: Pueblos Mágicos : a traveler's guide to Mexico's hidden treasures / Chuck Burton.
Description: First edition. | Houston, TX : Bayou City Press, LLC, [2025] | Includes index.
Identifiers: LCCN: 2025945895 | ISBN: 9781951331122 (paperback) | 9781951331139 (ebook)
Subjects: LCSH: Pueblos Mágicos--Guidebooks. | Cities and towns--Mexico--Guidebooks. | Historic sites--Mexico--Guidebooks. | Mexico--Guidebooks. | LCGFT: Guidebooks. | BISAC: TRAVEL / Mexico. | TRAVEL / Special Interest / Adventure.
Classification: LCC: F1209 .B87 2025 | DDC: 917.20482--dc23

First Edition   Printed in the United States

Dedication

To my best honey and best friend, Kathy,
who told me I had to write,
then followed it up by offering total support
and necessary criticism throughout the journey.

Contents

Dedication v
Part I: Foreword 1
   Why We Travel *1*
   Why Mexico? *2*
   The Pueblos Mágicos *4*
   On the Pueblos Mágicos Trail with the Author *7*
   Chapter 1: Practicalities of Visiting the Pueblos Mágicos 13
      Safety and Security *15*
      Transportation *29*
      Lodging *40*
      Food *43*
      Language *45*
      Money and Costs *51*
      Odds and Ends *55*
Part II: The Towns 59
   Introduction *59*
   Chapter 2: The Favorites 63
      10) Mexcaltitán, Nayarit *65*
      9) Orizaba, Veracruz *68*
      8) Xilitla, San Luis Potosí *74*
      7) Huasca de Ocampo, Hidalgo *80*
      6) Twin Towns *87*
         Coatepec, Veracruz *87*
         Xico, Veracruz (Bonus Town) *91*
      5) Huautla de Jiménez, Oaxaca *92*
      4) Palenque, Chiapas *97*
      3) Cuetzalán, Puebla *104*
      2) Real de Asientos, Aguascalientes (Hidden Gem) *108*
      1) Zacatlán de las Manzanas, Puebla (Hidden Gem) *114*
   Chapter 3: The Honorable Mentions 119
      10) Bernal, Querétaro *121*
      9) Capulálpam de Méndez, Oaxaca (Hidden Gem) *123*
      8) Twin Towns *126*
         Mineral del Monte (Real de Monte), Hidalgo *127*
         Mineral del Chico, Hidalgo *132*
      7) Pahuatlán, Puebla (Hidden Gem) *134*

6) Cuatrociénegas, Coahuila *141*
    Poza Azul *143*
  5) Calvillo, Aguascalientes *145*
  4) Malinalco, México *149*
  3) Valley de Bravo, México *154*
  2) Tepoztlán, Morelos *158*
  1) Tzintzuntzan, Michoacán *161*
    Isla de Janitzio *164*
  Pátzcuaro, Michoacán (Bonus Town) *166*
Chapter 4: And All of the Rest (Northern) 167
  Background *169*
  Todos Santos, Baja California Sur *170*
    Barranca del Cobre, Chihuahua *172*
  Batopilas, Chihuahua *173*
  Creel, Chihuahua *175*
  Parras, Coahuila *177*
  Santiago, Nuevo León *178*
  El Rosario, Sinaloa *180*
  Magdalena de Kino, Sonora *182*
  Jerez de García Salinas, Zacatecas *184*
  Nochistlán, Zacatecas *185*
Chapter 5: And All of the Rest (North Central States) 189
  Twin Towns: Salvatierra, Guanajuato, and Yuriria, Guanajuato *191*
  Salvatierra, Guanajuato *191*
  Yuriria, Guanajuato *192*
  Ajijic, Jalisco *193*
  Mazamitla, Jalisco *197*
  Tlaquepaque, Jalisco *198*
  Cadereyta de Montes, Querétaro (Bonus Town) *200*
  Jalpan de Serra, Querétaro *202*
  Tequisquiapan, Querétaro *203*
  Aquismón, San Luis Potosí *204*
  Pinos, San Luis Potosí *207*
Chapter 6: And All of the Rest (South Central States) 211
  Huichapan, Hidalgo *213*
  Tecozautla, Hidalgo *215*
  Zimapán, Hidalgo *220*
  Twin Towns: El Oro de Hidalgo, México, and Tlalpujahua, Michoacán . *221*
  El Oro de Hidalgo, México *221*
  Ixtapan de la Sal, México *222*
  Tepotzotlán, México *223*
  Angangueo, Michoacán (Hidden Gem) *225*

    Cuitzeo del Porvenir, Michoacán *228*
    Tacámbaro, Michoacán *229*
    Tlalpujahua, Michoacán *229*
    Chapter 7: And All of the Rest (Southern) *233*
    Tlayacapan, Morelos *235*
    Mitla, Oaxaca *236*
    Atlixco, Puebla *237*
    Twin Towns: Chignahuapan, Puebla, and Tetela de Ocampo, Puebla *240*
    Chignahuapan, Puebla *240*
    Cholula, Puebla *241*
    Huachinango, Puebla *242*
    Tetela de Ocampo, Puebla *243*
    Tlatlauquitepec, Puebla (Hidden Gem) *243*
    Xicotepec, Puebla *245*
    Coscomatepec, Veracruz *245*
Part III: In Closing **249**
    Author's Note *249*
    Guide to Mexico City *249*
    Mexico City Transportation *252*
    Mexico's Hidden Colonial Cities *253*
    A Few Suggested Itineraries *254*
    And for Those Who Like It Nice… *255*
Afterword **257**
Acknowledgements **261**
Glossary **263**
Photograph and Map Credits **271**
Index **273**
About the Author **281**
About Bayou City Press **285**

PART I:
Foreword

Why We Travel
Why do we travel? There are as many reasons as there are people. A few centuries ago, when modern tourism was invented, travel was only for the wealthy, and they did it in the highest of style. Before that epoch, there were the explorers and adventurers. And from time immemorial, there have been people who had nothing and left their homelands to look for a better life. And there were those fleeing famine, plagues, crusades, pogroms, and wars of all types. But if they had food, water, and shelter, people generally stayed close to home. It was a scary, unknown world out there, and besides that, it was a long and slow walk from place to place. Many people never went farther than a day's journey away from their village in their entire lifetime.

Fast forward to the present. Some voyagers are still motivated by restlessness and wanderlust. Others want to see the world or "how the other half lives." There are famous sights to see, and we thrill at the mention of certain places: the Louvre, Machu Picchu, Times Square, the Great Wall, Angkor Wat. A lot of people just want a restful beach vacation, to learn something on a curated tour, or to be pampered on a cruise or at an all-inclusive resort.

I grew up in the easy comforts of the San Francisco Peninsula in the fifties and sixties. Like so many well-off young men, I was sheltered from the draft by a student deferment, then graduated from the University of California in 1971. I had little ambition and even less idea of what to do next. In the end, I washed dishes for six months to get some money together, then strapped on a backpack and flew off to destinations unknown. I wound up spending nine months mostly hitchhiking and sleeping rough in Europe and Israel. There was no internet and no real information. I heard of a destination on the backpacker's grapevine and headed there to check it out. And gradually, I became addicted to the adventure and intense sense of freedom inherent in this style of wandering.

Yes, there are many forms of travel. I am a proponent of what is called "slow travel," and for seven years have been a moderator of a Facebook group that extols the pleasures of that kind of journeying. For me, the joy lies in entering a foreign culture, immersing myself in it, meeting the locals on their own turf, and sharing as many of their ways as possible.

I yearn and thirst for authenticity, and I am filled with the desire to get away from the straitjacket of conventional tourism. Perhaps you are like me, but don't know quite how to proceed—if so, this book is for you. I have written this small book to offer up the beauty and mystery of off-the-beaten-track Mexico, along with travel advice and guidance. And mostly, I hope to open the door for you to the greatest treasure Mexico holds: the friendly, welcoming, and generous people who await you in these beautiful and inviting places.

So, if you're ready, let's hit the road. I'm delighted to have you along.

Why Mexico?

Europe is chock-full of history, architecture, art, museums, festivals, and untold natural beauty. It is also thronged with tourists. Just recently, I walked in downtown Lisbon and found myself elbow to elbow with hordes that had descended on the storied city, jetting in from North America, Asia, and other European lands. And it felt as if the legendary Old Quarter had been magically redesigned. Rather than standing as a monument to bygone beauty and mysteries, it had morphed into a tourist trap, with garish establishments open until they could hungrily part the mobs from their money and then send them home for the night. The sights were still authentic, but not much else.

Enter Mexico. The fourteenth largest country in the world and the eleventh most populous, it also abounds with history, architecture, scenic colonial cities, ruins, museums, art, over four thousand registered archeological sites, untold numbers of natural wonders, and a thriving indigenous culture with a wide variety of mouth-watering cuisine. Mexico encompasses vast desert lands; most of the tallest mountains and volcanoes in North America; tropical jungles; and, of course, thousands of miles of gorgeous coastline with booming surf in the west and warm and gentle Gulf Coast waters in the east. Truly, Mexico has something for everybody.

What it doesn't have in its interior, however, is foreign tourism. Untold numbers cross over for some thrills in places like Tijuana and Juarez, but besides these border hoppers, over 90% of the foreigners who visit Mexico fetch up in a few resort locales, like Los Cabos, Puerto Vallarta, Huatulco, Cancún, Ixtapa, and the like. Many of them never venture away from these ersatz all-inclusive havens, or at best, they take expensive guided tours or drunken mini-cruises to nearby areas.

There are large gringo communities in lesser-known places such as the north shore of Lake Chapala outside of Guadalajara and in the UNESCO World Heritage town of San Miguel de Allende, but those people also seldom stray from a small number of locales. Meanwhile, the more adventurous types, younger and older, all seem to be heading for Oaxaca. Don't get me wrong—Oaxaca is a fabulous destination that boasts colorful indigenous markets, the world-class ruins of Monte Alban, and plenty of vibrant culture. But every backpacker I meet seems to be heading there, and pretty much only there. While Mexico is full of historic colonial cities with gorgeous and magnificent central districts, it is unusual to see a single light-skinned foreign face in many of them. Such is the irresistible magnetism of modern tourism: A few places get all the publicity, and the crowds follow. The industry is well aware of this tendency to herd and knows it enhances its ability to easily rake in vast profits. This is true in Europe, India, Southeast Asia, and other tourism epicenters just as much as in Mexico.

I am not naive. I understand the reasons why this amazing country is so under-traveled compared to Europe and Southeast Asia (namely, Mexico's portrayal in the media as a violent and crime-ridden nation). The question is whether these reasons are based in reality. The truth is that Mexico is one of the most misrepresented countries in the world. I will dive into this controversial subject when I discuss Safety and Security in the Practicalities section of this book.

The bottom line is that much of Mexico remains an undiscovered treasure trove of beauty, and nowhere is this truer than in the *Pueblos Mágicos*. That's what this book is about—helping readers discover the "real" Mexico, and illustrating how genuinely magical the country can be.

The *Pueblos Mágicos*

As I've alluded to, Mexico is a world-class destination and in no need of additional attractions. The country is overflowing with myriad riches and wonders guaranteed to please even the most discerning of travelers. But the icing on the cake is the network of *Pueblos Mágicos*, or, in English, the "Magic Towns." These towns are part of an exciting program, originally established by the Mexican government in 2001, with the stated goal of bringing attention to beautiful, relatively small, rural Mexican towns, many of them relatively unknown even by Mexican citizens. Each *Pueblo Mágico* is chosen because it offers something special, such as colorful traditions, festivals, sites of cultural or historical significance, and/or outstanding architectural gems.

In practice, the program's worthy goal has been admirably accomplished, albeit with some inconsistencies and contradictions (which is rather representative of Mexico's national character and culture—it is a land of paradoxes). For example, a number of the towns are not quite so "magical" in and of themselves, but they are surrounded by all kinds of natural wonders like caves, lakes, waterfalls, *cenotes*, hot springs, volcanoes, and more. In any case, the founders of the program wanted to give all of these communities both financial support and incentives to protect their heritage. And there is little doubt that they have largely succeeded in doing so.

There are certain criteria for being designated a *Pueblo Mágico*, one of which is a minimum population of 5,000. If accepted, towns receive funds to spruce up their infrastructure and attractions. The biggest perk is the permission to use the now-highly-recognizable *Pueblo Mágico* logo, which the towns can then include in advertising and put on highway marker signs in order to entice passing motorists.

Clearly, the Mexican government has a definite interest in attracting foreign tourism. Increased tourism is one of the cornerstones of the government's urgent plan to bring hard currency into the country. Their efforts to do so are easy to observe in the hundreds of millions of dollars spent to develop upscale tourist destinations such as Cancún, Huatulco, and Cabo San Lucas. What is far murkier is whether their priorities have extended to the *Pueblos Mágicos* program. Apart from the select minority of *pueblos* that have been well known for decades, I personally don't know of any government literature in English promoting these valuable but much more modest (and low-cost) attractions. For the most part, even North Americans of my acquaintance who have actually traveled off the standard Mexican tourism routes are still generally unaware of the program. As of today, it appears that the Tourist Department has only focused on boosting domestic tourism to the *pueblos*. I have been traveling all over Mexico, backpacker-style, for nearly fifty years, yet until fairly recently I had never heard of the *Pueblos Mágicos*. When I first went over the list of towns (at that time there were 132 of them), I was astonished that even a fairly savvy old Mexico hand like myself had never heard of about three-quarters of them!

Additionally, the *Pueblos Mágicos* experiment got off to a slow start. In the first decade, only 32 towns were added, and a substantial number of those were already well known and without the need for additional publicity (for example, Tequila, Taxco, and San Cristóbal de las Casas). These places were all doing fine and were already enjoying plenty of foreign business; they didn't really need a boost from the appellation. Another early recipient was San Miguel de Allende, which absolutely did not need any assistance, having been inundated with tourists for decades. It was removed from the program, however, when it received UNESCO World Heritage status in 2008. Other *Pueblos Mágicos* that are somewhat widely known include Todos Santos and Loreto in Baja California, Palenque, Tulum, Isla Mujeres, Cozumel, and Valladolid (home of Chichén Itzá) in the Yucatán, Sayulita, Teotihuacán, Ajijic, Zihuatanejo, and San Blas. The program expanded with new government funding in 2010 and grew by fits and starts to encompass 132 towns by 2021, which was when I started exploring them in earnest. Then, in rapid succession, 45 new towns were certified in the summer of 2023. Few foreign travelers, including me, had ever heard of any of these new ones. And this remains true to this day.

In a country little traveled beyond a sliver of popular destinations, these towns represent a precious mother lode of culture and atmosphere for those who choose to mine it. The intrepid travelers, the adventurers, the seekers of authenticity, and the curious wanderers who search for hidden gems have been gifted a sumptuous banquet to feast on. These towns are beautiful, clean, tranquil, inexpensive, and safe. And the majority of them are virtually unvisited by foreigners. They are, in a word, magical.

On the *Pueblos Mágicos* Trail with the Author

I first came to Mexico in 1975. I had a light backpack, a heart full of wanderlust, very little money, and even less Spanish. After graduating from the University of California in 1971, I traveled for nine months in Europe and Israel, often hitchhiking and sleeping rough. Now I was turning my attention to our more accessible southern neighbor. More accessible in distance perhaps, but culturally a total mystery to me. And, of course, I knew it was a place where one could get by for just a handful of centavos. In the fall of 1975, I rode my thumb from the San Francisco Bay Area to Calexico and crossed the border into Mexicali.

I was supposed to get a tourist card from some undesignated source, but I didn't know that at the time, and nobody asked for it. Actually, nobody in Mexico ever asked to see my papers. (They still very rarely do, unless you are flying in and out.) Someone had told me that the train was the cheapest mode of transport. At the Mexicali depot, I bought a ticket to Mazatlán for six dollars. Yes, the train was cheap, but it was also *very* slow. It took 36 grinding hours to reach the Pearl of the Pacific, as Mazatlán is known. Passenger trains had priority over absolutely nothing, and we spent hours on sidings hoping to hear the whistle of a freight passing in the other direction. I wasn't carrying food, but luckily, there were vendors at every tiny station. I seldom knew what it was that I was buying, but it was sustenance. Besides that, the cars were full of friendly families. The señoras passed out tortillas and beans, and as far as they were concerned, this pathetically skinny gringo was just another member of the family. The generosity of the poor in this country is practically unrivaled anywhere.

Finally arriving in Mazatlán, I made my way to the ocean.

Some other stragglers pointed me to the Mar Rosa, the hippie and Volkswagen Bus trailer park, where a spot on the sand for your sleeping bag went for a dollar a night. There was a nearby sheltered space with a bathroom and a cold shower thrown in. The kindly sisters who ran the show served meals of beans, rice, and tortillas for twenty cents. I carried a Spanish-English dictionary and a Castilian grammar book, and I spent painful hours attempting to chat with people. Thus, I began my decades-long struggle to achieve fluency. I spent a few weeks on that beautiful beach, living on just two dollars a day. And I began my lifelong love affair with Mazatlán, which is where I live in retirement today.

I next rode the rails to Guadalajara, where I had to switch to buses, which were slightly faster and slightly more expensive than the train. I headed south on a loosely defined hippie trail. The buses were definitely a challenge. Though my Spanish was slowly improving, understanding the rapid-fire responses to my hesitant inquiries was frequently beyond my abilities. And while you cannot get lost while riding a train (although I'd point you to the movie *The Darjeeling Express* for the exception that proves the rule), buses are a different story. And in Mexico, there are always hundreds of buses going in every possible direction. I often did not know the name of my destination, or how to pronounce it correctly, so the process was rather fraught, to say the least. The natives were invariably kind and helpful, but they couldn't help breaking into hysterical laughter at my fumbling efforts to communicate. One late evening, I bought a ticket and heard the woman tell me it left at *dos*, two in the morning. I probably should have been suspicious about this odd departure time. And of course, she had said *doce*, which means midnight. So, when I finally showed up, everything was dark and empty. I slept in a nearby creek bed. In the morning, she was kind enough to exchange my ticket at no cost.

Back in those days, there were a few destinations that my kind were heading to—Oaxaca and Puerto Escondido come to mind—pretty much like it is today with the backpacker set. But we had an excuse to keep to those areas, because all the wonderful places I will describe in this book were utterly unheard of. And to this day, a few are still a bit tricky to get to, even if one desires to do so. Back then, forget it. As the years passed and my language skills improved, I continued to wander around the country with more confidence. I followed whims, intuition, and word-of-mouth tips. So, when I finally became aware of the *Pueblos Mágicos* project, I found that I had already visited about twenty of them in the past, albeit mainly the better-known ones.

My days of aimless backpacking around the world and in Mexico persisted from 1972 to 1985, punctuated by sojourns back in California aimed at earning some cash in order to hit the road again. I got married in 1979, but little changed, because Barbara wanted the same thing. Otherwise, why would she tie the knot with a guy with no money, no car, and no regular job? She was 34 and I was 29. All of our friends laughed. "You two can't get married, neither of you wants to work," they said. I had more than my share of trailside romances, but up to then, no sensible woman wanted anything serious with a guy with nothing to his name and no prospects.

After defying the world and getting hitched anyway in 1979, we traveled from San Francisco to Santiago, Chile, and then back to Quito for six months on numerous buses. In 1985, we adopted our precious daughter, Marisol, in Colombia, and things changed. The responsibilities of conventional life slowly eroded the joys that had founded our partnership. We traveled, naturally (a lot of van life), but it wasn't quite the same. In 1998, we reached the end of the line, and I became the single parent of a 13-year-old girl. Five years later, Marisol finished high school, and I picked up my old backpack, dusted it off, and have been hard at it ever since.

In 2017, my incomparable partner Kathy and I bought our little heaven on the beach in Mazatlán. She was still working.

I was on the road for four or five months a year. I know, I know. You can't figure out my magic formula. Yes, I did work long and hard hours. But it was only for eleven weeks a year. It was lucrative and quite legal, but on these pages, I am acting as only a travel guru, not a career coach. For seventeen years, I had been spending the winter months traveling, primarily in Mexico, Southeast Asia, and India. In warmer months, I hit places like Eastern Europe, Turkey, and Japan. One secret I will share: Earn your money where the pay is good, then spend it carefully in warm, cheap countries. That has been my lifetime philosophy.

When COVID reared its ugly head, my happy routine ended with a thud. The other side of the Pacific was no longer possible to visit. Mexico, on the other hand, was pretty much the only country in the world with no entrance requirements. And happily for me, I had acquired permanent residence status and was free to go back and forth without restriction. At about the same time, I started to read about the *Pueblos Mágicos*, which sounded exactly like my cup of tea. On top of my other advantages, I had a Mexican Senior (IMAPAM) card that gave me half-price fare on all long-distance buses, and free entry to all non-private museums and archeological sites. And so, I set off on this new adventure, which has slowly evolved into a minor obsession.

The first big trip started in Guadalajara in October 2021. Things were not so easy. Masks were required everywhere, and many attractions and public spaces were closed. Though my normal *modus operandi* is to go places and hang out for a while ("slow travel"), these were not the best conditions for doing so, and I made that 2021 circuit primarily a survey trip to find which places I might like to return to when the world returned to normal. In seven weeks, I visited 26 *Pueblos Mágicos*, along with the cities of Aguascalientes, Zacatecas, San Luis Potosí, Tlaxcala, and Puebla. Most of these were for two or three nights, though a number were just day trips. Early in the trip, traveling north and east away from the heavily populated central zone of the country, I passed over four weeks without seeing a single other foreigner or speaking a word of English. My already solid Spanish took a major leap forward. I was hooked. (By the way, the 2,000-mile loop cost me all of $113 in half-price bus fares.)

At one point, I had been to 64 of the 132 *Pueblos Mágicos*. Then the government upped the ante and designated 45 new ones. I have now been to 79 of the new total of 177. It is a good thing that this is not a bucket list venture for me. I am too old, and the authorities keep moving the target. Also, I have done most of Central Mexico, and many of the others are quite far apart. Anyway, all of the towns have YouTube videos, which are very helpful when selecting my destinations. My preferences run to small towns, often indigenous, where I can dive into the diversity of Mexican culture and cuisine and experience authentic old Mexico. I also am attracted to beautiful and tranquil natural settings where I can spend hours hiking in the *campo* (countryside) and meeting country people. History, religion, and architecture are further down on my list of interests. So, when you read through this account of my travels, you will need to run them through a filter of your own interests. Some of the towns that I have bypassed or not yet visited may actually be better fits for you. And by the time you finish this book, you will have all the necessary tools to create your own itineraries.

The next section deals with practicalities, primarily safety, transportation, and language skills. After that, I'll take you with me to my favorite towns, the honorable mentions, the ones worth a look, and, just for good measure, a few of the (very rare) disappointments. In the future, I hope that I will be able to continue this journey. And I hope to meet some of you on the road. So, let's set out!

CHAPTER 1:
Practicalities of Visiting the *Pueblos Mágicos*

Safety and Security
Transportation
Lodging
Food
Language
Money and Costs
Odds and Ends

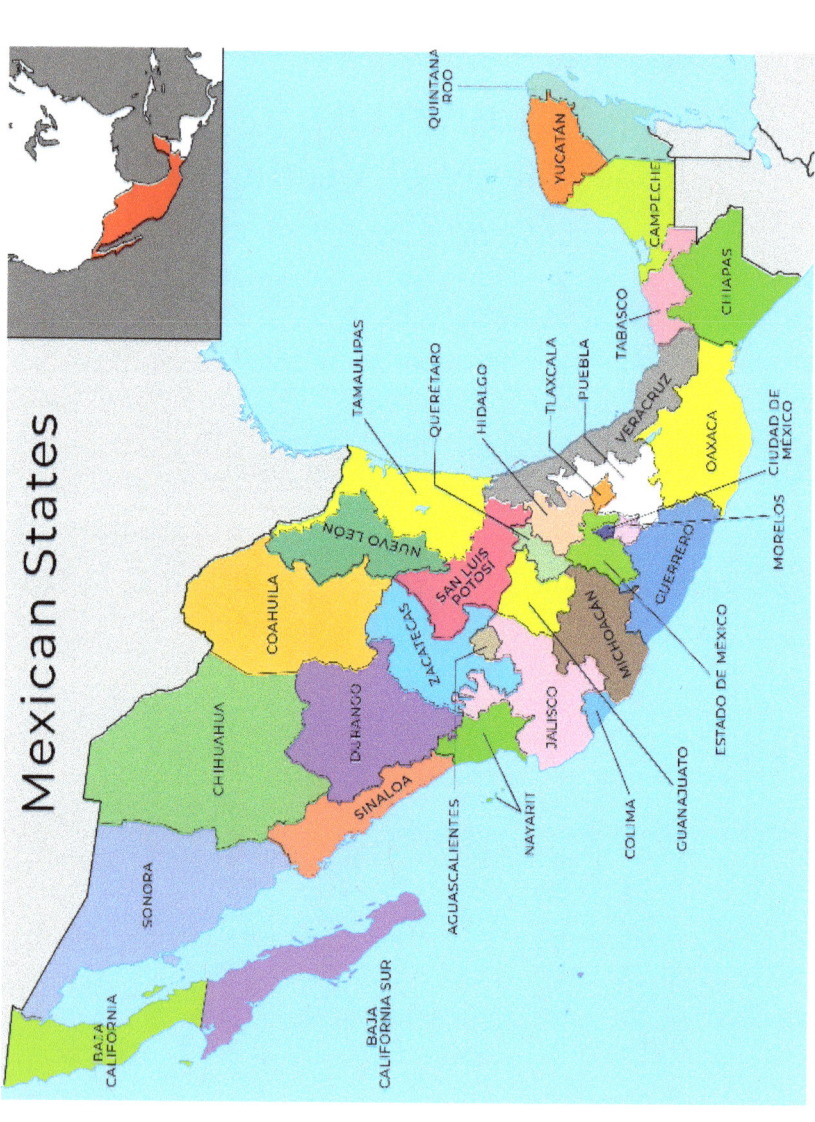

Safety and Security

"Safe" is an odd and rather ambiguous word. I moderate a Facebook group for retired travelers, and fairly frequently, there appears some sort of post from a clearly inexperienced person asking for suggestions for somewhere warm and "safe" to spend the winter. I wish I knew what they meant. So before presenting my opinions and conclusions on the subject, I propose to give the discussion of safety a good deal of context. And I also want to emphasize that it is hardly possible to characterize an entire country in simple terms of "safe" and "not safe."

First, some background. Mexico is a large and diverse country, full of treasures both manmade and natural. So why is there almost nobody foreign to be found in the great majority of this vast land? One reasonable explanation is that most of Mexico's wealth of culture and beauty is hidden and unpublicized. This is a little difficult to understand, considering how reliant Mexico is on tourism for bringing in hard currency. Why hasn't the government mounted a vigorous advertising campaign to attract international tourism away from the glitz?

To suggest one possible explanation, allow me to detour into pre-pandemic Thailand. Thailand has long been one of the preferred destinations for the young and adventurous international set. They probably represented and continue to represent about 90% of that country's tourism. They also infused a lot of money into the local economy despite their thrifty ways, if only by force of numbers. This did not please the ruling elite. They wanted foreigners to spend lavishly in deluxe lodgings and resorts, the ones that they owned, not waste their baht on small merchants. Thailand once had a very open entry system. Anybody could come in for a month, walk out into Malaysia, Myanmar, or Laos, and then walk right back into Thailand with another month stamped into their passports. Border runs were a major industry. Thousands of foreign residents of dubious legality, artistic types, and those with Thai partners took advantage of the system to stay on, often for years.

Eventually, the government responded to this kind of activity with various measures designed to restrict or prevent it. Giving a month-long visa to those arriving by air, but only fifteen days for those coming by land was one example. Limiting the number of times travelers could leave and re-enter was another. The elite resented that so many visitors were spending in ways that benefited the local economy but not them. They also disliked the hippie/druggie image of their country. (Which is interesting, because they don't seem to be concerned with the stigmatic label of sex tourism, which, even though greatly exaggerated, is a common Thai trope. Could this be because well-heeled foreign men restrict themselves to exactly the few places the authorities want to encourage?) Of course, these kinds of restrictive measures never work for long, and people always manage to find workarounds. Above all, Thailand is incredibly dependent on tourism. It has little in natural resources other than rice. There used to be a lot of valuable teak, but it is mostly gone. In any case, post-pandemic Thailand has learned its lesson and for the moment the easier old entry laws have returned.

The Mexican government has followed a model that bears striking similarity to that favored by the Thai elite. For example, before the movie *The Night of the Iguana* popularized it, Puerto Vallarta was an isolated fishing village. Capitalizing on the publicity generated by the film, lots of investment money poured in, roads were built, and the town grew into the almost strictly tourist behemoth that it is today. That phenomenon has recurred in Cancún, Zihuatanejo/Ixtapa, and Huatulco, all once tiny and unpopulated places with beautiful and pristine beaches. But big money came in and developed them all, adding basic urban infrastructure for the large number of poorer Mexicans who migrated in search of employment. Yes, a lot of common people eke out a living from these playgrounds for the wealthy, but all the real money pours into the pockets of those who need it the least. It always has and it always will. And it appears to me that the government is content with the way things are and has little interest in encouraging budget travel. As far as I can tell, there are exactly zero government websites in English touting the *Pueblos Mágicos* program.

The many towns that have sought *Pueblo Mágico* status crave the influx of federal funds, such as they are, and many have made the most of the opportunity. These towns tend to be much cleaner and more prosperous than their neighboring settlements, which actually have some of the same attributes. But if the *pueblos* are only lightly visited, these nearby cousins get no traffic at all. Life goes on the same as it always has, and gringos are as rare as unicorns. So outside of the few best-known places on my list, there is no incentive for big money to enter the scene, or big cartel money either, for that matter.

However, in many *Pueblos Mágicos*, boutique-style lodging and fine dining are coming increasingly into vogue. Inside the region which lies in easy proximity to Mexico City, and to some extent around large cities like Guadalajara and Monterrey, the rich and upper-middle classes are flocking to these lovely and vibrant places on weekends and holidays, bringing their tastes along with them. Towns like Valle de Bravo, Tepoztlán, Malinaco, Bernal, Tequisquiapan, Santiago, Mazamitla, and Tapalpa, among others, fill up rapidly. As a seeker of authenticity, I don't have any personal interest in any of this fancy stuff, but there is little doubt that it would be a draw to many with different tastes, and still another reason to add some *Pueblos Mágicos* to your itinerary.

The dearth of publicity does not extend to Mexican nationals. Many aspiring YouTubers travel around the *Pueblos Mágicos* circuit, and thus there are videos of all of the towns. And some of the more enlightened communities advertise, leveraging the value of the logo, which is becoming better known every year. For those who care to browse, these videos should further whet your appetite. Just find a list of them (Wikipedia has all 177 by date of entry) or type in a state name, i.e., *Pueblos Mágicos* Sinaloa. On YouTube, search for one such as Cosalá *Pueblo Mágico*. Very simple, and you'll get a great sense of the beauty of these towns.

All this brings me back to the original subject of this chapter. Foreign travelers, even the young, intrepid backpacking types, simply aren't visiting old, authentic Mexico, even as they flood Southeast Asia, Europe, and India. Mexico's beautiful small towns aren't being promoted, so there's a profound dearth of travel guides upon which foreigners can draw—which means that people remain uninformed and, by default, are likely simply to be intimidated by Mexico's scary reputation. But should they be? And is the reputation warranted?

Mexico, like Colombia forty years ago, has a terrible image. Many travelers who would welcome and appreciate the *Pueblos Mágicos* are likely daunted or, even more likely, just plain scared.

So how much of this fear is warranted? I am just offering up my opinions, but they're opinions grounded in fifty years of experience. Still, you're completely free to take them with a grain of salt. And here's a disclaimer: There is a slight bias to my experiences, as I am a small, brown man, conversant in the language and culture. I carry almost no luggage save for a small, old, beat-up backpack. I look nothing like a tourist or a gringo, and there is nothing about me that suggests I am carrying anything of value. In many ways, I am essentially invisible, walking the streets without drawing any attention to myself. My advantages are even more evident in a country like India, where I tend to wear native garb. Nobody ever bothers me or even speaks to me uninvited. But when Kathy came to visit me in India for three weeks, she was beset with hassling attention. But almost none of that pestering has happened to her in Mexico, where she also sticks out like a sore thumb.

In Mexico, people are much more prone to mind their own business. So, although it is possible that I am minimizing risks that I have never personally experienced, my gut—and all my experiences—tells me that I am not.

Most of you will be much more visible than I am, but the great majority of Mexicans are completely non-aggressive and often a bit shy. The *Pueblos Mágicos* are, for the most part, unaccustomed to foreigners. Your chances of being bothered in any way, much less targeted, are vanishingly small. Also, remember that Mexico City has hundreds of thousands of light-skinned citizens. Out in the sticks, you are about as likely to be taken for one of them as for a foreigner, at least until you open your mouth. The truth is that you are far more likely to be hassled in a very touristy locale in Mexico than in any of these out-of-the-way towns. By their very nature, tourist spots draw petty thieves, scammers, con artists, high-pressure vendors, and all the troubles that accompany modern tourism. Obviously, these unsavory characters prefer to target unsophisticated neophytes. You will very likely never encounter bad actors like that in your standard *Pueblo Mágico*. They have no reason to be there. On the other hand, you are much more likely than I to be addressed by someone who wants to practice their English! Sounds to me like a plus.

Few North Americans know very much about Mexico, and what they do know is often wrong. Millions of people cross into the border towns, mostly looking for a good time or perhaps some inexpensive dentistry. Such places are hybrids of the U.S. and Mexico, neither fish nor fowl. You won't get any real sense of Mexico in hassling, hustling Tijuana, which is anything but laid-back. To highlight the fact that the border towns are "different," just note that the national daily minimum wage in these international zones is twice that in the rest of the country.

The border aside, the great majority of visitors stay in resort destinations. You will not learn a great deal about the United States at Disney World; don't expect to do so regarding Mexico when you're in Cancún. Snowbird communities are a slight step up. They hold significant minorities of North Americans who speak at least basic Spanish and know something about the culture. But it's still a minority. I live in such a place, in a very gringo building of beachfront condos, because Kathy is happy and comfortable here. Very few of my fellow residents show any interest in authentic Mexico or even in trying to learn basic Spanish. And few of them ever venture outside of a limited comfort zone. They shop at Walmart and eat at restaurants that cater to foreigners. Inland expat communities like Chapala, Ajijic, and San Miguel de Allende are similar. Many of their residents do know more about their expat home than a casual visitor, but not necessarily that much more.

As I stated earlier, there are many travelers who do venture into the real Mexico and do know something about it. Still, they also tend to "herd." Most adventurous young European backpackers head for Oaxaca, San Cristobal de las Casas, the Yucatán, and then possibly into Belize and Guatemala. But I virtually never see anyone like that in a *Pueblo Mágico*. The more academic types frequent Mexico City, Guadalajara, and Puebla. But many of the other wonderful colonial cities are ignored. I have heard that Zacatecas, often acknowledged as the prettiest city in Mexico, is one of the most visited by domestic tourists. But by foreigners? Forget it.

All of the groups I have mentioned have at least been in Mexico. So, if they know so little about the country in general, imagine the ignorance of Americans who have never set foot here and likely never will. Whatever ideas about Mexico they may have probably come from media coverage and movies or television, if they bother to pay any attention at all.

Unfortunately, media coverage of Mexico is generally quite clueless. In the United States, we have tens of millions of people conditioned to distrust the media, but that distrust is mainly based on political issues. They usually have no problem accepting the media mythologies when it comes to the subject of Mexico. And that same media culture follows the old rule: If it bleeds, it leads. Even though Mexico is a highly diverse society with a large population, how much of the coverage regarding it concentrates almost entirely on cartel activity and its attendant violence? Without a doubt, these are serious problems, but they represent only small pieces of the Mexican jigsaw puzzle. As an example, what percentage of North Americans are aware that Mexico has a new woman *Presidenta*, and a Jewish one at that? I would wager that the number is very low. In addition to that, the country is brimming with exciting innovation and groundbreaking progressive programs. Why do we hear so little about any of that?

At least the press sometimes provides a modicum of broader and more factual coverage, scanty as it may be. But the American entertainment industry is truly a shambles. How many movie scenes have you seen featuring scowling men with long mustaches and sombreros, armed to the teeth and exuding menace? Naturally, this image is almost always heightened by scary music. I have traipsed around Mexico for half a century and cannot recall meeting anyone who fits this description. Pancho Villa has been dead for over a hundred years, but his stereotype lives on. Anyone traveling in Mexico encounters many policemen, army checkpoints, and other examples of officialdom. Besides the fact that they might be well-armed, these men and women are invariably courteous and pleasant. I have no fear of approaching a cop in any of the places I visit, looking for information or directions. I can't remember a time when these authorities were not friendly and helpful.

I am a fan of the series *Weeds*, but the scenes that take place in a rustic Mexican country village are total fiction and vigorously propagate the aforementioned stereotypes. The Tijuana Cartel episodes are not a whole lot better, as they're deliberately hyped-up for America's jaded television audience. I really enjoyed watching *Weeds*, but I was well aware that the entire series was way over the top. Yet for uninformed viewers, and especially those who have never been to Mexico or learned anything about the country, the series simply reinforces media-instilled prejudices and timeworn negative tropes.

Scenes in many modern movies, such as when the intrepid foursome from *Sex and the City* visits a Mexican resort, are genuinely cringe-inducing. In the *Sex and the City* film, the women are terrified of drinking anything, especially the water. Of course, they get the runs anyway. Two observations here: Traveler's diarrhea is common among those who travel quickly from north to south and vice versa, due to the introduction of unfamiliar gut flora to the body. Mexicans can encounter the same problem when flying to the United States. People often ask me about the changes I have seen in Mexico over all these decades, and one of the most prominent and welcome is the tremendous improvement in standards of hygiene and sanitation. More and more, the "turistas" are a thing of the past. The Carrie Bradshaw experience is anachronistic, as even contemporary tourists to all-inclusive resorts quickly come to realize, but old stereotypes don't disappear easily.

There is also a recent and authentic Netflix documentary called *The Guardian of the Monarchs,* set in Michoacán, about one man's struggles to defend butterfly nesting sites from the depredations of the cartels. The film is realistic and accurate, but, again, it depressingly focuses mainly on the bad. As I said earlier, if it bleeds, it leads.

I absolutely detest the popular and controversial novel *American Dirt*, about a woman and her son fleeing the Acapulco cartel. I have never seen a darker and uglier portrait of Mexican life. Yes, plenty of poor people and immigrants do suffer the kind of horrendous trials and tribulations the author chronicles. But if all you know derives from reading this one book, you would not be blamed for believing that it is an accurate representation of the entirety of this vibrant, colorful, and friendly land. It decidedly is not. The entire storyline is preposterous and full of ludicrous inaccuracies. I am not going to spend any more time addressing *American Dirt*, other than to say that it is practically all hole and no cheese. I do not recognize the Mexico described in it. But if it were all I had ever read, I too would never have come here.

It's important to note that this is not just a Mexican problem. Sensationalized and stereotypical images abound everywhere. India is depicted as desperately poor and filthy, end of story, which is an absurdly simplistic summary of a nation with a rich and ancient culture and which is a vast, diverse land, home to about twenty percent of the world's population. And as I said above, one of the first things that comes to people's minds when they think about Thailand is sex tourism, which is actually located in only a very few places. The novel *The Beach* begins on the main tourist street in Bangkok, Khao San Road, where a sinister figure emerges from the shadows and menacingly offers the protagonist a drink of cobra blood. Never going to happen in a million years. (By the way, I once had a glass of this unpleasant stuff under entirely different circumstances in the Mekong Delta of Vietnam.) And there is also a Netflix video about a Thai serial killer preying on young backpackers. It is based on a true story, but has extremely little relevance to Thailand, a country where violent crime is very rare, particularly with regard to occurrences targeting foreigners. My message is that you should be wary of any and all broad-stroke, generalized descriptions of an entire society. And that goes double for Mexico.

Last but not least are the U.S. State Department travel advisories. Their reports are replete with dire warnings and advice to avoid, well, pretty much the whole country of Mexico. Once, I read an article that described a slew of scary kidnappings, carjackings, and other horrors directed at American citizens. And who authored this fantasy treatise? A security company that rents out employees to protect travelers. No conflict of interest there. I was stunned to find some of this article's rhetoric repeated almost verbatim in the official government advisories. The bureaucrats who write these reports have likely never visited the places they are warning us about and probably know as little about Mexico as the rest of the American populace. The government's main concern, in my humble opinion, is to minimize liability. Discouraging people from coming to Mexico seems to be their main objective.

In my fifty years of backpack-style travel to every sort of Mexican locale, I have not once felt threatened or in danger. I have been victimized by petty theft, which can happen anywhere, but that is it. In my younger days, I had a few unpleasant encounters with drunks, which is also an experience more or less common to every country. You can trust me or the U.S. government and the media circus. That is your choice. Everybody's knowledge is limited, but I am happy to pit my knowledge about Mexico against almost anybody else's.

So, is Mexico a dangerous place or not? Can one travel safely to the *Pueblos Mágicos* even though one knows little about the country or its language? "Finally!" I can hear you muttering. "How much have I had to pore over here without the author getting to the point?" If all that you have read and heard about Mexico comes from the sources I noted above, then you are justified in feeling fearful and intimidated. And what other reason can there be to explain why a country so full of wonders and treasures is empty of travelers? Here is my answer, and I bet you can guess what it is: a resounding "no" to danger and an emphatic "yes" to safety. And nobody is paying me to write this!

There are dangerous parts of Mexico, and enough scary statistics and reports of horrifying violence to give anyone pause. But let me explain why none of this pertains to you. There is violence in Mexico, but it is largely confined to a relatively small number of localities. These are the places where gangs and cartels are competing for turf, market control, and transport routes. A small town in the highlands of Puebla contains nothing of interest to them, and that's true of nearly all of these *Pueblos Mágicos*. Moreover, the cartels are fighting each other, not poor civilians, and certainly not foreigners. Cartel-style crime just isn't part of traditional Mexican culture. When I was traveling fifty years ago, before the U.S. war on drugs created huge profit incentives (all while the U.S. supplied the demand and the arms), the few murders one heard about were almost always crimes of passion, often involving alcohol—just like in any country. So today, away from the areas of turf conflict, violent crime is very low—lower than Canada, in fact, and *definitely* much lower than the U.S. Take the state of Zacatecas as an example. According to the State Department, it's one of the most dangerous states in the country, and you are urged to avoid it. But beautiful Zacatecas city is tranquil and safe. Go forty miles north to the city of Fresnillo, a major transportation hub, and you could find yourself in the middle of a cartel zone. Easy fix: Don't go to Fresnillo. (And even there, I would not be concerned walking around during the day).

Two major forces in Mexico, the government and the cartels, share one viewpoint in common: Don't mess with the tourists, particularly the older ones. The government has three sources of hard dollar currency, although maquiladora manufacturing is rapidly becoming a fourth. The standard three sources are oil, tourism, and remittances (money sent to families by Mexicans living and working up north). Once upon a time, there was quite a bit of petty corruption aimed at foreigners, such as little bribery shakedowns at the border. But the government eliminated all that decades ago. Mexico has traditionally granted everyone 180 days upon entry. (Note: There are currently some reports of people being given less time when arriving via certain airports, with immigration laws in flux. Check your papers before leaving immigration.) The paperwork is simple and straightforward. They want us here. They have built resorts for us. For those who are already in Mexico, when is the last time any official has asked to see your papers other than at a bank, an airport, or the border? For most of us, never.

As for the cartels, they maintain a strict "hands off the tourists" policy. They have hundreds of millions of dollars to launder, and they sink the money into hotels, resorts, restaurants, and the like. So don't ask too many questions in your plush resort digs! You may be enjoying the benefits of cartel investments or perhaps their version of Social Security. In other words, we are their customers, and the last thing they want to do is gin up bad publicity or scare us off.

A year or two back, a group of four people entered a border town for purposes of medical tourism (i.e., cheap prices). For some unknown reason, they met with tragedy instead. Nobody knows whether they were specifically targeted or if it was just random bad luck, which again can happen anywhere. It was a huge story everywhere, whereas this kind of crime is so commonplace north of the border that it generally does not even make the news. Also unmentioned was that hundreds of thousands of people visit Mexico for medical treatment every year without anything bad happening to them. And what was the response by the cartel to the incident? They tracked down the culprits, something the police couldn't do, and tied them to a police vehicle with a sign saying that this outrage was not the work of cartels. Like I said, they don't want the bad publicity. I'm not trying to say anything good about the cartels (they're horrendous criminals); I'm just suggesting that if you mind your own business, they have no intention of messing with you. And that is something you surely want to know for your own peace of mind.

The lesson is that you are a protected class in Mexico. And remember, the *Pueblos Mágicos* don't have any bad guys who prey on tourists in the first place. After all, there aren't any of us around to be preyed on!

I live most of the year in Mazatlán. Unlike Puerto Vallarta or Cancún, this is a fairly large working city, the largest port between Panama and Long Beach, and the center of the Pacific shrimp industry. Tourism is just another business here, not "the business." In fact, outside of cruise ships, there is not that much traditional tourism. Most of the foreigners in residence tend to be snowbirds. In many ways, it is a close-knit community with its own districts, hangouts, websites, and Facebook groups. Even now in late 2024, in the middle of a "mini" Sinaloa cartel war, everyone I know feels as safe as they have for all the years they have been coming here. The strife happens far away from the beach, and mostly at night. It is not part of our lives. If one of our group happens to fall victim to crime, we all hear about it quickly. The grapevine and rumor mill operate quickly and efficiently. So, if we are not hearing about things like that, which we rarely do, it probably means that they aren't happening. Even with the present unpleasantness of cartel conflict in our state of Sinaloa, I absolutely, unequivocally feel safer here than I do in the United States.

Here's the thing: Crime is mostly targeted in Mexico, not random. If you are minding your own business, you will be just fine, barring some sort of freak occurrence. In the United States, guns are everywhere, but in Mexico, only the government, the army, and the cartels (courtesy of the U.S., of course) have them. It is extremely difficult for a private citizen to acquire a firearm. Nobody in Mexico shoots up a school, a church, or a mall. Never have and never will. Nobody walks into a private business and kills their former co-workers. I hate to say this, but if the bad guys have you in their sights, it is likely that you have been messing around in the wrong place. And as for *Pueblos Mágicos* mostly tucked away in the mountains, cartel crime is nonexistent.

Just follow a few common-sense rules: Don't wear expensive clothes or sport fancy watches and jewelry. Keep your money out of sight. Walking about in the daytime in small towns and cities is completely safe. Even in the evening hours, plenty of people walk around without concern, including single girls and women. If you are concerned about your safety when going out at night, ask at your hotel.

As long as I can remember, when I told people that I was going to Mexico, the most common responses were "Aren't you afraid?" and "Isn't it dangerous?" Depending on the circumstances, I might have either laughed lightly, asked if they were serious, rolled my eyes, given a sarcastic retort, or, occasionally, tried to give a straight and serious answer. Not that it's ever done much good. It is very difficult to break through the propaganda, and people are going to believe what they believe. There is also kind of "cognitive shield" at work here. Most people think of their home turf as pretty safe and secure, and mostly they are right. Those who watch a lot of television consistently believe that U.S. crime rates are much higher than they really are. But ask them about their own neighborhood, assuming they don't live in an inner city, and they usually feel pretty good about it. And that belief system extends to the entire country. The U.S. may have plenty of problems, but it is home and a known entity, whereas the rest of the world is "poor, dirty, dark, and scary." The fact is that the United States is one of the most dangerous and violent countries in the world. It is awash with guns, and the most frightening thing is that the violence seems almost random. Somebody might start shooting anywhere.

But I do feel safe enough in the United States, because I summer in a small town and spend most of my time in the woods. But even there, when I hear something that sounds like gunfire, I shudder inwardly. I never feel that way in Mexico. Here, you know it almost has to be fireworks. So as long as I am going about my quiet and unassuming daily routines, I simply take my personal security for granted.

I will close this section with a short shaggy dog story, although the friend who originally told it to me insists it's true: An old Texan and a similarly retired Canadian couple were sitting around their patio by the beach, chuckling at the foolishness of all the people who think that Mexico is dangerous and would never consider coming here. The Texan paused for a moment and then said, "Well, in a way, they might have a point. It is a lot more dangerous for you than it is for me."

The Canadian pair were confused. "How can that be true?"

"Well, when I am ready to drive down here in the fall, I get in my car, soon enough cross the border, and go on my way. But you, you have to drive across America." Of course, my Canadian friends laugh at this story a lot more than my American friends. Which is telling. Canada, like Mexico, has strong gun control laws.

And one final word on safety. The most dangerous things that many people do every day are spending hours watching television without moving around, while drinking alcohol and eating lots of processed junk food and sugar. The next most dangerous thing is getting in a car. But there is little point in living in fear. I, for one, am a big believer in living life to its fullest.

Transportation

Now that I have finished my little safety pep talk, I'll move on to transportation, which can be a relatively complex part of independent travel here, particularly if one is short of language skills. I'll give you more of my insights, all garnered through lots of exploring and sweat, honed over decades of figuring out how to travel around this vast country. And I believe that after reading this section, you too will find the prospect of independent travel less daunting. In a country where the majority of the citizenry lacks private cars, public transportation is highly developed, and with a bit of practice not all that complicated.

One transport possibility is driving your own car. The two main advantages are that you will enjoy easier access to all kinds of natural wonders and that you will have somewhat more control over your travel schedule. But as a lifetime slow traveler, the latter has always been of little interest to me. Meanwhile, the disadvantages are numerous. For one, driving your own car is far more expensive. Besides sky-high gasoline prices, most of the main highways charge tolls—often substantial ones. It's also very easy to get lost, as destination and road signs can be very confusing. Even more annoying, Mexico, particularly rural Mexico, is rife with speed bumps. The biggest problem with the speed bumps is that there are often no warnings on the approach to these omnipresent menaces. Believe me, it can be plenty rough on your suspension. Driving through small towns and cities can also be a nightmare, as they were not built for motorized transport. One-way streets are the rule, not the exception. Traffic can be horrendous. Parking is often nonexistent. And if you are limited to lodgings that provide parking, you'll miss out on a ton of attractive alternatives. My guess is that one long and relaxing ride on a comfortable Mexican bus will sell you on the biggest advantage. It is much more relaxing and much less stressful. Or as the Greyhound ads once announced, "Leave the driving to us."

I did drive to and around Mexico frequently in my younger days. The only gas was called Nova, which the Mexicans called *No va* ("It doesn't go"). It was leaded, and the government banned it decades ago in their long struggle to clean up the air. Gas was also relatively cheap, unlike today. There were hardly any toll roads either, and much lighter traffic. However, the roads were two-lane only, and at times crammed with trucks and buses belching diesel, particularly going uphill. The challenge was to pass them—safely—which was often an adventure. Warning signs proliferated along many stretches, sporting the words *Curvas Peligrosas*, or dangerous curves. (Even today, when I see one, I keep my eyes peeled for distracting señoritas!)

In those days, you also had to be aware of eccentric driving habits. Cars didn't signal or stop when they turned left; they just veered off slowly when it was safe. Driving at night was considered crazy; there were no floodlights and plenty of roving livestock. The worst hazards were the Mexican drivers themselves, who refused to turn on their headlights. I asked why they did this and was told it was easier to see the other guy when yours were off. When I enquired what happened when two cars going in the opposite direction followed this practice, they looked at me like I was crazy. Logic is not always a straight line in these parts. Traveling by car was all good fun back then, and we were seldom in a hurry, but I no longer have any desire for that kind of travel.

The best way to travel within the country is to take advantage of the incredible Mexican bus system. Numerous buses go almost anywhere you might want to visit, and on a frequent basis. After all, the majority of the population can only dream about owning a car. And they need to get about somehow. In our advanced North American systems, bus lines like Greyhound are considered transportation for the poor. The routes are driven infrequently, and the buses fail to service many destinations at all. They are not particularly pleasant or clean compared to Mexican buses, either. Long-distance buses here on major routes are ultra-comfortable. The seats are spacious, they recline, and there are plenty of movie screens. The restrooms are clean. These buses operate on the toll highways and make decent time, though they can get bogged down when navigating the nightmarish city traffic. The slightly more expensive direct buses do not even have this problem, except when leaving or arriving. Above all, the buses are economical, especially for me with my Mexican Senior card, which gives me a 50% discount. In fact, it costs me more to take a taxi 15 miles to the Mazatlán Airport than it does to ride a first-class bus 300 miles to Guadalajara.

Using this system is not that complicated, but it works nothing like the way we are conditioned to think. The first thing you need to do is throw away any preconceptions based on how our North American systems function. Naturally enough, Mexico has its own rules. The first time you go to a bus station in any big city, you will be astounded to see how many vehicles and boarding lanes there are—usually in the dozens or more. In fact, Mexico City boasts four enormous terminals, each offering hundreds of routes. They cover all the cardinal points and are conveniently located on the various Metro lines, cheap and fast if you are only carrying one bag, as I do. (I will address the fabulous Mexico City Metro in the appendix. By the way, it is free to all riders over 60, including foreigners.) The new Guadalajara central is not so large, but it has about six halls spread about a very large parking area. What does this tell you? On all the major routes, including all the cities along the toll highways between Mexico City and Tijuana, a distance of nearly 1,500 miles, there is no need to check either departure times or make reservations. Just show up at the bus terminal. There will be many competing companies, and the most time you will have to wait for a bus might be half an hour. More likely, you will be sent onto a departing bus almost immediately.

Travelers being travelers, you may want to go online and check departure times, no matter what I say. But this can actually be very frustrating. First of all, you have to determine which bus line goes where you want, and there are tons of them. There are various booking websites that help with this, but they come with a premium. Or you can ask Google which buses go from Mazatlán to Durango, for example, and you might find that information. However, the keyword is "might," because that will often not be the end of your search. A company website will give you the departure times you are seeking *if* there is a bus that originates where you are and passes through or goes to your destination. And this can be a big if. Most of the time, this kind of route is not available online from where you are leaving. All too often, there are no buses that originate at your location. Worry not. The reason is that, much of the time, a route is by a *bus de paso*. In other words, your bus starts somewhere else and is just passing through where you happen to find yourself. Here is the best way to go about this, assuming you are visiting one town, then intending to move on to another, as I usually am: When you arrive at your first destination, simply check on connections to the next before you leave the terminal. Even if you will only be taking a *bus de paso* route, at least you will know approximately what time it will be passing through. You can arrive a little bit early if you are the anxious type. Just know that a *de paso* bus is almost guaranteed to arrive a little late, and they're almost never early.

There's another important wrinkle. I just went onto Greyhound's website and searched for a ticket from Dallas to Seattle. It obliged me by giving me a price, a transit time, and the information that there would be four transfers. That is the way it works in North America. In Mexico, do not try this if your destination is not in a straight line from where you are. Even at the terminal, you will almost never find any bus route that does this. Again, no worries. Look at the map and find where you will be changing highways. Take a bus to that point. At that terminal, there will be another bus going where you want. I guarantee it. However, one caution: If you are heading way out in the sticks, you may have to wait. This happens. But that can be a good thing. Sometimes I like the look of a town that I have never heard of and spontaneously decide to spend the night there, leaving for my actual destination refreshed and with no wait at the station. After all, not every beautiful place gets to be officially rated as "magic." At least not until you make it so.

Here's an example of this type of wrinkle: Many people go on an expat Facebook group here in Mazatlán and ask how to take a direct bus to Puerto Vallarta. There are no flights unless you want to make a lengthy detour to Mexico City. In this case, it happens that there is one company that offers a luxury bus trip once or twice a day. But aside from a slightly higher price, that also locks you into a reservation and someone else's schedule. I personally don't care to travel that way. The easiest way to get to Puerto Vallarta is to just show up at the Mazatlán terminal and get on a bus to Tepic, the capital of the neighboring state of Nayarit. They go by *De Paso* all day long, every twenty minutes or so. And Tepic is on the main line from Guadalajara to Puerto Vallarta. So, when you get there, you will quickly find a *De Paso* to Puerto Vallarta. No fuss, no muss, no reservations, no being locked into a schedule. If you decide to spend the night in Tepic, there is plenty to see and do. It's a pretty city and, like most of its kind, devoid of foreigners.

In Mexico, there is always a way to get almost anywhere. But most of the time, you cannot plan it ahead in detail the way many modern travelers insist on doing. I am a slow traveler, generally with no set itinerary, so this kind of thing does not bother me. The difficulty of making plans in advance is particularly true with the *Pueblos Mágicos*, which can be out of the way and not on any major bus routes. I try to remember that getting there is part of the adventure, besides allowing you to rub elbows with the Mexican people and see lots of beautiful scenery.

One time I was in Jalapa, the capital city of the state of Veracruz, and my next destination was the *Pueblo Mágico* of Tlatlauquitepec, in the state of Puebla. One of the idiosyncrasies of Mexican travel is that at times there is no direct route between towns in two different states, even if they appear fairly close together on a map. More often than not, the problem is a mountain range. In any case, state capitals tend to be hubs from which you can get to any reasonably sized town in that particular state. The stress-free route for me was to take a bus to Puebla, then switch to one to Tlatlauquitepec. But that entailed many extra hours of travel and a much higher expenditure. Examining the map, I saw a large town named Perote at an intersection with a numbered road (meaning more than a windy stretch of gravel), which led to another named Tezuitlán (population of 60,000, per Google). And from there it was only about 20 miles to my destination. So that was my first plan, to go to Tezuitlán. That would probably mean one bus change, but checking at the Jalapa terminal, I made the happy discovery that there was actually a direct bus to Teziutlán three times daily, even though it was in another state. Aha! No topographical obstacles.

There was no online information about how to get from Teziutlán to Tlatlauquitepec (what a mouthful). But in Mexico there is always a way—collective vans, shared taxis, or, as a last resort, a private taxi (which for that distance would likely cost about $10-12). In the end, any fretting and stewing was a waste of energy. I arrived in Teziutlán without incident and found that there were onward minibuses every thirty minutes. The whole transit was fast and cheap.

I don't want to make this seem too easy, particularly if you don't have good Spanish as I do, but there is always a way, and there are generally people eager to help you. I will discuss the language situation at length in the next section. The point is to be flexible and light on your feet, and also to have faith that you will manage to get where you are going one way or another. While poor Mexicans speak perfect Spanish, they are without all of our financial options—yet they get where they are going.

Here is another example of thinking outside the box: I was in Oaxaca city and wanted to visit the *Pueblo Mágico* of Huautla de Jiménez, which is extremely isolated in the mountainous northeast part of the state. I saw on the map that there was some kind of direct road. But checking at the bus terminal after coming up empty online, I was told that there were no buses to Huautla. It must not be much of a road, I thought to myself. I did discover that there were buses from the city of Tehuacán, Puebla, to Huautla, though that meant a considerable detour and much more time spent, in theory anyway.

My next stop was the State Tourist Department in Oaxaca. But I was unsurprised to find that they had no clue. Huautla is a fascinating town (actually, it will turn up on my Top Ten list), but the girl said nobody had ever asked before, and they had no information. This was just more reinforcement of how unknown most of Mexico is to the tourist infrastructure. She did direct me to a small bus station elsewhere in the city that served local destinations. It was not very easy to find either, but when I did, they also did not have any bus available for a place 140 miles away via a small, winding road.

I don't tend to give up easily. Before settling for a long, detoured journey via Tehuacán, I had one more card up my sleeve, thanks to the ease of modern communication. My next step was to research lodging. (I will also cover this in a later section.) After deciding on a hotel, I called them. After saying I wanted to stay with them on selected dates, I said that I was having trouble finding transportation. The señora gave me the name of a small company that ran minivans nearly right to her door, and some landmarks to help find them. She did not know the street name. I passed this little tidbit on to the tourist office later that day, though it didn't seem like they cared much. When was the next time some crazy gringo would ask a question that nobody ever had before? Anyway, that was that. After some bumbling around, I found the enterprise and bought a ticket for the next morning. There was quite a bit more to this adventure, but you will have to wait for the rest of it when I take you to the town of Huautla in the main section of this book. And by the way, you don't have to speak Spanish to use this hack, though it is simpler if you do. Your hotelier will be glad to assist you. Maybe even the girls at the State Tourist Office. Or not!

So, you have arrived at the bus terminal. There are a bewildering number of different companies, and crowds of people milling about. Numerous signs flash long lists of destinations. If yours is a large and prominent one, you are bound to spot its name on many of the competing boards. If so, you can determine for yourself which bus has the earliest departure. However, today you are not going to these famous places; you're off to a humble *Pueblo Mágico*. Do not panic! Write the town name clearly on a piece of paper. Find an open window with a clerk who is not selling tickets. Say "*Voy a*," and show them the paper. Generally, they will tell you the right company and wave in its direction. The good news in smaller places is that there is only one window and one door.

You have surmounted the first obstacle. You have found the correct company and ticket window. You've named your destination or shown them your paper if you are concerned with your pronunciation. On first-class buses originating at the terminal, they might ask you to choose your seats. You pay (*efectivo* means cash, and a *tarjeta* is a credit card). Your ticket is in your hand. Congratulations! But don't relax just yet, particularly if you are in a big city with a busy, enormous terminal. There are numerous departure areas. This is no time to be shy or worry about annoying the clerk. The most important thing is to make sure you know how to locate your bus. First, determine if your destination is the ultimate one for your bus. Particularly with small towns, it likely isn't. Ditto for *De Paso* routes. You should first inquire as to what destination name will appear on the front of the bus. The second is which *sala* (departure area) you need to go to. Generally, this is right behind or close to where you buy the ticket. Next is the parking lane number. Remember, there can be over one hundred in big cities. Finally, ask for the bus number. They'll likely know it if it's a direct bus, but not with a *De Paso*. Make them show you all of this on the ticket, because if they talk, it will likely be too fast for you to understand. This can be true at times, even for me, a fluent speaker. When a Mexican gets going on a full head of steam, it can sound just like a completely different language. One hack is to say "*Mas lento, por favor,*" which means "Slower, please." This will get you a knowing smile, and possibly maybe even some reduction in the velocity of speech. At least for ten seconds or so until they forget and revert to normal. Also, you will want to confirm if your bus is *De Paso*, because when you get to the correct departure lane, it will often be empty or house a different bus.

You're not quite done yet. Go to the correct waiting room. If your departure time is more than fifteen minutes away, sit down and relax. Otherwise, go outside and scout around. If your bus leaves from your departure city, it should be waiting in the correct lane. *Should be.* There are no guarantees in Mexico! But there are lots of ways to check. Stall number, bus number, destination sign. If you haven't found it, show your paper to someone who looks like they know, such as a driver standing near another bus. They will point down the line, say something about not here yet, or shrug helplessly. Just persevere. In today's Mexico, there's sure to be someone who speaks at least broken English.

If you are not a Spanish speaker and are engaged in learning basic traveler's vocabulary, concentrate on your objective. Your goal is not to learn how to speak the language. If you are starting out as a typical retiree, this is not going to be achievable, barring heroic and intense effort. What you do need to do is learn basic communication skills. Your first task is to work on the simple phonetics, especially of the vowel sounds. I will discuss all this at length in the upcoming section on language. After pronunciation comes basic vocabulary. In terms of bus travel, I supply these in an appendix at the end of this book.

The majority of the *Pueblos Mágicos* will have some kind of regular bus service, which means there will be little need for the kind of improvising mentioned above. But the farther out a place is, the less like it is to be serviced by one of the super-comfortable buses that ply the main routes. But neither will they be the "chicken" buses of yore, though I can think of one that did bear a bit of resemblance to those "good old days."

Even when there are no buses, there are collective vans, shared taxis, and the regular taxis that I mentioned earlier. You might have to scramble a little bit to find them, but again, Mexicans tend to be very helpful. At times, a bit too helpful. The biggest hazard in soliciting this kind of assistance on the street is that people can be overeager to assist a little lost lamb, and they really hate to admit that they do not know the answer to your question. In fact, they may make something up rather than disappoint you! I have been at this for a long time and am pretty good at knowing when someone really knows what they are talking about. In fact, it is usually pretty obvious. Just be aware that if someone is hemming or hawing, or perhaps looking around desperately in search of someone else to deal with this foreign lunatic, they are less than likely to be a reliable source of information.

If you are the type of traveler who actually takes me up on the offer to visit these wonderful *Pueblos Mágicos*, I expect that you will also be patient, resourceful, and adventurous. And that is really all you need. But in any case, there is one fairly simple way to get your feet wet: Do some research, pick one state, and plan to base yourself in its capital. From there, you can easily go out on day trips or arrange two- or three-night stays depending on your preferences. Particularly in the region surrounding Mexico City, where much of the country's population lives, there are numerous mountain towns easily accessible by bus in a few hours or less. I will make some more specific itinerary suggestions later on, also included in an appendix.

Lodging

Finding a suitable place to sleep will be one of your easiest tasks. Except in a few of the most remote and lesser-known towns, there is something for everyone. You will find basic, inexpensive local hotels and guesthouses, hotels in lovely old colonial buildings covered in flowers (my preference), and standard middle-class hotels with the usual amenities but significantly less charm. There is also a plenitude of private places either listed on Airbnb or on sites like booking.com. Particularly if you are staying for a while, these can be spectacular bargains.

In some of the *Pueblos Mágicos*, which are more like domestic resorts, there are plenty of deluxe and boutique lodgings, including cabins out in the forest and hills. In other words, you have a good chance of finding what you want.

You are always free to book ahead, but it is generally not necessary. Unless you are heading to one of the better-known and popular towns, or there is a holiday or special festival going on, you will find a world of vacancies. Weekends can also be competitive in these busier destinations. Otherwise, supply heavily outweighs demand.

It also depends on what amenities you desire. I am seldom in my rooms during the day, and what I value most is cleanliness, quiet, comfort, a friendly atmosphere, decent plumbing, and good internet service. When I took my first extensive *Pueblos Mágicos* journey in 2021, the internet signals were at times erratic. They sometimes did not reach my room, forcing me into the lobby. And in some of the smaller and more isolated places, reliability was sometimes an issue even right beside the router. I confess to being addicted to my iPad. It is my camera, my music, my library, my news source, my visual entertainment, where I write my novels, and where I'm now writing this book. (I have come to terms with recognizing this addiction, even while wondering how I would live without it.) The good news is that internet service has improved appreciably in just the last three years, and 5G is standard. During my five weeks of travel in the fall of 2024, only once did I experience an unreliable signal that did not reach my room.

All the other amenities I mentioned are usually present, except for peace and quiet, which is always a bit hit-or-miss in Mexico. If I have any inkling that there might be a problem, I ask for a room away from the street. But noise is unpredictable. What you get when you check in can be radically different after dark. Fortunately, most of the *Pueblos Mágicos* are not known for nightlife, so quiet is more the rule than the exception.

Besides the internet and noise pollution, the only other items that can be problematic are water pressure and water temperature. That is also gradually getting better all over Mexico, with new technological progress, but a lot of places where I stay are older. It is very rarely bad enough to bother me, as long as the water at least gets warm. When I think of my youthful traveling days, hitchhiking and sleeping rough, I realize that I have nothing to complain about.

Unless I happen to be on some kind of schedule, I seldom make reservations too far ahead. One reason is that I do not know in advance how long I will spend in any given town. Booking ahead leaves my itinerary in charge of me, rather than the other way around. There are many online websites available. I like to use booking.com because it has an excellent inventory, and also because, with regular use, I get significant discounts, often below a hotel's rack rate. My general practice is to browse my next destination. After identifying my first lodging choice, I wait until I know when I intend to arrive and often reserve a day or two in advance. As I said, supply usually outweighs demand, so unless I know something to the contrary, I don't expect and have almost never had any problems. Once, I arrived at a hotel and found their price to be higher than what was quoted on the website, and they just told me to book online while I was standing there. They clearly preferred that option to losing the business. Besides that, I think they get pretty much the same amount either way. It is the facilitating website that pays the difference because of my status as a preferred customer.

In some of the lesser-known and more isolated towns, there are no listings on any of the regular booking sites. No problem. I simply type into Google the name of the town, followed by the word lodging in English (or in Spanish using the words *alojamiento* or *hospedaje*). These searches bring up nearly everything available, including the most economical, which do not want to pay a commission to anybody. I'm not sure about their arrangement with Google. However, many of these listings do not show a price. The first thing to do is confirm that the address is actually in the town you want. Next, read the reviews, so you have a sense of the property. When you enter a date asking for a quote, it never works; instead, it tells you to contact the property directly. If you don't speak Spanish, find someone to help you telephone.

I have stayed in some perfectly adequate, even quite nice rooms for under $20. In the isolated town of Pahuatlán, the most expensive place ran $35. But a block away, I found a family hotel called *El Jardin* (The Garden) with a nicer view and a more pleasant ambience. My room was furnished simply, but this happy haven had very good internet and plumbing, plus a television in the room. The price per night? $15 USD.

I visited the town of Angangueo in Michoacán, which is known for its beautiful monarch butterflies. The YouTube video looked very pretty, but with the mariposas out of season, there did not seem to be a lot to do there. Still, it was just off my route from Mexico City to Morelia, so I decided to make a day trip to scope it out. The first step was to leave the inter-city bus in the large town of Zitácuaro. The cheapest hotels are generally by the bus stations. Since in this case I needed little more than a bed, I found a place quickly. It was 200 pesos, or $10. That included internet, a hot shower, and cable television. I definitely got my money's worth.

There has been inflation in Mexico for sure. Three years ago, my rooms were generally in the $20-30 USD range. Now they tend to be between $25 and $35 USD. Or perhaps I am just staying in nicer places now. I do have an affinity for old, pretty buildings that have been updated in terms of amenities. For many readers, the best news about these prices is that the rates are almost always meant for a double room. For a couple, lodging in real Mexico is still extraordinarily affordable.

I prefer to rent hotels near the town's *zocalo* (main plaza). You are probably going to spend the majority of your time in that vicinity, and you can find more restaurants in the town center, so it makes a lot of sense to stay there. And it is usually the prettiest part of town. The smaller *pueblos* generally are not surrounded by horrible contemporary strip mall ugliness, but the larger ones generally are. But whether you're in a magical town or a larger city, the historic section is bound to supply a visual treat.

Bottom line: Don't sweat lodging in the *Pueblos Mágicos*. Except for special events and festivals or long weekends, you are very unlikely to run into any difficulties.

Food

Mexico is a true foodie paradise, and particularly Mexico City, which boasts world-class international cuisine along with a spectacularly diverse array of domestic favorites. In the United States, the food in Mexican restaurants runs traditionally to the Tex-Mex style—you know, tacos, enchiladas, burritos, tostados, et cetera. All of these are mainly variations on one theme, with the same small range of ingredients. So, for most Americans, that is what Mexican food is. But in the last fifteen or twenty years, with the influx of immigrants from farther south (including refugees from Central America), a wider range of Mexican cuisine has arisen all over the US, rich in different fresh ingredients, condiments, and cooking styles.

Northern Mexico, called *Pocho Mexico*, is still primarily Tex-Mex, with a preponderance of meat. This is desert country, with little access to locally grown fruits and vegetables, or to the wide range of native herbs and spices. The southern and eastern regions of Mexico, with their mountains, forests, jungles, and diverse indigenous traditions, offer a staggering diversity of cuisine. "Cuisinology" is not my specialty, so I will not try to catalog it all here (insects, anyone?), but if you travel the backcountry in these regions, you will discover an entire new universe of tasty treats. Two of my personal favorites are mountain trout and wild mushroom soup—they're to die for.

I mainly travel alone, as I have for decades. There are numerous fine restaurants along the *Pueblos Mágicos* trail, but after all this time, I have little enthusiasm for eating by myself in fancy places. Thus, I have likely missed out on some excellent eating opportunities. My preference, particularly for breakfast, is to eat in central markets—fresh, hot, and traditional food lovingly prepared by señoras with lifetimes of experience. Did I mention it's also extremely cheap? And one of the best parts is being surrounded by the vibrant color and bustle of authentic Mexican life. Later in the day, I often waver between small local places and higher-class restaurants if something on the displayed menus appeals to me. I have to confess that I often take my later meal at Chinese buffets, which are becoming more and more common. This has nothing to do with any food preference. Most Mexican restaurants are light on greens and vegetables. In the Chinese places, I can pig out on lots of fresh broccoli.

In the midday heat, I enjoy *licuados* (smoothies), juice, nuts, and fruits. One of my favorites is a glass of *jugo verde*, which is orange juice combined with whatever fresh greens are available. It may be a bit bitter, but it smacks of health and virtuous living. Another good one is the aptly named *vampiro* (vampire)—orange juice and beets. And *jugo de zanahoria*, carrot juice, is always a standby, brimming with vitamins.

Did I mention cheap? Yes, indeed. I delve into this more in the money and costs section, but you will never go hungry in Mexico. In my younger traveling days, I was a vegetarian, and I thrived on a diet of bananas, avocados, fresh fruit, rice, beans, and tortillas. Plenty of delicious, sometimes tongue-scalding homemade salsa also. And finally, I would be remiss if I neglected to mention the mouthwatering array of *pescado* and *mariscos*, fish and seafood, on both coasts. I eat some of this in the mountains at times, but it is not quite the same thing. Be sure not to miss all the scrumptious street foods, vended from carts in the main plazas in the evening or on market days all over town. I personally don't worry about getting sick. Most items on sale look fresh and clean, and in today's Mexico, merchants tend to be fastidious about hygiene as national infrastructure continues to improve.

Language

When I was a young traveler, language was often a bigger issue than it is today. By attrition, the English language has become the lingua franca of travel almost everywhere in the world, which is fortunate for all of us for whom it is our mother tongue. Back in the day, I visited a lot of places, like Greece, Morocco, most of Western Europe, and many parts of Latin America, where not that many people spoke English. I did have decent French from high school and university, which was very helpful. Today, after fifty years of concentrating on Spanish, my French is sadly rusty, but I know that it is inside me there somewhere. My usual process back then was to get a Collins Phrasebook and learn the basics, such as numbers, food, pleasantries, et cetera. That, along with creative sign language, often got the job done. I did suffer some confusion in Greece, where yes is *neh*, no is *okie,* and an upward jerk of the chin signifies a negative, but it was all good fun.

A lot of this difficulty in communication is a thing of the past in contemporary travel. My personal opinion is that this is not some wonderful sign of progress, but I'm a dinosaur. One of the things I always loved about travel is that it turned you into the equivalent of a five-year-old having to learn customs and communication from scratch. That was a major part of the adventure. Whether I approve or not (I don't), it is now child's play to skip across the globe without learning any native language whatsoever. Many people tell me that they don't bother trying because it is completely unnecessary. Everyone speaks English, so why make the effort? This is, of course, a fallacy. It might work in most of Europe, but in Mexico, Thailand, Vietnam, Costa Rica, and a host of other hot destinations, no, everyone does not speak English. If you are visiting tourist locations and doing tourist things, they do. But as soon as you wander off the beaten track, assuming that you ever care to, they don't. Or not nearly as much. Before being specific to Mexico, I want to emphasize the value of learning at least the basics of Spanish, and particularly the pleasantries. The smallest effort on your part will reap rich dividends and will be greatly appreciated everywhere you go. It will also gain you more respect and make it less likely that someone will try to take advantage of you as someone who just fell off the banana boat.

As an aside, many of my older contemporaries do try to learn Spanish, generally using old textbooks or modern apps like Duolingo. Though this effort is admirable, the results will probably fall far short of what they want to accomplish. Let me explain why: In Mexico, the well-educated minority are the exception. Most common people do not speak anything close to formal or grammatical Spanish. Their vernacular is full of slang, dialect, and indigenous vocabulary. They speak very fast and often do not enunciate well. As I said earlier, even a veteran like me is challenged to understand "street" Mexican Spanish. In fact, I have a friend who grew up in Spain who confesses that she also, at times, has no idea what someone is saying.

As an example of why poring over books may be less than helpful, every form of older printed matter will probably tell you to use a formal phrase such as *"Como esta Usted?"* for "How are you?" If there exists a contemporary Mexican who actually ever says this, I have yet to meet him. It is just not a formal culture. If you do use this phrase in an attempt to be polite with someone, she will probably cover her mouth and smile. And you will definitely be marked as a greenhorn.

I have no interest in, nor do I try to teach Spanish, which I don't feel qualified to do anyway. I try to teach communication skills like proper pronunciation, basic phrases, pleasantries, and the like—all the things that can smooth one's travels. You can learn some of this from books and apps, but there is no substitute for speaking up and engaging with the locals. Our generation is often hesitant to follow through on this, fearing to appear foolish. I urge you to resist this impulse. Mexicans are exceedingly gracious, hospitable, and helpful people. They may giggle a bit, a cultural trait that I personally find endearing, but their appreciation of your efforts cannot be overstated. Oh, yes, and above all, speak up and don't mumble!

I am writing this book to tell you that visiting the *Pueblos Mágicos* is neither difficult nor intimidating. But I also do not want to minimize the language issue. Yes, this is all fairly simple for me with my long experience and fluent Spanish. But I am fully aware that it will likely not feel that way for you. And despite my language skills, I do still commit gaffes. That is also part of the fun. A good laugh from others is not meant maliciously; tongue planted fully in my cheek, it's just another opportunity to go home and make fun of the gringos.

The more Spanish you know, the easier your passage will be and the more chances you'll have for pleasant contacts with your hosts. I would not recommend setting off with *zero* Spanish, but it can still be done. Even in the hinterlands, plenty of Mexicans know some English. All the modern young people study it in school. A hotel owner is bound to know the minimum basics needed to run her business. Ditto for clerks selling bus tickets. Scattered all over are men who have spent time, sometimes a lot of time, working in the United States. You will be able to buy a bus ticket, rent a hotel room, and eat a meal without any Spanish. ATMs usually have an English button. You will be able to get by. As for attractions and activities, there are piles of information on the internet. Tripadvisor is an excellent resource, but there are many others. And taxi drivers are also included in the ranks of those likely to know a bit of English. Finally, every town has a Tourist Office. Some of them have been enterprising enough to put up bilingual signage around their attractions, even if nobody is coming yet to enjoy them.

However, if you are starting from zero, I strongly urge you to learn the basics of traveler's Spanish. The grammar is difficult, but that is pretty irrelevant. The best thing is that Spanish is a completely phonetic language. There are some challenging consonant sounds, but the vowels are completely consistent. Once you know these five sounds, they will not change on you. Practice pronouncing them correctly over and over; they are the main key to making yourself understood. This is important. If you pronounce these vowels wrong, you will not be understood. Otherwise, you can foul up the language as much as you want, and people will likely still be able to figure out what you're saying.

There are thousands of cognates, words that are similar or identical in both Spanish and English. That includes nearly all modern and technical terms. There are also a very few bad cognates, or false friends, but not enough to worry about. Don't tell someone you are embarrassed unless you want them to think you are pregnant. "Sensible" means sensitive. There are a few other examples. The standard way to ask if someone has something is to say *"Hay?"* (pronounced with a silent *h*) which means "Are there any?" It's better to use that than *"Tiene?"* which means "Do you have?" You don't want to ask a man if he has *chiles* or *huevos* or a woman if she has *leche* (hot peppers, eggs, and milk). To do so can have some unwanted sexual connotations, though this is not so true as it once was. As for food and menus, you already know a lot of it unless you have never been to a Mexican restaurant. The basics, including numbers, are not all that challenging.

    Most of us realize that languages are difficult, especially for older people. I am of an age where bits of English fall out of my head at inopportune moments. Learning and retaining a foreign language are hard, very hard. The best idea is to tamp down your expectations and be kind to yourself. By the way, Mexicans are well aware that the great majority of "tourists" make no effort to learn Spanish. This makes them sad, and perhaps a bit frustrated. My advice is to be one of the good guys. If you do it, you will be richly rewarded.

    If you already speak adequate or even good Spanish, the news is even better. Strangers rarely start up conversations with me on the street because they don't notice me or pick me out as a foreigner. If you are a North American reading this book, it is likely that you are more noticeable. Once, I ran across an American on my traveler's Facebook group. We were both in Zacatecas and decided to meet up for a day. He was driving around Mexico, so we made an easy day trip to a nearby *Pueblo Mágico*. I was my usual anonymous self, but he was light-skinned, with long and wild white hair. So, I too went from my usual inconspicuousness to getting plenty of attention. My friend was also fluent in Spanish from growing up on both sides of a Texas border town, so we got into a number of spirited conversations. In most of the *pueblos*, the inhabitants see few if any foreigners, and they are friendly and curious. Though they seldom initiate contact with me, I have no such inhibitions. During my 2021 tour, I passed an entire month without seeing a single other foreigner or speaking a word of English. That kind of immersion can do wonders for your language skills.

Mexican Spanish is very rich in slang, dialect, and loan words from indigenous languages. There is still a significant population for whom Spanish is a second language. I was thrilled in the market of Pahuatlán to hear a covey of colorfully dressed old women twittering like birds in an indigenous language. What fun!

The most common indigenous language is Náhuatl, which is descended from the nation's dominant group, the Aztecs. An example of Náhuatl word-usage is the name of my own home base, Mazatlán, which means "place of the deer." But our baseball team's name is *Los Venados,* which is the Spanish for deer. Numerous place names are derived from native languages, as well as the names of many birds, animals, plants, and other parts of the natural world. In the broader Hispanic world, these terms are unique to Mexico. The Spanish words for peanut, owl, vulture, and turkey are *mani, buho, buitre,* and *pavo.* In Mexico, they are *cacahuate, tecolote, zopilote,* and *guacalote.*

In any case, a majority of the *Pueblos Mágicos* bear indigenous, non-Spanish names. Many are quite long and difficult to pronounce, like Tlalpujahua. Try wrapping your mouth around that one. It's too much for me, and I am fluent. Or perhaps Tlatlauquitepec. Even after I practiced saying it, I discovered the locals themselves do not even bother, and they shorten the name by omitting the "tepec." By the way, *Tlal, Tlat,* and *Tlan* are just variants of the suffix meaning "the place of." Finally, one of my favorites is the lovely *Pueblo Mágico* of Tzintzuntzan, located a few miles from Pátzcuaro. The Spanish word is *colibri,* but the Purepécha language version is pure music in its meaning—hummingbird.

You don't really need to commit these crazy names to memory or have an anxiety fit trying to pronounce them. But if you are trying to arrange your transportation, it would be an excellent plan to write them on a piece of paper. Unless, that is, you would enjoy the hilarity of the locals watching you trying to pronounce them.

Money and Costs

In most of Mexico, cash is still king. Most small establishments and many family guesthouses and family hotels do not accept credit cards. The larger supermarket chains, upscale restaurants, and classier hotels do. So, particularly in the outlying *Pueblos Mágicos*, be prepared to be asked to pay in *efectivo*—cash.

Due to fees and add-on charges, cash U.S. dollars are a very inferior mode of exchange in Mexico. Meanwhile, Canadian money can be exchanged easily enough in tourist areas, but often not in small towns where they are seldom seen. I would not consider them suitable for *Pueblos Mágicos* travel. Cash has two drawbacks: The first is that it is inconvenient to carry large amounts of it if you are on a slow journey. And in today's world, I don't consider doing so to be a sound practice—not in Mexico nor in any other country. Opportunistic petty theft can happen anywhere. The second reason is that the exchange rate for cash is significantly inferior. Banks and *casas de cambio* (exchange booths) charge a significant premium that can run to five percent or higher.

Try to avoid changing cash in an airport, unless you don't mind throwing away ten percent of your money. And for that matter, don't buy pesos before you travel. You are sure to take a beating on the rate. Rates may be better away from these very pricey options, but it can also be a hassle to exchange cash in other venues. Banks are not always open, for example. The *casas de cambio* generally offer the lowest rates.

The only truly efficient way to get cash is via an ATM debit card. You get the top daily exchange rate, and many banks cover 100% of your ATM fees. The machines are everywhere, so you don't have to take out large sums, as you can always easily replenish. The biggest drawback is the lower security protections of debit cards compared to credit cards. I keep my available balance fairly low since I can transfer funds in one day, minimizing my risk. Get in the habit of carrying passports, cash, cards, and anything else important inside your clothes. In Mexico, particularly in small towns, the risk of theft or snatching is relatively low, but there is no reason to take a chance. Don't carry any of these valuables in an external bag of any kind. Again, this is not true just for Mexico, but almost anywhere, perhaps even in your own home country.

Here's some ATM guidance: Exchange during the day when there are lots of people around. Most, if not all, machines translate instructions into English. This may or may not be true in the small towns. I do not know for sure, because since I speak Spanish, I never look. The first screen asks for your PIN. It is usually hooded so that nobody else can see the screen. On the next screen, choose *retiro de efectivo*. Be wary of machines that let you choose between being charged in dollars or local currency. You always want to choose local currency. Anywhere in the world, this is true. You want your exchange to be in the country's own currency, in this case, the peso. If you allow them to use a dollar conversion rate, they will be fleecing you of 5% immediately.

On the next screen, select *cheques* if you are withdrawing from a checking account. Then the next screen will give you a selection of withdrawal amounts. Usually, you want more than the choices they post, which are geared to poorer locals, so select *otra cantidad* (a different amount). This is a bit tricky. Every bank has different limits—sometimes it is the limit that your own bank allows, sometimes it is much lower. I personally use Charles Schwab Bank because it allows me one thousand dollars a day. Particularly at home in Mazatlán, I like to transact as infrequently as possible, because I can take the money right home and store it safely. I also much prefer ATMs of common banks, such as Banorte, because their machines are fast and easy to use, and because they allow me the full amount that Schwab allows, which most of the other banks do not.

The next screen asks you to accept the ATM fee from whatever bank you are using. I don't really care that much, since my bank refunds all of it to me at the end of every month, but I like them, so why should I make them pay more? Banorte is charging a relatively low 58 pesos at the time of this writing. A much larger and more widespread bank, like BBVA, charges around 200 pesos. Ten dollars seems usurious to me, but this is typical of their business model, so I try to avoid doing any kind of business with them if possible.

The following screen often asks you to make a small donation. Follow your own conscience. Now is the most important point: They will supply you with a conversion rate and ask if you wish to accept it or decline it. Generally, the decline button is on the bottom left, whereas accept is on the bottom right. They hope you unthinkingly hit it out of rhythm. This is a worldwide banker's scam to rob innocent people blind. Many people are afraid to hit decline because they fear that their transaction will be rejected. Don't worry. The bank still wants its ATM fee. Once you hit decline, the machine shrugs its shoulders and pays you. Never ever accept the conversion rate unless you feel like gifting the banksters 5% of your money.

Some machines ask you if you want a receipt. And at the end, they ask if you want to make another transaction. Say no, and your card comes out. Don't forget this important last step. Someone near and dear, the absent-minded type, left his card behind at the airport, at his first hurdle, and practically wrecked his whole vacation!

As for credit cards, many charge 3% on all foreign transactions. I use Capital One cards that don't. In fact, I use my card whenever possible, as it gives me cash-back rewards everywhere. It goes without saying that you should use this kind of card whenever possible for larger charges like hotels, fancy restaurants, and bus tickets. You get the best rate, perhaps some cash or air miles, and it cuts down on the money you need to carry. I said earlier that I avoid reserving lodging too far in advance if it is practical. But when I am ready to pull the trigger, I do prefer to use my card.

Everywhere North Americans congregate, there are expat Facebook groups. Recently, I saw a comment bemoaning how expensive everything has gotten in Mazatlán. The poster closed by asking plaintively whether there were other places in Mexico which are still cheap. Someone replied that no, that is a thing of the past. It is expensive everywhere, he wrote.

Such spoiled and entitled attitudes make me want to tear my hair out in frustration. If you are wealthy enough to keep a winter vacation home in another country, your moaning turns my stomach. Why don't you look at all the poor Mexicans barely eking out a living in these inflation-ridden times? But of course, they are invisible to some expats. Just part of the furniture. Sorry, rant done.

However, what I find most ironic is these people's utter cluelessness. As I explained in the introduction, tourist Mexico constitutes only a tiny sliver of the country. And yes, prices have moved much higher in tourist Mexico. The locals charge what the traffic will bear. It's called business. In small-town Mexico, there is also some inflation, but it is far more moderate than in Cancún or Cabo San Lucas. The local service economies and crops have not gone up all that much. And Mexico, the real Mexico, is still quite cheap and quite a bargain. I described earlier how I easily find comfortable and pleasant rooms for $25-35. And that is generally the same for a couple. Markets and local restaurants are more than affordable. In Mexico City, recently, I consistently found full breakfasts of eggs, beans, tortillas, orange juice, and coffee for $4. In one of the *Pueblos*

Mágicos I visited, I had a big plate of the same, with coffee but no juice, for $2.25 in a pleasant hole-in-the-wall. Because I spoke Spanish, the indigenous old lady master cook twittered away in her native tongue. I hardly understood a word she said. Thus, the minuscule price of a great breakfast was complemented by some free linguistic entertainment. Again in Mexico City, I found an all-you-can-eat Chinese buffet for $3.50. And in a market, a plate of five small bean-and-cheese tacos for $0.75.

So, don't go telling me that there are no cheap places in Mexico!

Odds and Ends

Once upon a time, you could walk into a pharmacy in Mexico and buy almost anything. You might not have been sure of its quality or if it had expired, but you could purchase it. Times have changed, and many more pharmaceuticals do require a prescription, particularly anything to do with opioids, the production of meth, etc. There is still a workaround for getting your medicines without going through a lot of hassle, locating a doctor, and making an appointment: Look for one of the common pharmacies that have a doctor on-site in an adjoining office. You discuss your condition and explain why you have a legitimate need for the pharmaceutical you are seeking. If she agrees, which is generally so, she will write your prescription, and you can take it back next door to get it filled. Most of these doctors speak at least some English. And the fee is minimal, perhaps fifty or one hundred pesos, depending upon the time spent and your own level of gratitude and generosity.

Smoking is not legal in any public space in Mexico. This would go as far as including the beach. This provision is neither enforced nor enforceable, but it is a good idea to be aware of it. I generally see very little smoking in Mexico. Maybe it is just too expensive.

This is something that is not particularly publicized, and perhaps the government wants to keep a low profile, but possession of small amounts of all drugs (5 grams or less) for personal use has long been decriminalized in Mexico. That even includes heroin and cocaine. Possession of cannabis, or growing it for personal recreational use in quantities less than 28 grams, is now completely legal. There is a hidden provision that you are supposed to apply for a certificate. I don't have any personal information on this, but my bet is that the number of Mexicans who have actually applied for such a certificate is likely to be in the neighborhood of zero. I often smell the distinctive odor of the plant. Despite its legal status, I would suggest discretion. That is just common sense. Prior to 2009, smoking dope in Mexico as a foreigner, particularly a young and long-haired one, was legally somewhat akin to the risk of playing Russian Roulette. But like anywhere, smoking weed (called *mota*) has always been around. Gummies that contain a small amount of THC are also legal, and there are cannabis stores here and there. But currently, you still cannot buy actual marijuana in the shops. As it is in the United States, this area of law is in flux.

Statistically, the most dangerous drug in any country in terms of death and societal destruction is still alcohol. The legal drinking age in Mexico is 18, though questions are seldom asked. Generally, you cannot purchase alcohol after 2 PM on Sunday. Do not drink and drive.

Perhaps you have heard about the less-than-rigid concept of time in Mexico, exemplified in the term *mañana* (literally, *tomorrow*). It is true. Mexicans, in general, are far more flexible regarding time than North Americans. If you are late (well, not too late) for an appointment, it is likely that nobody will notice it, much less mention it. (For that matter, if you blow off the appointment completely, they might not even mention that either. It might be considered rude, and Mexicans are extremely conflict-averse.) So, if you make a date with someone, they may show up. Then again, they may not. This can be frustrating, but the best thing you can do is to train yourself not to get too upset about it. The same ethic applies to repairmen and businesspeople. Some are reliable, others are not. Opening hour signs can be more of a suggestion than a guarantee. There is, however, one small step that you can take to protect yourself from life's little disappointments: When you make a date or an appointment, ask if it is *tiempo mexicano* (Mexican time) or *tiempo americano* (American time). If it is the latter, then the individual is truly committing to showing up and will likely be no more than five or ten minutes late. After all, traffic and transportation issues can be problems.

Another lovely Mexican tradition is the word *ahorita* ("little hour"), supposedly defined as "right away." Perhaps you are waiting for your name to be called in a line or in an office. Your schedule is tight, always a foolish thing to do in Mexico, and you decide to ask the receptionist when you might expect to be seen. Invariably, she will reply "*Ahorita*." This means that your turn will happen today, probably.

The best advice is to learn not to be in too much of a hurry. If this proves too challenging, you may want to reconsider Mexico as your happy place. The people here take all this much more fatalistically than we do. Tardiness or even standing someone up is not considered a big surprise. Best not to get too upset and do what the Mexicans do: Shrug your shoulders and say, "*Ni modo*." What can you do?

Noise. Mexico is a very noisy country. The people love loud music, fireworks, boisterous conversation, and parties any time of the day or night. Mexicans tend to be very courteous and even formally polite depending on the circumstances, but this does not necessarily extend to common courtesy. If they are engaging in a loud conversation outside your room window at 4 AM, they are not trying to be rude. In fact, they are not thinking about you at all. This can extend to loud televisions in an adjacent hotel room. The good news is that most of the smaller *Pueblos Mágicos* have little nightlife. The better news is that noise pollution regulations are beginning to appear.

Sometimes they are even being enforced. When you are renting hotel rooms, check for nearby churches and cathedrals. If you hear loud bells ringing during the day, you are going to hear them at night. Barking dogs can also be a nuisance. I have no suggestions for that. Perhaps packing a long-distance water spray bottle? Or shrugging your shoulders and saying "Ni modo." I have been coming here for a very long time and wish I had something more substantial to offer. But I don't.

PART II:
The Towns

Introduction

I will now get down to providing stories, descriptions, and anecdotes from my explorations along the *Pueblo Mágico* trail. These are not meant to be used as any kind of standard guide, nor will they generally include reviews of hotels and restaurants. What I wish to do is give the reader my impressions of a place, what I liked or disliked, and, I hope, a general sense of each town.

Out of curiosity, I consulted the top budget-traveler resource, the *Lonely Planet* guide (aka the Bible, aka the Very Reliable Source). These slightly sarcastic nicknames are mine as a longtime user of the guides. I call it the Bible because too many travelers take it to be the gospel truth. I have actually seen some get very upset if they couldn't find a certain restaurant or if a price had gone up, which is not too surprising with the significant time lag between a reviewer's visit and the appearance of their findings in a revised edition.

Specifically, the "Bible" sobriquet came about this way: Two Singaporean boys got on a bus in India. The driver asked for 80 rupees. "But it says 75 here," wailed the distraught victim, showing the book to someone unlikely to read English and less likely to care. When I was much younger, I would have been likely to intervene. Now I know better. Why should I detract from the boy's obvious pleasure in mourning his lost ten cents? *What is this book, the travel gospel?* I wondered. (Note: Haggling is a popular blood sport between budget travelers and merchants all over Southeast and South Asia. I have witnessed extended screaming arguments involving tiny and insignificant amounts. Once, I foolishly inserted myself in an argument between a fellow passenger and a tuk-tuk driver because I was waiting for my ride to continue, and so I offered to pay the difference. Both parties turned upon me in a fury for spoiling their fun.)

As for the term "Very Reliable Source," I find myself imagining a young backpacking reviewer working on commission and hurrying around trying to turn a dollar as quickly and easily as possible. What level of credence should you attach to their information? Sadly enough, one hotel might receive a surge in patronage following a glowing *Lonely Planet* review, while its equally pleasant neighbor might be ignored. I stopped using the *Lonely Planet* guide long ago for specifics, but instead I find it valuable as a general guide to attractions and big-picture information on where to go and what to do in any given country.

The unintended consequence of total reliance on guides like *Lonely Planet* is what I alluded to earlier as "herding." Not only do travelers wind up in the same popular destination countries and regions, but when they get there, they tend to clump together in the exact same attractions.

Therefore, if it is not mentioned in the *Lonely Planet* or a similar major guidebook, a town simply does not exist in today's world of tourism. But I do want to give them some minimal credit. They are one of the few information sources that actually mention the *Pueblo Mágico* project, and they do recommend some towns that never turn up in more standard guides or in flashy "Where to Visit in Mexico" YouTube videos.

All of this preamble is to explain some tricky decisions I had to make in terms of which places to feature. Some places like Taxco, San Cristobal de las Casas, Zihuatanejo, Tulum, and San Miguel de Allende have been on standard tourist circuits for many years. They do not need any kind of a boost, and in my opinion, should never have been included in a program whose original concept was to increase awareness of smaller, rural communities with something special to offer. The next "tier" (as I think of it) of *Pueblos Mágicos* includes towns that are definitely on the map, but which may not be instantly recognizable to foreigners. A few of these are Palenque, Pátzcuaro, and perhaps Tlaquepaque. Despite my elitist self-image of "being in the know" about very out-of-the-way places, these more popular towns continue to rank high on my list of personal favorites. After some reflection, I have decided to include them. After all, perhaps they are not quite as much on the travel circuit as I imagine, and it would be a shame to deprive my readers of their charms. Then there is my third tier, of even less well-known towns. These include Valle de Bravo, Malinalco, Cuetzalán, Tepoztlán, and others (all of which are at least cited by *Lonely Planet*).

In this book, I've included close to 75% of the *Pueblos Mágicos* that I have ever visited. With a couple of exceptions, I have chosen not to include the ones that I stumbled upon long ago, before I became aware of the *Pueblo Mágico* program. After all, things have changed a lot in the last thirty or forty years, and my memory suffers from the same deficits that plague most of us old codgers. I've divided the towns into my ten favorites, ten "honorable mentions," and then a larger number of towns that I've deemed "worth a look." That still leaves almost a hundred towns that I have not yet visited. Many are far from Mexico's central region and will require plenty of long-haul bus transportation. Another forty-five were just recently named, giving me - and you - future opportunities for brand-new adventures. For the moment, the chances of running into another foreign traveler in most of them are very remote!

As I mentioned earlier, these accounts are by nature subjective. I know exactly what I like and what I have little interest in, and my tastes will, of course, not always conform to those of readers. The *Pueblos Mágicos* have a wide array of attributes that have led to their inclusion in the program. In approximate order, here are the town traits that most appeal to me:

1. Indigenous peoples and their traditions and culture
2. Lovely pastoral surroundings where I can easily wander off into the countryside and make discoveries
3. Distinctive local cuisines and unusual foods
4. Vibrant contemporary art, including street art
5. Beautiful colonial architecture
6. Local crafts and artisans
7. Political history
8. Religious history and art, including Renaissance art

A few final notes: 1) I visited many *pueblos* during the pandemic, when many museums and other places of interest were closed to the public. Particularly during 2021, even main plazas and town gardens were yellow-taped and off-limits. Obviously, it can be challenging to judge a place's true value under such trying circumstances. 2) An observant reader may notice that I have credited six towns as being Hidden Gems. As this is already a book of "hidden treasures" overall, why have I done this? To me, this is simple. These towns have hit a kind of Daily Double. Not only are they fabulous destinations, but they also share the commonality of being virtually unknown, even to Mexicans. Outside of typing their names into your search browser, I challenge you to find them mentioned anywhere. (Yes, dear reader, buy my book and you can be in the vanguard.)

And now, on to the *pueblos*!

CHAPTER 2:
The Favorites

10) Mexcaltitán, Nayarit
9) Orizaba, Veracruz
8) Xilitla, San Luis Potosí
7) Huasca de Ocampo, Hidalgo
6) Twin Towns:
Coatepec, Veracruz
Xico, Veracruz (Bonus Town)
5) Huautla de Jiménez, Oaxaca
4) Palenque, Chiapas
3) Cuetzalán, Puebla
2) Real de Asientos, Aguascalientes (Hidden Gem)
1) Zacatlán de las Manzanas, Puebla (Hidden Gem)

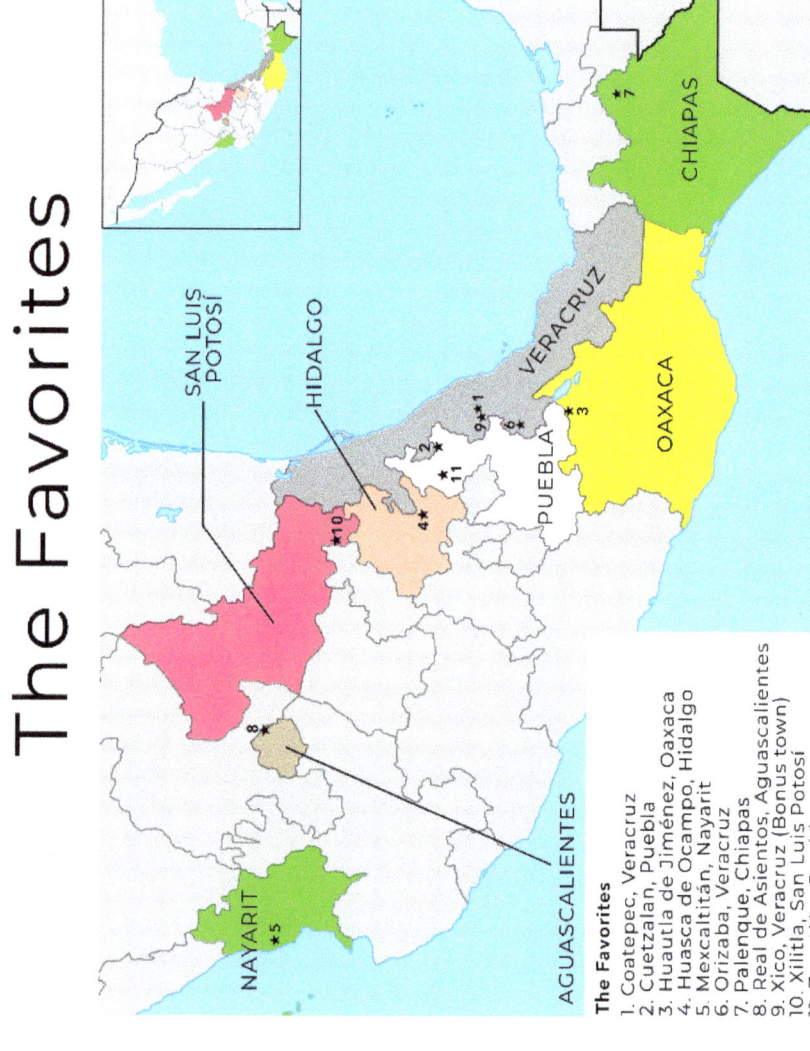

10) *Mexcaltitán, Nayarit*

This tiny fishing village does not contain a lot of special sights. What packs a punch is its unique locale and ambience, along with its role in Mexican history. It is also one of a couple of *Pueblos Mágicos* that were on the initial program roster, lost its status for some mysterious reason, and then was reinstated in 2020. Since its population is only 2,000, Mexcaltitán does not meet the technical requirements, and thus possibly was under review and then finally granted dispensation. In my view, it would indeed be a shame to disqualify it on simple technical grounds.

The name Mexcaltitán translates to "House of the Mexicans." Some historians believe that the site is actually the original Aztlan of mythology, a Náhuatl name for "House of the Egrets," from which the initial residents journeyed to found the island of Tenochtitlan (present-day Mexico City) in the pre-Columbian Aztec era. And to my genuine amusement, the place is also at times called by a third name, the "Venice of Mexico." Similarly, the lovely lake town of Catemaco in the state of Veracruz has at times been referred to as the "Switzerland of Mexico." As far as I am concerned, both of these appellations are silly hyperbole. The only resemblance of Mexcaltitán to Venice is that during the rainy season, the island is prone to flooding. As for Switzerland, all I can say is…no.

Mexcaltitán is not the easiest *pueblo* to get to, but once you arrive at the parking lot by the dock, all misgivings regarding the effort required to reach the town disappear rapidly the instant you take in your initial view. From this moorage, men with motorized launches compete to ferry you across. The day we visited, we were charged a bit over two dollars for the service—be sure to tip. Instead of taking us directly to the town tie-up, our guide first circumnavigated the island. The stellar vistas, along with the abundance of avian life, made this ten-minute circuit a thrilling one. And even from a distance, it was lovely to take in the vibrantly colored houses with their distinctive roofs and stilts, which give the town so much charm.

Mexcaltitán is without doubt a town dependent on tourism. Without that income, it would just be a poor fishing settlement. There are numerous establishments selling souvenirs, and plenty of attractive places to eat, with tons of seafood at bargain prices. But when I say tourist town, I mean for domestic visitors. We saw no other foreigners other than a Mexican-French couple traveling around making YouTube videos, and one other quirky exception, I will get to shortly. Due to the town's relative isolation and lack of guidebook mentions, you are not likely to run into other outsiders here.

The diameter of the island is 1,100 feet (340 meters), laid out like a wheel with spokes leading to the central plaza. It is a very compact place. Kathy, our friend Nancy, and I wandered along the main lane leading to the Centro, concentrating on stands and boutique-like art and clothing stores. Well, at least they did (in the list above of what most intrigues me on my voyages, shopping and souvenir buying are notable for their absence). There were some lovely and unusual goods on display. Neither of them is a big walker, and it was already quite warm in early May, so they soon settled into a pretty outdoor restaurant for drinks and lunch, allowing me to explore at my leisure.

The hour I spent walking around was enough time to explore most of the nooks and crannies of this tiny place, and it was an unalloyed pleasure. It is hard for urban North Americans to imagine the serenity of a venue without automobiles. The only pavement was on the avenue from the dock into and on the main plaza. Everywhere I explored was full of color and humming with a sense of village life far removed from modernity. Almost everywhere, anyway. The town is far from poverty-stricken. Most young women were dressed stylishly. Like the rest of the world, almost everyone had a cell phone. Mexcaltitán is off-the-path but certainly not off-the-grid. The people were friendly enough, without any of the staring that can occur in towns where seeing outsiders constitutes a major event. There were plenty of dogs, all completely non-aggressive, which tends to be the rule in Mexican towns, but not always in the countryside.

There was some scenic architecture in the Centro, including the small Museo del Origen and some municipal buildings. The small Catholic shrine was a jewel. Sitting in front of it was a stringy-haired elderly man with light skin, clearly not a local. Except he basically was—he turned out to be an itinerant Italian monk who had mysteriously arrived in Mexcaltitán decades earlier and stayed. We chatted in Spanish, his accent still noticeable. The only other outsiders I spoke with, assuming he could be considered such, were the couple making the YouTube video.

A short walk off the plaza stands the Hotel La Gran Tenochtitlan. It is very colorful and charming, full of flowers, and definitely clean and well-kept. It is also the only accommodation on the island. We were unable to stay, but I would very much like to return and spend the night in such quiet and serene surroundings. I would be more than happy to spend at least a full day soaking up Mexcaltitán's enchanting ambience.

Getting There: Definitely not the easiest of *Pueblos Mágicos* to reach. It is the only one I have driven to, since it is just over one hundred miles from my home in Mazatlán. We took the toll road, which was fast, expensive, and boring. We returned on the Libre, the free highway, which passes through many interesting small towns, but it added an hour to the trip. Watch the road signs at small country intersections, which are not all prominent. Also, stay vigilant for *topes* (speed bumps) if you value your suspension. From Tepic, it is forty-seven miles to Mexcaltitán, and you pass near the very well-known *Pueblo Mágico* of San Blas, if you wish to do both. By bus from either Tepic or Mazatlán, you can get to the nearby town of Santiago Ixcuintla. From there, you need a taxi to the dock. Facebook says there are combis or colectivos all the way to Mexcaltitán from Tepic, but I cannot verify this.

9) *Orizaba, Veracruz*

This town should probably be called a "Magic Small City," as it has a population of over 123,000, making it a bit too large for my usual tastes. But its joys and delights far outweigh its urban feel. A brief aside: Ironically, Orizaba is only half an hour away from an even larger *Pueblo Mágico*, Córdoba, which has 139,000 inhabitants. During my 2022 circuit, I found a small bus route right out of Orizaba to a third town, Coscomatepec, then went north on a small road through the hills to Xalapa (also known as Jalapa), the capital of Veracruz state. This is exactly the type of ultra-authentic bus adventure in which I delight. My original intent before discovering this "back door" route had been to travel from Orizaba to Veracruz (the city), and then double back to Xalapa. This would have taken me right through Córdoba. But would I have even seen fit to stop and check it out? The answer is likely no. And why not? At the time, Córdoba had not even been designated a Pueblo Mágico. It was one of the big "drops" of the summer of 2023, which suddenly added 47 new towns to the program, also succeeding in pulling the rug out from under my slow but steady progress in visiting as many as I could. The unstated lesson here, once again, is that Mexico is replete with wonderful, undiscovered gems, and I will never do more than scratch the surface.

But back to Orizaba. It is an absolute jewel of a town. A major asset is its stunning location, at the foot of its eponymous volcano, the Pico de Orizaba, which at 5,636 meters (18,490 feet) is the third tallest mountain in North America (behind McKinley/Denali and Mount Logan), besides being the continent's highest volcano. The states of Veracruz (where Orizaba is) and Puebla, east of Mexico City, are situated in the high hilly terrain above the Gulf Coast, marking them as my strong favorites for natural beauty. Blessed with a temperate springlike climate, there is plentiful rainfall, and the region is thickly vegetated and full of flowers. Orizaba town sits at 1,235 meters (4,000 feet). The only drawback to this relatively low altitude is that clear views of the majestic Pico de Orizaba are hard to come by. Fortunately, this was remedied for me when I visited the more mountainous Coscomatepec.

Interestingly enough, in my fifty years of visiting Mexico, I have never spent a summer in the country, and have in fact only visited one single time during that season, when I attended a meditation retreat in August 2005. (The problem then was cold, not heat, as the monastery was very high up in the mountains.) Summers in Mazatlán are wet and torrid, and I am content to escape to the Pacific Northwest. But if the time comes that I decide to stay in Mexico, Orizaba, with its much more agreeable weather, is very high on my list of possible summer refuges.

I cannot recall another town with such a concentration of pretty parks and plazas. They are dotted everywhere in the western half of the municipality, which abuts the mountain's slopes. You can walk aimlessly for hours and be guaranteed shady respites, complete with statuary and monuments. There are also quite a few quaint bridges, owing to the fact that the Rio Orizaba bubbles down from its high source and traverses the town. Unlike your typical Mexican urban watercourse, this river runs clear and cold, with neither litter nor pollution. It is bordered by nature trails on both sides, and the promenade is one that I could easily walk daily without any risk of tedium. If that were not enough, there is an actual small zoo alongside the path with clusters of cages devoted to different groups of fauna every few minutes. And it is all absolutely free of charge. In fact, writing this passage is making me want to go back for another visit and perhaps even raise Orizaba's ranking in my list!

For those looking for a challenging hike, there is a small, paved footpath at the edge of town leading upward to a scenic viewpoint of the volcano. It climbs the Cerro del Borrego, the "Hill of the Sheep." This trail is reasonably steep, with a 1,500-foot elevation gain, and at nearly ten kilometers (six miles) the round trip is no joke. To top it off, it was drizzling on my first full day in town. Under such conditions, no sane person would choose the hike. However, my online profiles are headlined by the sobriquets "Wanderer," "Hill Climber," and "Storyteller," so what choice did I really have? I can't let my imaginary fan club down!

Wet and tiring it was, but a considerable payoff came to me in the form of a couple of long, deep conversations with some fellow "old guys" I bumped into along the way. One of them was particularly noteworthy, a man who had lived in New Mexico for thirty years, working in an auto repair shop. He had returned to his birthplace in 2020 to visit his mother, who was dying of COVID, then decided to stay and begin his retirement. I guess I am not the only eccentric around. He said that he made this hike nearly every day. The other guy was an ethnobotanist with long and wild silver hair, whom I mainly listened to expounding about nature lore for nearly thirty minutes.

Few normal people make this trek on any regular basis. For less intrepid readers, I am happy to report that there is a popular *teleférico* (cable car) on the banks of the river, which whisks you up with great views (on a dry day), and relieves you of only about five dollars round trip. So, despite the fog, mist, and drizzle, there were plenty of Mexican tourists at the top. Besides the undependability of getting any clear view of the volcano, the whole area is a kind of open-air museum, with an old chapel and a small fort from the War of Independence (well, one of them—Mexico seems to have enough Independence Days to make your head spin). There are also some snack and souvenir stands, of course, and a small cafe. My New Mexico friend was sitting there, having arrived well before me after I dawdled with my other new acquaintance, and insisted on buying me a *cerveza*, whether I wanted it or not. I have to admit that I was content to escape the steady drizzle. And happily, it soon ceased, making my downhill passage far more pleasant.

So, is all this enough to make Orizaba a truly "magical" place? I think so—but there's lots more. The plaza area boasts an array of stunning architecture, including the cathedral and the storied Iron Palace. There are also many old churches and temples scattered throughout the town. Orizaba and Córdoba lie along the route Cortez took from Vera Cruz to Tenochtitlan, so the Spanish-style architecture is as old as you can get in Mexico. In fact, Orizaba was named the best *Pueblo Mágico* for its surprising architecture in 2022.

Finally, to frost the cake, there are the museums. Orizaba boasts about fifteen, mostly compact and many theme-oriented, such as the Cinema Museum, the Beer Museum, the Soccer Museum, the Modern Technology Museum, and the Hotel Museum. I don't want you to accuse me of making this up, but in the Tourist Office, I bought one booklet of tickets for the whole shebang and all for the princely sum of 50 pesos, or $2.50! I wasted some of my hard-earned cash, only visiting eight or nine for lack of time. I actually did not feel the need to see them all. After decades of traveling, I am somewhat "museum-ed out" and fairly picky. Have you ever walked through a museum dutifully reading the descriptions on all the exhibits, only to realize that you have no use for all that information? For better or worse, I came to that conclusion many years ago.

Historic center of Orizaba

Anyway, to make matters worse, the first museum I walked into, which was almost right outside the tourist office, was the Beer Museum, where I was soon greeted with a full cup of a brew of my choice, naturally, at no charge. So I decided to pretend that I had purchased the beer, and that all my other visits were gratis. But then again, where in the USA can you get a glass of beer for two and a half bucks? I also have to confess that the gratis part is not wholly inaccurate. As a permanent resident, my Mexican Senior Citizen card entitles me to free entrance to most public museums and ruins in the country. By the way, the Beer Museum was surprisingly one of the most interesting to me. I live in the home of the Pacifico Brewery, and it was fascinating to trace the history, interrelationships, and corporate ownerships of so many of the brands that I have sampled over the years.

There are advantages to being in a bigger place. Many of the smaller *Pueblos Mágicos* have limited restaurant and cuisine choices. That's not the case in Orizaba. In this rich, hilly agricultural region, there is a full spectrum of fresh foodstuffs. Always drawn to the small, local, and authentic, rather than fine dining, I discovered some working-class eateries where I could get a full meal for $2-3. (I know you think I am making this up. Inflation is real in Mexico, so three years later you probably will need to spend $3-4.) For those who enjoy it, there is nightlife too. But I am an old man, so nighttime almost always finds me in my room.

Did I mention the flowers? Most Mexican towns have many stalls or entire flower markets. Orizaba's goes on for a full square block. The quantities of beautiful blooms are astounding. I have often wondered what happens to the loads of bouquets that are not sold before they lose their freshness.

Despite its size, Orizaba has a typically laid-back Mexican vibe. The streets are wide and uncluttered, with only light traffic. There is no hustle and bustle. The whole town is fastidiously clean, as are most mountain towns in the country. I have mentioned its desirability as a long-term summer escape. Yet for a foreigner who is not wedded to beach life or English-speaking social activity, one could do far worse in terms of a prospective full-time residency.

I spent three days in Orizaba and wished that my itinerary allowed for more. And in those three days, I never saw one single person who stood out as a foreign tourist. Not one. How can this be true in such an amazing destination? I do hope that I am not letting the cat out of the bag, as I greatly appreciate the place just the way it is. But I doubt that this little book is going to change things much. Ah, but I can dream.

Getting there: Orizaba and Córdoba are easily accessed from Mexico City, Puebla, and Veracruz.

8) *Xilitla, San Luis Potosí*

The Huasteca, where the Xilitla *pueblo* lies, is an extensive region once dominated by the indigenous Mesoamerican Huastec tribe, who still make up a significant portion of the population here. It covers parts of many states mainly northeast of Mexico City and is primarily known for its highlands full of caves, canyons, wild streams and rivers, waterfalls, and exuberant and exotic flora and fauna. This enormous area belongs to nature, not humanity. With its wealth of scenic wonders, native heritage, and outdoor activities, one would expect it to be a big draw for tourists, both domestic and international. But there aren't any of that latter tribe, at least that I have ever run into.

I visited Xilitla, which means "Place of the Snails" in Náhuatl, in the seventies on another traveler's recommendation, in order to see the handiwork of the English artist Edward James and his crazy jungle sculpture garden. Nearly fifty years later, that was all I could remember of the town. Back then, I was close to penniless, sleeping in the cheapest *casas de huespedes* (humble, family-oriented guesthouses) and subsisting on beans, rice, tortillas, bananas, and avocados. So, I looked forward to a revisit with anticipation.

The bus trip into town was long, slow, and spectacular. The mountain jungle roads are narrow and winding, and the buses have seen better days. No chickens on them, though. The scenery and vistas are breathtaking. At about 700 meters (2300 feet) above the Gulf Coast, the hill country's tropical rainforest is green and mist-shrouded, and there are brilliantly colorful flowers all about. And don't forget, the journey is also part of the adventure. Just arriving in town, with its views of so many habitations clinging to the verdant hillsides, I felt the town's aura of magic. Still, times have changed, and boutique sensibilities have crept into what was once a truly isolated village. I don't begrudge these invasions, which add plenty of colorful crafts and fusion restaurant menus to the scene. And still, few or no foreigners.

Beautiful vista from Xilitla Centro

And now for a bit of a public service announcement: Do not trust Apple Maps in rural Mexico. The app does all right in the cities (usually) in leading you to the best-known spots. But in the sticks, Apple will have you chasing your tail. It took me forty minutes of lugging my backpack up and down many false and mislabeled streets and alleys before I finally found my hotel. In my opinion, Google Maps is more reliable, if not perfect. (Disclaimer: I just read a piece by some folks who visited the town in 2017 and couldn't find their lodging using Google either. Get a phone number before you go.) As to Siri or Alexa or whoever she is who is supposedly guiding you, "her" Spanish is so atrocious that it borders on ludicrously hilarious. Spanish is a phonetic language. Why can't these obscenely wealthy corporations find some AI that can pronounce it correctly?

The layout of Xilitla features numerous elevation changes, resulting in a daily routine with more than enough stairs. My hotel, once I finally found it, was located in a natural basin on the south side of town. Back and forth, stairs all day. The Centro is above the highway in a large, level area. There can be found all the civic buildings and the zocalo, along with trendy hotels, restaurants, and one excellent attraction which I will discuss later. A number of lanes open onto the plaza from the north and south. I was fortunate to be in town on Sunday, when all of these arteries were filled with a street market bursting with produce, drinks, snacks, artisans, and an array of household goods. I love these markets, which are a weekly occurrence in many large towns and fill the day with vibrant life and festivity. Xilitla is not actually a large town, but as the only one in the general area, it serves as a hub. From the Centro, the views are magnificent - and via a long walk straight down into the jungle, you can visit the estate of Las Pozas, Edward James' eighty-acre refuge from the world.

James, sometimes known as the Mad King of Xilitla, was an English poet and the founder of the surrealism movement. He exiled himself from Britain to the USA during WWII and bought his land in Mexico in 1947. Sometime after that, he began creating his sculpture garden, a process which continued until finally halted by his death in 1984. On my first visit in the late 1970s, the place was barely known. I don't have many memories of coming to Xilitla or of getting to the garden. By road, it is 3.6 kilometers (just over two miles). There are two reasons I know for sure that I walked there back then: first, because I would not have been caught dead in a taxi, and second, because any taxi would have been considered an unaffordable luxury even if I had wanted it.

Sculpture garden

Upon arrival back then, there was almost nobody around. The caretaker asked for 10 pesos, less than a dollar, and gravely cautioned me about the slick, muddy trails up and down the waterfall. I spent about two hours wandering around, appreciating the wild foliage, flowers, singing waterfalls, and mystical aura of this garden paradise.

On the other hand, the famous-but-bizarre oversized cement creations, which seemed like grey dinosaurs in the jungle, failed to delight me either back then or more recently. Delightful or intrusive, the entire scene is quite different today, and by my lights, not in a good way.

This time around, when I visited the town, it was the second season of COVID. Mexico had been hit very hard, and the ambience was quite subdued for this particular culture. Nobody was resisting mask usage, although too many had pulled the masks down from their noses, greatly reducing their efficacy. I asked around for the best walking route. Of course, everyone recommended a shared taxi instead, but that is not for me, generally. Old habits die hard, and I would never want to miss the lovely downhill "shortcut" walk with its last stretch along a jungly dirt road. In any case, I was directed to a kiosk in the plaza. As this was a Saturday, there was a line to the window.

The line was all Mexicans, naturally. A sign advised me that I must buy tickets in advance right there, at a price of about $2.50. When I reached the girl, I discovered that I also needed to choose a time slot, and that entrance was only available with guided group tours. See what I mean about the old days? So much more free and fun. This is even more striking to me as I am well aware that Mexicans prize their individuality and are less than fond of rules, regulations, and regimentation.

An hour later, after eating a sandwich and buying a bottle of cold water, I set out. And yes, the hike was gorgeous and not too strenuous, though during the first leg I had to watch my step carefully for loose stones on the old cobblestoned byway.

When I finally reached the entryway to Las Pozas, there was a small crowd of visitors milling about, waiting for their entry time slot. There were some artists' tables. I struck up a conversation with a long-haired young man with the glossy brown skin common to indigenous ethnicities. He spoke the most beautiful Spanish I had ever heard in Mexico—clear, grammatical, and literate. We talked about life, art, and philosophy for about thirty minutes while I awaited my own entrance time. It turned out that he was a local boy who now lived in Mexico City. His art was luminous, fashioned from thin silver wire and beads, each creation folded into various astronomical shapes. I had to buy one for Kathy.

The tour was anti-climactic and disappointing, pretty much in accord with my expectations. I loathe being in a crowd, particularly when it's moving slowly and I feel like we're crawling around like snails. The tour leader droned on, with far too much detail regarding James and his work, much of which I already knew (thanks, Google), and, frankly speaking, had little interest in, adding to my already overstuffed mind. On top of that, many of the old sculptures were in the throes of a slow erosion. The jungle always wins in the end. Still, it was an extravagantly beautiful spot and a feast for the senses.

After an hour on the tour, I was thrilled to get away. I don't know if you can call it claustrophobia if you are outdoors, but that's how it ended up feeling. Outside the portal, I sampled the snack and drink tables. One sold a very scrumptious sorbet made from tropical goodies, like the passion fruit flavor I selected. It turned out to be a specialty of the region—yet another reason to come to this part of the Huasteca. Finally, I took a shared taxi back to town. No more excuses. I am far from poor in my old age, it was dead uphill, and I had already sampled the scenery. Besides, my fare was less than a dollar.

It turns out that the real spectacular art is back in the center of town. Leonora Carrington, another expatriate Brit who was also active in surrealism, had joined James in Xilitla for a period.

As well as being a big mover in the early feminist epoch, she was an amazingly talented sculptor and painter. I don't know how well known she is, since I am not a student of art, but her work blew me away. I had first seen her large sculptures in a museum in the beautiful city of San Luis Potosí, a week before coming to Xilitla. But the tidy and well-kept Carrington Museum in this *Pueblo Mágico* features many of her stunning small pieces and turned out to be the highlight of my visit. Truly, Xilitla meets all the requirements for a genuinely magical place and is well worth your time and energy, despite its relatively isolated location.

7) *Huasca de Ocampo, Hidalgo*

One of the most pleasant "starter" *Pueblos Mágicos* circuits is accessible just a couple of hours north of Mexico City, from Pachuca, capital of the state of Hidalgo. Of the colonial cities in central Mexico, Pachuca offers fewer attractions than most. The number one draw is its famous clock tower. Other than that, Pachuca's *Centro Historico* is fairly pedestrian.

But Pachuca easily makes up for its deficits by offering three excellent *Pueblos Mágicos* in close proximity, with the farthest from the city, Huasca de Ocampo, located only 37 kilometers (23 miles) away. The two closer communities are Mineral del Monte and Mineral del Chico, which both hold spots in my Honorable Mentions group. I have one important heads-up for this particular mini-tour: Carry warm clothes, especially in the cooler months.

Drawn both by the towns' proximity and the appealing YouTube videos about them, I had tentatively planned to visit all three in my first and most extensive *Pueblos Mágicos* circuit. But an unexpected complication derailed this plan during my night spent in Mineral del Monte, which sits at an elevation of approximately 2,700 meters (8,900 feet). In a word, it was cold. More than cold. At that elevation, the night was absolutely freezing, and I had only packed warm-weather clothing. I ended up beating a hasty retreat from the town and decided to skip Mineral del Chico, which lies at about the same elevation. I moved right on to Huasca, farther east. It was an easy ride in one direct combi. And Huasca, at just over 2,000 meters (6,800 feet) elevation, seemed almost balmy in comparison. In fact, it is lower than Mexico City, and I enjoyed perfect weather during my three days there.

Huasca has one important distinction and pride of place: It was the very first town to be designated a *Pueblo Mágico*, all the way back in 2001 during the infancy of the program. That would lead you to believe that it is a truly worthy choice, and you would be correct in thinking that. In fact, a few miles outside of town is a UNESCO World Heritage Site, the *Prismas Basálticas* or Basalt Prisms, which alone merit its selection. And there is plenty else in Huasca to delight in, besides enjoying it as a welcome refuge from freezing to death. The town center is flat, without surrounding slopes, so it cannot match the ethereal views of its two nearby cousins, but the setting is open and handsome. It is clear that being a longtime beneficiary of the government program has paid off. The municipality exudes an aura of prosperity, and there are few signs of the rural poverty that can be seen in other parts of Mexico. But Huasca's is an old-fashioned kind of prosperity that radiates charm and is completely laid-back.

I had not investigated lodging yet, as I was arriving a day or two earlier than intended. I might have done so early in the morning, while shivering inside my Mineral del Monte hotel, but the WiFi signal was almost nonexistent there. As detailed in my Lodging section in the Practicalities, this is very rarely a problem in these towns, but it does occur. So, after arriving in Huasca, I walked up a side street from the plaza, where I glimpsed a couple of hotel signs. While I was eying the first one, a man sprang out of its neighbor and offered me a room for 400 pesos, a bit less than $20 at that time. Later on, I noticed the rack rate of 800 pesos above the reception desk.

Even though the weekend was starting, there were clearly far more rooms than prospective lodgers. I was more than pleased with that price and checked in.

The room was fairly basic and uninspiring in its decor. In 2021 you could generally get a lot for your 800, so that sum would have definitely felt pricey. Of course, I was only paying half that. Still, my space was clean, quiet, and comfortable, with plenty of light. And as I have stated, I don't spend much time indoors during the day, so all I need are the basics. This time, there was even a bonus. To my great pleasure, the room had its own router, the first time I had seen this on the trip (and to this day, the only time I've seen that in Mexico). Thus, the WiFi signal was strong and reliable. The shower had low pressure, but the water was hot and did not run out, which is a frequent hazard with older places in Mexico. In short, for what I was paying, the room was a fabulous bargain.

I spent the afternoon and evening strolling around the town. The Centro was filling up with domestic visitors coming in for the weekend, including a good number of couples and family groups wandering aimlessly about. The best adjective for the ambience might have been rural chic. There were plentiful rows of food and art stands (the most eye-catching being those offering heaps of toasted little creatures, i.e., insects), though not packing the arena like they would during a full-on weekend market. And similarly to most of the main plazas in Mexico, there were outside restaurants all around the perimeter, with people drinking beer and snacking.

Getting back to the six-legged variety of snack food, what is your reaction? A big yuck? Of course, what we eat and how we feel about it is really just a matter of cultural conditioning. Muslims don't touch pork, devout Hindus would rather die than harm a cow, and the Vietnamese have dog restaurants—which I admit is a bridge too far for me. But insects are just a mini-bite of nutritionally rich toasted protein.

Market food stall

I was first introduced to insect cuisine in Thailand. Walk around any night market in that country and you see them being sautéed in sizzling woks before being sold in small paper bags like french fries. I had encountered this sight frequently, but as a semi-vegetarian, I had never sampled them. That failure came to an end one New Year's Eve in the northern enclave of Chiang Mai.

I found myself in the company of two much younger American girls. The witching hour was drawing near. Passing a stand, we started daring each other to indulge. Abstaining did not seem like my best option. Wimping out would certainly completely eliminate my already very slim chance of getting lucky. We bought and shared a baggie, crunching them down, while chasing each mouthful with a swig of beer. My biggest impression was saltiness with a slight bitter aftertaste. Not my favorite, but not a big deal either. (Daring or not, I still slept alone that night.)

In Mexico, you find insects as condiments in traditional recipes in the state of Oaxaca, primarily grubs and worms. In the highlands north and east of Mexico City, in places like Huasca, the grubs are accompanied by crickets. The stands were offering free samples, though with the deep piles of them available, the quoted price seemed practically free anyway. I tentatively munched on one. No worries. You can floss out the wings and legs, I suppose, but one cricket was enough for me. All in all, I prefer chomping on tiny frog legs, no matter how grossed-out Kathy was the last time I indulged in them, also in Thailand.

Huasca was also wonderfully quiet. Living in a beach vacation town, I have to put up with loud salsa and mariachi, and I try to avoid them on my travels. Up in the hills, there is little or none of it. In the evening, the air was filled with gentle modern rock and pop, or lovely classical music. I'm sure that this would come as a surprise to tourists in Cancún and Puerto Vallarta. I really would love to have a megaphone to shout out to these unsuspecting hordes that Mexico is not what you think it is. But I don't.

Everything was still festive in the morning. After breakfast, I hung out watching the street singers and dancers who were performing for crowds all around the plaza. Then I was ready to head out to the area's number one attraction, the Prismas Basálticas (Basalt Prisms) Park. The map said it lay six kilometers (four miles) outside of town. I approached the tourist kiosk looking for information on public transportation. The girl told me that there was no bus, only taxis. I knew from experience that asking her was likely a fool's errand, but I thought I would try anyway. Few foreigners visit here, and well-to-do Mexicans either have their own vehicles or will use a taxi. The idea of riding a public bus or, heaven forbid, walking somewhere is not part of their cultural mindset. Of course, I soon learned there was a regular bus that passed the turnoff to the park, less than a kilometer's walk away.

You already know by now that I am a walker, and that distance was hardly imposing. As always, the hike was well worth the effort on this warm, sunny day, and I met a lot of fun people and saw a lot of sights I would have missed had I taken motorized transportation. And anyway, I rode the bus back to Huasca after a short stroll to the turnoff.

A twenty-minute walk out from Huasca, pretty much in the middle of nowhere, there were two vendor tables by the side of the road. At one, an elderly couple was selling homemade honeys and jams. At the other, there were piles of used books. Don't ask me why. The people were very kind and friendly, and they urged me to try samples of the honey and jam, even though I told them that I could not really fit jars inside my small traveling pack. I did buy a slim old copy of *The Old Man and the Sea* in Spanish, for all of ten pesos. And I had some great conversations. Like so many things in Mexico, why these people chose to be where they were, and how they expected to make any real money was a mystery. I was the only pedestrian, and no passing cars stopped while I visited.

A little farther down the road, I passed a house whose lawn was bordered by flower bushes; a lovely palette of tropical colors. In the front yard was a menagerie of chickens, ducks, turkeys, dogs, cats, and goats, a riot of farm creatures coexisting in easy harmony. This is why walking in the Mexican countryside is such a joy—you never know who you will meet or what you will see next. And you'll miss out on all of it if you whizz by in a vehicle. That's my main argument against destination-based "bucket list" travel. In your haste to get to the "main event," you forget to stop and smell the roses.

Ah, but what a main event the Basaltic Prisms are. The complex is expansive, filled with open lounging areas, restaurants, and pulque and drink vendors. Finally, you come to the ravine, or *barranca*. Once a part of a vast hacienda, this stupendous natural wonder was encountered and popularized by the German explorer and naturalist Alexander von Humboldt in 1803. The natural walls, which go on and on, are lined by polygonal columns of rock up to 50 meters (164 feet) high. Cascading waterfalls are scattered throughout. Wherever you choose to walk in the area, you are rewarded by awe-inspiring vistas. Fittingly, I ran into the first recognizable foreigners I had seen in over four weeks, an older German couple. It almost felt odd to speak English after not having done so for so long. It seems likely that Huasca was chosen as the very first *Pueblo Mágico* based upon this stupendous attraction.

After another delightful Saturday evening in town, after breakfast the next day, I walked to the exquisite village of Santa Maria Regla, which was once the seat of the old hacienda mentioned in the previous paragraph. It lies partway between Huasca and the Prisms, and I had no hesitation about repeating a bit of the short, pleasant walk. The village is absolutely gorgeous and full of character, hearkening back to a forgotten era. In fact, it would not be a bad place to base yourself if you're looking for utter tranquility. A short distance away from the village is a small lake functioning as a working trout farm. I was particularly amused by a sign forbidding bicycles and horseback riders there. What kind of past problems had the equines caused, I wondered to myself? Finally, there is a circular amphitheater-like area featuring about 18 mostly identical restaurants and some souvenir stores. I never understand how this kind of setup can support so many indistinguishable enterprises and suspect that the first two eateries on either side of the entrance portal hog more than their share. Nevertheless, I sat down and relished one of the best meals in memory, an entire fish with rice, salad, bread, and a beer for under $9.

All in all, you could do far worse than spending a few days in Huasca de Ocampo.

Getting there: Huasca is less than an hour east of Pachuca, Hidalgo state's capital, with frequent combi service that also passes through Mineral del Monte.

6) *Twin Towns*

On its own, this lovely town would not have made my Top Ten list. But as they say, location, location, location. This *Pueblo Mágico* gives the discerning traveler a true "three-for-one." 14 kilometers (9 miles) to the north of Coatepec is one of the prettiest and least-visited colonial cities in Mexico, Xalapa, the capital city of the state of Veracruz. And 10 kilometers (6 miles) to the southwest is Xico, another tiny and charming *pueblo*. Public buses whiz between the three along scenic lanes, and you can traverse the whole area for about a dollar (well, half of that for a senior like me!). It would be easy to while away a relaxing week or two in these environs, and I was lucky enough to score one of the most pleasant hotels in the area. More on that later.

Coatepec, Veracruz

Coatepec also received a bit of an unfair advantage in my ratings by virtue of the fact that my visit coincided with the *Día de Muertos* (Day of the Dead), the celebration of which goes on for days. This could easily be considered the most colorful holiday event in the Mexican calendar, with public spaces filled with vibrant, fantastical images akin to our own Halloween decorations. Though it is a feast for the eyes, the holiday is actually otherwise fairly subdued by Mexican standards, without wild revelry, loud music, or fireworks. Instead, the people become introspective and reserved while honoring their departed loved ones.

Google Maps got me off the bus—correctly this time—close to my lodging, the Hotel Miguel Arcangel, a short walk from the center of town. The hotel was a delight. Clean (as in, eating off the floor clean), with a wonderfully friendly staff. In fact, the owner designated herself as my *tía* (auntie) following our first conversation (I know that I am older than she is. This stuff just happens. In Gdańsk, Poland, I stayed at the Mamas and Papas Hostel. The enthusiastic girl who checked me in said that everyone called her dad Papa. When he first greeted me, there was that awkward moment when the ramifications of how he introduced himself to me sank in.) It was also extremely quiet, give or take the occasional early-morning rooster. The serenity made the walk from the Centro well worth it. The old building sported bright and colorful new paint, which blended in well with the hotel's charming antiquity. My room was a bit small for two, perhaps, but very comfortable with a wonderful bed. And everything worked great—WiFi, hot shower, television. Each room had a nice view of the pretty garden area. The final touch was waking up to resplendent sunshine pouring in and framing the window. Talk about an inspiring way to start the day (see photo). Finally, the price was ridiculously low, at only $23 US, although as I'm writing this, I see that it has risen considerably since the fall of 2022. I had booked for two nights but wound up fitting a third into my schedule.

This wonderful introduction to Coatepec set the tone for my visit. Leaving the hotel, I found myself on a spacious and lightly trafficked boulevard heading downtown. The first thing I saw was a crystal-clear view of the Pico de Orizaba (Peak of Orizaba) in the distance, which had been hidden by clouds back when I was in the town of Orizaba. Looking westward, the peak of Cofre de Perote, also snow-covered, was clearly visible. The serene and spacious feeling elicited by those views permeated the whole town. The central garden was verdant and shaded, as are so many in this rainfall-rich region of Mexico. Resplendent Day of the Dead decorations full of color and mystery filled the space, watched over by a number of monuments to historical figures. Across the street was a lovely old cathedral flanked by large, graceful trees. The whole scene made for a chill hangout in the warm and sunny afternoon, and it gave way to festivities that lasted long into the evening, with families strolling about in their holiday best.

Coatepec Plaza on Day of the Dead

Coatepec is not the most exciting of *Pueblos Mágicos* in terms of things to see and do, with few memorable attractions. But it sure felt good to be there. Many small *Pueblos Mágicos* have little in the way of diverse dining options, but here, with the town's population at a healthy 50,000, there was a surfeit of good places to eat, and the prices were more than reasonable. Wandering about, I located an elegant establishment with tables inside a courtyard with a garden, and light classical music filling the air. The food was excellent. As for the prices, you can see them featured on the sidewalk sign in my photo. (Photographic evidence seems to be the only way to convince anyone that the prices I mention are real!) And this was no basic mom-and-pop cafe. Breakfast with a main course, orange juice, coffee, and bread for $2.75. A main meal for a quarter of a dollar more. This is why I scoff when people complain about high prices in Cabo or Cancún. Your Mexico, maybe, but not mine.

My first afternoon was a profound and leisurely break from the grind of travel. Not that this kind of trip is much of a grind, but it does have its moments (which will be clear when you read about the fifth town in this Top Ten list). The next day, I visited Xico, and on my last day, the most interesting place that Coatepec has to offer: an old hacienda, plantation, and coffee museum.

There were frequent five-peso combis that covered the three-mile trip, so I compromised and walked there one way and returned as a passenger. An attractive wooden mansion housed the museum, which featured every historical implement and machine needed to grow, harvest, and process coffee beans. As I've said, some things interest me, and others not so much. This one definitely held my attention. When I arrived, there was a large group of teenage students on the premises, but by the time I had finished looking at the exhibits, I was pretty much alone. I was assigned a guide to the grounds, a bright, well-spoken, and very knowledgeable seventeen-year-old boy.

He took me around, regaling me with more detailed specifics than I really needed. But it was a pleasure to see all of the coffee plants in their natural habitat. I am not one of those who can taste much difference between coffees and wines. But I now know plenty about the former. The Coffee Museum is well outside of town, but not to be missed.

Xico, Veracruz (Bonus Town)

Xico, formerly known as Xicochimalco, is an ancient Náhuatl place, founded in 1313 according to the stone marker in the main plaza. It is a very quiet village which exudes a sense of antiquity. Despite representing an earlier era, the zocalo and cathedral are as handsome as most of their counterparts in other towns. After looking around in the area, which I had pretty much to myself, I hiked down to the river. Google had marked the location of an old stone bridge. Decrepit and falling apart, it was a good lesson about the way things were in those pre-modern times.

Back in town, there were a few small museums. I toured the Dance Museum, which held many exhibits and photos from the town's main festival in July. I had witnessed the killing of six bulls in Torremolinos, Spain, when I was twelve years old. That had been plenty for me, so I skipped the Bullfighting Museum. The History Museum was closed.

The main attraction in Xico is the Cascada de Texolo (Texolo Waterfalls). Without a vehicle, the round-trip hike through lush countryside was a bit over two hours, which was right up my alley. Nearing the falls, I ran into and chatted with three bicyclists from Mexico City who were touring the region. The walk presented no challenges until the last stretch, which ran down steep stone steps to the river. Though it did not faze me, the cyclists struggled as they were forced to carry down their metal beasts loaded with all their possessions. And I'm sure it was even less of a picnic coming back up!

The falls were as impressive as advertised. I spent a while

lallygagging and chatting with my new friends before returning to town for a hearty early afternoon meal of fresh fish before grabbing a combi back to Coatepec.

While I am not detailing colonial cities in this book (but will briefly note them in Chapter 8), one colonial city, Xalapa, is more than worth its own visit. Its impressive archeological museum is one of the finest in Mexico. And Coatepec, Xico, and Xalapa, when considered as a unit, constitute an excellent stopover on the *Pueblos Mágicos* trail.

Getting there: Xalapa is on the main highway between Mexico City and Veracruz. There is also service through the hills from Orizaba and Cordoba. Buses to Coatepec and Xico leave from the Xalapa market, west of the Centro.

5) *Huautla de Jiménez, Oaxaca*

I like to say that getting somewhere is half the fun. Unfortunately, getting to Huautla de Jimenez was no fun at all. But most of the best travel tales spring from horror stories. And this one is no different.

In my introduction, I wrote about my trials and tribulations in merely locating some transportation to this *Pueblo Mágico*. But after a lot of aimless effort and brainstorming, I had an inspiration—that calling a hotelier in the town would be the most likely way of finding out how to get there. I was actually rather shocked when this desperate strategy worked, and I will be trying it again in the future. At last, I found the right bus company in the maze of the Oaxaca market district. And with no more drama, I had a ticket for the following morning.

I arrived at 8 AM for my 8:30 departure, already knowing that a punctual start was against all odds. The usual chaos reigned. It seemed like a lot of people had the same plan as me. The transport was not actually going to be a bus either, the only vehicles around being large colectivo vans. The next thirty minutes crawled by while the management tried to get ahold of three serviceable road warriors. Next came the calling and checking of the roll and assigning everyone to a vehicle and a seat. Then followed the distribution of the luggage, stacking it on the racks and tying it securely under tarps. Better than India anyway, where there would likely be no tarps and your bag would be returned to you coated in dust. However, I was not sure why they were so assiduous in making sure each bag was traveling with its owner. After all, the three vans were going to travel in convoy. I wondered what disaster they might be expecting.

At 9:00 we were ready to depart. These vans can be reasonably comfortable. The three front rows had padded and tilted seats with a decent view. I was out of luck, however, despite my white hair and decrepitude, and had been rudely deposited in the rear on a hard bench with an equally unforgiving shelf to lean against.

On my left was a fellow in the middle seat who at least could stretch his feet into the aisle. On my right was a rather portly teenage girl clutching a fidgety infant. I was booked to spend the next five and a half hours—plus a merciful meal break—being periodically poked in the ribs by this duo, while trying futilely to find a niche for my feet and knees. Good thing I am a little guy, or it would have been a lot worse. I also had the impression of a lot of gorgeous scenery passing by. Too bad I could hardly see any of it. The good news: I did eventually get to Huautla, living to tell the tale.

Huautla is located at a fairly high altitude and is isolated in the rugged Sierra Oriental of northeastern Oaxaca state. It is the only good-sized town in the region. The district gets a lot of rainfall, though this time I was fortunate enough to enjoy three pleasant days. Luxurious, deeply green vegetation and a riot of flowers were omnipresent. I am aware that I say this a lot. The entire rugged region high above the Gulf Coast is a visual treat worthy of any redundancy in description. Soon I felt as if I were in the marigold capital of the world. And as Huautla lies well above the surrounding countryside, it boasts vistas that go on forever.

Occasionally, I arrive in a place that feels like it is unmoored in time and space. This one was probably the most heavily indigenous of all the towns I have visited. I heard many people speaking a native tongue. Despite its isolation, this *Pueblo Mágico* is best known as the home of the eminent shaman Maria Sabina, who introduced the Western world to *hongos*, the magic psilocybin mushrooms whose name means the Flesh of the Gods. The first known outside visitor to Sabina was the ethnomycologist Gordon Wasson, who made the trek in 1955. Later on, the pilgrims who came to see her included the Beatles and the Rolling Stones. It is hard enough to get there today; I can hardly imagine how difficult it was sixty years ago.

The center of the town is built into the side of a hill, so, like Xilitla, this is a locale where you walk up and down lots and lots of steps. But who would want to complain about a little exercise, considering how pretty the whole place is? One peculiarity was the heavy police presence. But the feeling was anything but that of an armed camp. Almost every 50 meters (150 feet) on the two main streets stood young, spiffily uniformed women. They blew their whistles and waved their arms at the thin stream of motorized vehicles, the drivers more or less ignoring them. I bet the policewomen were enjoying their fairly low-stress work, considering that the serene and utterly laid-back ambience obviated any need for their presence. There are many more tedious and backbreaking jobs involved in earning a few pesos, and this one had the virtues of plentiful fresh air along with opportunities to socialize.

The central market area spreads along the length of the upper avenue, which is also home to all of the combi stops. It was as vibrant as the rest of the community, with an array of goods of clearly local provenance. I am not a shopper, as can be testified by my minimalist luggage, but this would be rich ground indeed for a collector with more acquisitive tastes. And of course, there were flowers, heaps of them everywhere I turned. The other items where supply undoubtedly overwhelmed demand were the hundreds of aromatic loaves of whole wheat bread piled up in many of the stalls. On my last day, a Sunday, an even bigger market filled the main plaza, which fronted on the cathedral and encompassed a busy basketball court. An odd mix of activities indeed. Amid the antiquity, there were also some chic modern eateries.

Huautla de Jiménez is absolutely a magical place. As long as the weather is temperate, it would be agreeable to spend many days hiking around, breathing the pristine air, and basking in the rich indigenous culture. But its placement on the government list is mainly due to its best-known attraction, the house of Maria Sabina. And here comes the standard warning: Do not trust your well-being to Apple Maps. My phone told me that it was about a kilometer out of town. In fact, it was about seven times that length, along a road that snaked ever upward. Mind you, I would have walked anyway, but without the gnawing fear that I had somehow inadvertently missed my destination. There were no signs until I finally reached the last tiny lane that forked off the main road. I did keep asking locals, who looked at me oddly as they pointed straight up, always straight up. Why is this crazy gringo walking? The views and local color were worth it, naturally.

One of the loveliest sights was a small chapel festooned with the "*hongo*" theme, which was also prevalent all around town. It was intriguing to observe how seamlessly Catholicism is interwoven with the animistic practices of the earlier inhabitants. As always, if I hadn't walked, I would have never noticed any of it. (But I did design to take a combi back to town.)

A rural hongo-themed chapel, one of the prettiest sights in a very pretty town

Maria Sabina lived to the ripe old age of ninety-nine years and ten months. Her descendants live in a pleasant farmhouse in a settled clearing on the mountaintop, with a couple of rooms devoted to a fascinating little museum filled with relics and photographs. There were copious fruit trees and chickens, and I imagine that the family lives quite comfortably on the revenue provided by the modest entrance fee, supplemented by the sale of homemade souvenirs. The extended family was enjoying a midday meal when I arrived. One granddaughter in her twenties stood up and attended to me, providing a tour and answering my questions.

Getting there: If you want to follow in my footsteps, walk west from the Oaxaca Centro, turning into the slightly seedy district north of the municipal market. There are plenty of small transportation companies in the area. If you can't pronounce Huautla (oo-out-la with a breathy out), write it on a piece of paper and keep showing it around until you find your goal. Don't forget to request actual seats instead of the back bench. For the faint-hearted, you can take a bus from Mexico City (or even Oaxaca, although the distance is considerably longer) to the city of Tehuacán, which is known for its mineral waters. From there, it is a four-hour trip on a real bus, which covers the 127 km (80 miles) of stupendous views and scenery. Still, this is Mexico. On my trip back out to Tehuacán, the bus stopped by a pretty waterfall while the driver and his accomplice descended and spent five minutes chatting and taking pictures. This type of unscheduled break was routine in the old Mexico, but I had not experienced its like in many a moon.

4) *Palenque, Chiapas*

I began this project with a few primary objectives: promoting Mexico as an under-appreciated travel opportunity, introducing the *Pueblos Mágicos* program, and featuring hidden gems—little or even completely unknown destinations worthy of the attention of discerning travelers. From the book's inception, I have been undecided about what to do with Palenque. It is quite well known and certainly not a "hidden gem." Members of the psychedelic generation have been magnetically drawn here for decades. Yet what is obvious to one person may be completely unknown to the next. Can I really be a good judge of a town's popularity or lack thereof?

My decision to include Palenque ultimately came from my personal history. In the end, I could not bear to leave it out. I have been to this small town four times—in 1976, 1979, 2000, and 2012, more than any other on the *Pueblos Mágicos* list. It is a personal power spot that calls to me with force, and about which I wrote a long chapter in one of my novels. However, placing Palenque in fourth place was a fairly arbitrary decision. For me, the town exists on a plane all by itself.

My travels have taken me to numerous famous ruins, including Angkor Wat, Machu Picchu, Tikal, Ephesus, Chichen Itza, and Teotihuacan, just to name a few. As stated earlier, I am somewhat "museum-ed out," and in a similar fashion, I am also somewhat "ruin-ed out." After all, I have always been far more interested in living people and culture as opposed to their ancient relics. And as far as ruins go, at times they just feel to me like a pile of rocks. I would love to hear them singing to me as some others claim happens, but I don't. Perhaps I could use the services of a good ruin-whisperer capable of hearing voices emerging from antiquity. A good example would be Machu Picchu. The structures did not really grab me when I visited in 1980, but the setting is one of the most spectacular in the world. In any case, for those who do resonate to the music of the past, the Mayan king's tomb complex in Palenque, which only fairly recently put the town on the map, is one of the prettiest ruins anywhere. (Various Spanish expeditions noted the site beginning in the 16th century, but it was not until the 1950s that there were any serious excavations.)

When I first followed a siren song to the town in 1976, Palenque was indeed little known to the conventional outside world. At the same time, it was a storied stop on the hippie trail. In that small subculture, it was steadily gaining fame as the place to go for those seeking "magic mushrooms." As I have said earlier, location is everything. The town is situated at an elevation of 60 meters (200 feet) above sea level, where the loam-rich agricultural lands of the Gulf Coast meet the first rising slopes of the emerald, jungle-blanketed hills. No doubt this is the very reason the Mayans selected it as a propitious venue for their memorial to a king. The township itself is replete with greenery, both wild and cultivated. It is also filled with flowers, as is the entire region, but it is otherwise unremarkable. But even a pedestrian community here in the humid southland is far easier on the eyes than its dusty, desert cousins in the north. Fifty years ago, it was unremarkably *tipico*, typical for the region, but today it is atypically touristic. Palenque's neighbors offer none of its upscale lodging, restaurants, or boutique shopping. From the urban center, a road snakes its way on an upward slope for a few miles to where those rich agricultural fields give way to the untamed jungle. The immediate area below the ruins offers a number of lodges, mostly in the "glamping" category. But back in my day, there was almost nothing here other than the legendary Maya Bell Campground.

I find myself overcome with nostalgia while writing these words, looking back on my almost fifty-year-younger self from the perspective of the "late autumn" of my life. Back then, the May Bell was dotted with Volkswagen buses and tents. I owned neither of those niceties, only a sleeping bag and a rolled-up rubber pad. The community was long-haired and outfitted in all the colors of the rainbow. There was a small office attached to a veranda restaurant, where the Señora doled out beans, tortillas, and local veggies for pennies. The campground was surrounded by a jungle full of fruit trees, their bounty free for the picking. In the back of the communal building were a few cold-water showers—hot water being unnecessary in the tropical climate—and some basic latrines dug into the soil and flushed by bucket. Clear, cold water emerged from a stream bubbling out from the hills. It tasted wonderful. There were few other amenities out there. If you wanted some other basic foods or gear, you had to trek into town and back on foot, unless you were lucky enough to score a ride from the infrequent motorized traffic. It rains a lot in those parts, but fortunately, management had a few ragged tarps to lend out to exposed indigents like me. Finally, nearby roosters acted as a handy alarm clock—although after becoming fairly habituated to them, I sometimes managed to sleep through their crowing. But snoring through the barrage of howling monkeys, who pierced the dawn air with roars that sounded like those of ravenous lions, was almost impossible. My minimal lodging fee there was a dollar a night, six dollars for a week. Many of us stayed on for that amount of time or longer. It was a hard place to leave, particularly for those of us with no worldly responsibilities and at least a minimal stash of money.

From the campground, there were two ways to get to the ruins: You could follow the road for a short distance until it made a hairpin turn into the main entrance, where a guard sat dozing in the soporific heat of his small booth, only to be roused by the occasional car or itinerant pedestrian. At least that was true back then. (Today, there is a steady stream of cars and tour buses.) Entry back then was not free, but it wasn't a lot of money either. In 1976, these ruins were just emerging as a standard tourist destination. And there were fairly few tourists, because the hike from town was a very hot, humid, hour-and-a-half trip each way for those who lacked a private car or wanted to avoid the expense of hiring a round-trip taxi.

The majority of the non-motorized visitors came from the campground, and most of us used the "unofficial" entrance. From the corner of the campground, a muddy path ascended through the thick vegetation until it reached the first of a series of natural pools. From there, it was one delightful bathing spot after another, all connected by a melodic stream punctuated by numerous small waterfalls. For many of us, this watery wonderland was the main attraction, where hours could turn to days and days to weeks. The pools were crystalline and refreshingly cool. Clothes were optional, meaning rare. In most of Mexico, shedding your garments was perilous and meant risking arrest. But here, there weren't any cops patrolling the remote and sacred grounds, which were reachable only by steep and slippery trails. Free entertainment was provided by raucous tropical birds harmonizing with a plethora of buzzing insects, along with an occasional roar if a howler felt the need to add to the cacophony. Like the ticket seller, residents passed long stretches in this Eden, snoozing or, in our case, canoodling and carousing.

Mayan ruins

First-time frequenters, who had not yet gotten the word, often bypassed this wondrous paradise (generally returning through it on their way out if a veteran had clued them in) via a dilapidated fence which separated the carefully groomed grounds of the ruins from the ever-encroaching jungle. Most of the time, the park was staffed by only one man in the booth, who had little interest in traipsing around in the heat searching out trespassers. On weekends, he was reinforced by a companion who wandered around checking tickets. If you didn't have one, you were sent back to the booth to remedy the situation, paying the regular fee along with a penalty of about a quarter. One busy day, I was high up on one of the pyramids surveying my kingdom when one of these overseers walked by. He gave me a good, hard look while I returned the favor—looking away would have only confirmed his suspicions. Then he shrugged and turned away. Climbing steep stone steps was not part of his job description. On bright moonlit nights, beneath a canopy of brilliant stars, we snuck in and climbed the pyramids carefully with flashlights, sitting atop the mounds along with the gods and goddesses, howling like wolves at the spectacular celestial display. Still, the main draws were the pools and waterfalls. How many times can you check out even the prettiest of ruins?

But the place is nothing like that today. Everything is scripted and organized. There are lots of those omnipresent tour buses in the parking lot. The price has come up considerably, to about three dollars, plus a parking fee. Naturally, seniors like me with a credential are free. Between the grounds and the water now stands an actual barbed-wire fence. (It is not guarded. The powers that be are likely not worried about the small number of miscreants who might come this way. No doubt they consider a fence to serve as an adequate barrier. Last time I was there, someone had naturally enough cut a hole in it!)

In the past, as if the gorgeous ruins and pools were not enough, there was another draw for the young and the restless. In the seventies, Palenque was ground zero for hongos—the magic mushrooms I described earlier. They were so prevalent that nobody even bothered to sell them, which they do today, of course. The peasantry considered them to be a sacrament, and they were happy to allow us colorful hippies to roam around the pasturelands, as long as we promised to shut all the gates behind us. As noted, this is a warm and moist climate. All that is needed to grow this species of fungus is cow paddy, a little rain, and a sunny day or two. Before you can blink, the fresh psilocybin caps are craning their succulent heads toward the blue sky. Many an ambitious travel itinerary disintegrated there in the Maya Bell Campground. Someone would go to bed vowing to pack up in the morning. Then, the next day, they would stretch, rub their eyes, and look around, then climb back into their sleeping bag. Tomorrow for sure.

The modern town is a nice, leafy place to hang out, with lots of crafts for sale and wonderful, fresh food. It is as pleasant a place to stay as any, particularly since it has become quite prosperous. It's just no longer authentically rural and forgotten by the world.

A little anecdote: On the evening of December 31, 1999, I was sitting in the town plaza early in the evening, watching the world go by. Palenque just happened to be where I found myself on that fateful evening before the advent of the year 2000, also popularly known as Y2K. On that date, hundreds of millions waited in trepidation, fearing the possible end of civilization as we knew it, and all for the lack of a couple of binary digits.

Across the street, I glimpsed two twenty-something lovelies consulting a thick book and looking around questioningly. Then they walked away. Such "kids" have always made up a significant portion of visitors to Palenque. I was 49, recently single after a lengthy marriage, and the sight of these maidens evoked a mix of complicated emotions in my heart (and loins), most particularly a strong nostalgia for my own youthful days. About five minutes later, they were back again, book in hand, engaged in voluble discussion. "It says it should be right here," I heard one say. It was clearly time for an intervention. I had seen this movie before, more than once. I approached with a smile, asking if they were having a problem. They showed me their *Lonely Planet* guide with a restaurant listing, wondering why they couldn't find it. I gently explained the vicissitudes of "*Lonely Planet* World" and the restaurant business. "Whoever wrote this was here two years ago. The place you are looking for is no more." Then I suggested an alternative, my current *palapa* of choice, and asked if I might join them, to which they agreed. The two women were from New York City, it turned out. At dinner, I embarked, primarily with one of them, on a spirited and fairly raunchy discussion. This is not uncommon among travelers, where inhibitions can be casually discarded, knowing you will never see each other again. It quickly became apparent that there was a definite spark lighting up the evening between me and this one favored lass. After the meal, I led them to a crafts market a couple of blocks away. You know I am not much for souvenirs, but I happened to chance upon a shirt which strongly resonated with me. It was definitely on the effeminate side, but that sort of thing has never concerned me (I like pretty, flower-child-like clothes and buy a lot of my casual wardrobe while traveling, primarily in Asia). Meanwhile, the two of us were paying plenty of attention to each other, the vibes were intensifying, and soon the friend said, "See you later," and wandered off. Long story short, we woke up on the morning of January 1, delighted to discover that the state of the world had not altered, and that we would not have to walk all the way back to the USA. I have always loved Palenque and always will.

Getting there: I used to ride the Mexican trains to Palenque station on the Mexico City line to Merida. Sadly, this system was dismantled in 1997. Today, you take a bus to the capital of Tabasco, Villahermosa, then switch to a local to Palenque. You can also arrive by slow and twisty highways from San Cristobal de las Casas in western Chiapas. Not too far from Palenque are the awesome cascades of Agua Azul, which are definitely worth a day trip.

3) *Cuetzalán, Puebla*

I have long considered Cuetzalán to be one of the most interesting and atmospheric towns in the Republic of Mexico.

I was first there in the early eighties with my ex-wife, again in 2002 with Kathy, and a couple of years ago on my 2022 *Pueblo Mágico* tour. I have often wished to spend more time there, but there's one fly in the ointment. When the weather is pleasant, it is a heavenly place to be. Unfortunately, nice weather is not a thing you can rely on. Cuetzalán is situated high in the foothills above the Gulf Coast, and as such is subject to plenty of fog and precipitation. Be prepared and bring some winter clothing, particularly rain gear. The community is somewhat isolated at the terminus of a rural highway, three or four hours due north of the state capital of Puebla. This is truly the "end of the road," but what a fabulous final stop it is.

Gorgeous main plaza of Cuetzalán

The town has everything a traveler's heart might desire. Yet when thinking of Cuetzalán, I tend to thrill the most about one fairly inconsequential item—a bowl of steaming hot wild mushroom soup, which I can hardly wait to dip my spoon into every time I arrive. It is one of my favorite exotic delicacies anywhere. Apart from this personal obsession, Cuetzalán is a majority-indigenous community that also features stunning Spanish architecture, nearby ruins, an excellent botanical garden, cascades and springs, adventure sports, and loads of art and cultural activities. On top of this, indigenous peoples from the surrounding countryside and villages pour into town for its famous weekend market, which spills out into all of the central streets. And naturally, this cultural cornucopia also provides a rich banquet for foodies.

This is probably not the best destination if you don't care to walk up and down the old and occasionally treacherous cobblestoned streets. But even if your stamina is low, you can stay and eat in the Centro and hire taxis for the rest. Sunny days are indeed a joy. But when it is damp, be advised that you should watch your step at all times, as the cobblestones, smoothed by centuries of precipitation, can be devilishly slippery. The architecture in the Centro, highlighted by two gorgeous old cathedrals, is spectacular. And, as in Huautla de Jiménez, the omnipresent views of the hilly countryside are magnificent. It is easy to pass hours sampling the diverse edible and artistic wares on market days. Cuetzalán is a homey and very friendly place. I have heard that the town does have a following among the hip minority in the know (*Lonely Planet* even notes it), but I have never seen enough foreign visitors to spoil either the locals or the locale. As I have remarked from the start, even the somewhat known parts of Mexico are still rarely visited. Getting to an out-of-the-way spot like Cuetzalán requires both motivation and effort. And it's well worth it in my opinion!

The people of this part of the country are truly beyond friendly and helpful. One day on my most recent visit, I tripped on an uneven sewer grate and fell down. Within seconds, a couple of policemen were on the scene, extremely solicitous and concerned about my well-being. Fortunately, I escaped with a minor cut and a few bruises. This had nothing to do with the weather, just bad luck. The grate appeared to be smooth, and I never saw the rough, protruding edge. (It is always important to watch your step in Mexico, and that is something that is not likely to change. The country is full of ancient and uneven byways, and upgraded infrastructure is not anywhere close to cheap. So, it always pays to watch where you are going.)

I thoroughly enjoyed walking around the Xoxoctic Botanical Gardens, less than 3 kilometers (2 miles) out of town. The name means "non-native" or "exotic," and there is a large selection of surreal-looking tropical species as you walk the extensive grounds (I was accompanied by a very knowledgeable young guide who definitely knew his stuff). Farther afield are the well-kept ruins of Yohualichan, which can be reached by taxi or combi. I visited them in 2001, but I skipped the ruins this trip for reasons I have noted earlier.

I was fortunate enough to lodge in the simple Hotel Posada Sernichari, which felt more like a homestay than a hotel. The proprietor, her family, and the dogs and cats were exceedingly friendly. The room, more than reasonably priced, also included a homemade full breakfast, cooked to order. The Sernichari is just down the slope from the main avenue, a few minutes' walk from the Centro.

I don't mean to discourage you with concerns about the weather, but it is good to know what you are signing up for. That at least applies to contemporary travel. Back in my heyday, you almost never had that kind of information, which had both pluses and minuses. But that intriguing subject will have to be left for another book. My next title might be High Times, Free Love, and the Open Road: A Memoir of the 60s and 70s. Ready for it? Anyway, in Cuetzalán, depending on the season, sunshine is more common than wet and grey days. And if that kind of thing does not bother you one way or another, Cuetzalán is another place that never bores nor disappoints.

Getting there: Basically, at the upper terminus of the paved highway, there are frequent straight-shot buses from the Puebla city terminal. (I recently arrived from the nearby *Pueblo Mágico* of Tlatlauquitepec on a series of combis which connected a number of tiny villages. It was a wonderful and scenic adventure and also a bit wild and woolly, but I can't in good conscience recommend it to non-Spanish speakers. In fact, I am only mentioning it because if you ever get the yen to see the Mexico that nobody else does - well, all I can say is if there is a will, there is a way.

2) *Real de Asientos, Aguascalientes (Hidden Gem)*

A confession: I almost didn't visit Real de Asientos. At the time, there were two *Pueblos Mágicos* between Aguascalientes city and my next destination of Zacatecas. One, San José de Gracia, is a popular weekend resort on a pretty lake. But it is also mainly known as a Catholic shrine, which isn't something in my particular sphere of interest. I was just beginning my first *Pueblo Mágico* circuit in October 2021, and I had not yet discovered many applicable websites that could help me in choosing between destinations. There are more now, and as I have already mentioned, YouTube videos are an excellent resource.

Thus, I could not find a lot of information to whet my interest in Asientos. Another factor was that the people at the main city bus terminal told me there were no real buses going there, despite the fact that it is only 61 kilometers (38 miles) from the capital. They did explain to me that *colectivos* left from a lot north of Centro, some distance away. At the time, being new to this very Mexican travel style, it all seemed a bit vague and dubious. Knowing what I know now, I should have boarded any non-direct bus on the main road between the two state capitals and gotten off at the crossroads. From there it is a much shorter *colectivo* ride. But I was indeed still new to this type of back-road Mexican travel. Four years later, such improvisation has now become routine.

In any case, the photos of the place seemed nice enough. With little to lose, I decided to unpack my adventure shoes and give it a shot. My hotel told me how to find the colectivo station, more or less (get used to vague directions in Mexico, they are more common than not). The day before departure, I walked in that direction for around half an hour, nearing the correct district, then enlisting the help of passersby. Remember, if you can communicate with them, Mexicans are more than eager to help. In the end, it was not a big deal to find the hub and return the next day. At the extensive lot, there were rows and rows of vans heading out to small towns around the state. As usual, I looked for drivers sitting by or washing their vehicles whom I could ask for information. Soon I was at the right departure point, and fifteen minutes later, on my way.

This was during the height of COVID. The van was crowded from the beginning. But at least everyone was wearing a mask, and I was well vaccinated. Apple Maps said it was about an hour's drive. We passed uninspiring scenery and many poor and dusty villages. After constantly stopping to take on and offload literally scores of erstwhile companions at any byway along the road, the trip ended up taking well over two hours (a virtue of transport in rural Mexico is that you can descend or board pretty much everywhere). In the end, I was the only passenger who traveled from the beginning all the way to Asientos, which speaks a lot to the town's remoteness. My first glimpse of the settlement was a bit uninspiring, as it was surrounded by pleasant-looking but monotonous high desert scenery. However, walking around town after checking in to my hotel, I discovered that first impressions aside, things were much more intriguing.

This old mining town, founded in 1548, feels somewhat forgotten and left behind by modern life. It is clean and handsome, with broad avenues, a wide-open plaza, and negligible traffic. Walking down the hill to Centro, there seemed to be only two hotels. One appeared a bit more attractive than the other, but just before noon, the door was locked and there was no one about. So, I crossed the street and received a friendly welcome at its competitor. The place was basic, but clean. The shower ran hot water. The price, at $12, was certainly a plus. But something immediately came up that filled me with disquiet: for the first and possibly only time in Mexico, there was no WiFi. It wasn't the hotel's fault, at least according to the proprietor, who suggested that I investigate the situation further at the tourist office. It turned out that a cable had broken or something, and the entire town was likely to be cut off from the World Wide Web for the whole time I would be there. But as I said, I didn't know that yet. Actually, my first fear was that something was wrong with my iPad. Could I survive for two days without connectivity? I did have a downloaded book and plenty of music, and naturally, I had my camera in both my devices. This might prove to be a good test of the severity of my technology addiction, I thought to myself. And I was certainly not anywhere close to turning tail and running, thank goodness.

    I walked a half block to the plaza, where I immediately noticed a well-marked tourist kiosk. The girl explained the situation—connections were out all over town. Thinking about outages back home, I asked if the problem might not be soon remedied. She went on a bit wistfully that this was unlikely, and that the community might have to come up with a sort of ransom in order to be reconnected. Actually, she relieved my anxiety. At least there was nothing wrong with my iPad. Even my phone was more or less useless, though I was later able to find some hotspots high above and outside the town limits. I am here to report that I did survive and was absolutely enthralled by Real de Asientos. Without electronic assistance, the girl actually wrote down some suggested itineraries on paper for me. What a novel idea!

The town itself is a study in contrast. Despite the nearly monochromatic high desert scenery, there is a bubbling spring feeding a meandering stream that passes through the settlement not far from the town center. The entire area around this source of life-giving water is thick with decidedly non-desert vegetation. Taking the thin dirt path along the stream, I discovered many hidden nooks and clearings, perfect for meditation. Overall, I found the juxtaposition to be stunning and delightful. I imagined that this place was somewhat akin to a Saharan oasis, something I have never experienced.

Looking out from town, high desert scenery

The whole community has that totally laid-back and serene feeling that I'm always searching for. There was hardly any traffic noise, and nobody seemed to be in any hurry at all. The tourist girl said that visitors, even domestic ones, were scarce—perhaps a few weekenders from the capital, and that was all. I felt like I had the whole place to myself. As always in Mexico, there were plenty of basic *fondas* in which to get simple and typically regional meals and snacks. But there was only one real restaurant. It, however, was a jewel—beautifully decorated, with the walls sporting numerous cooking school certificates of culinary excellence for the proud owner and master chef. Her specialty was *Chichimeca* (the region's indigenous tribe) rabbit stew. I ordered it and it was scrumptious.

The natural beauty of Asientos would have kept me happy enough during my involuntarily tech-free sojourn, but this historical place has far more than its share of other attractions, especially given its diminutive size and total lack of notoriety. First is the beautiful cathedral and its adjoining small museum, which was quite fascinating due to the antiquity of the relics, including both the first and the largest bells in the state. But the main interest for me at that site was the hidden trap door opening to a staircase descending to some dark, cramped rooms and tunnels. This was where the small Spanish population repaired to conceal themselves when periodically attacked by aggressive *Chichimeca* bands.

A short walk out of town leads to a handsome old aqueduct in excellent condition. But along the street leading to this antique monument stands a unique structure, I never like to use the word "unique" lightly—but this house was truly one-of-a-kind, per the actual and precise meaning of a word that has suffered so badly in modern parlance. (Unique does not mean unusual or even extremely unusual. It means one and only, and may not be modified. End of another rant.) A gentleman who was sitting on his front porch brightened up when he saw me walking by, clearly an outsider, and beckoned me over. He had spent thirty years building his house from old rocks and gemstones. Inside and out, his home was a sparkling, shimmering shrine to his artisanship. The bathroom, with modern accoutrements, felt particularly surreal. His richly deserved pride in his achievement shone through the entire tour.

And there is still more. An hour hike out of town lies a finely preserved former convent. I have asked a number of Mexicans why they are called convents rather than monasteries. To me, convents equal nuns, but almost all the "convents" in Mexico housed only monks. As with many other questions in this often-confounding country, I have never gotten a good explanation, so we will leave it at that. When I arrived after a brisk forty-five-minute walk, I found an empty parking lot and a lone university student at the desk. Without phone service, she was bored and bereft, and more than enthusiastic to find a live human companion to converse with. She led me across the grounds and into the maze of the ancient structure, explaining everything in detail. I learned quite a bit about monastery life circa the 18th century and took in a number of interesting exhibits. The most fascinating one was when she played an old indigenous instrument reminiscent of an Australian didgeridoo, which I managed to video. Meanwhile, the most eerie and intense interlude occurred when she sealed me inside the pitch black "punishment" room for a couple of minutes. It felt like a very long two minutes where I deliberately refrained from imagining what it must have been like to suffer this form of penance for an extended period of time.

There turned out to be no fee for all this, and I had to practically force a fifty-peso tip on her. This might sound odd to readers who have mainly visited "tourist" Mexico, where the locals have grown jaded. But in a town like Asientos, where this girl may have never before met a foreign visitor, her modesty was characteristic of these people's humble generosity.

With the exception of Mexcaltitán and Asientos, all of my

other Top Ten *pueblos* are in the moist green east of Mexico, and those are the regions I prefer. So, this town, which clearly merits the appellation of a hidden gem, was an enormous and delightful surprise to me. I thoroughly enjoyed my two days here, full yet so very tranquil, and look forward to revisiting someday. Perhaps the internet connection will have been restored by then, but I can't swear whether it would be any improvement.

Getting there: If you are looking for gritty authenticity, you are welcome to follow in my footsteps and travel from the Aguascalientes combi station. But probably the better way is to take an Aguascalientes-Zacatecas bus (not a first-class direct bus) and make sure the driver understands your destination. At the crossroads, you should be able to find taxis and a combi happy to convey you to Asientos. Coming from Zacatecas, just reverse the process.

1) *Zacatlán de las Manzanas, Puebla (Hidden Gem)*

Zacatlán is, in my opinion, *Lo Mejor de Todo*, the "Best of All" of these 62 towns.

Many people travel in search of the amazing and spectacular. Perhaps that is part of our hyper-sensational entertainment culture: wilder car chases, more eye-catching explosions, more swoon-inducing romances, you name it. You can't have your audience getting bored, their eyes glazing over. Experiencing authentic Mexico is a much quieter but ultimately far richer endeavor than the kind of bucket-list tourism that I think may partly be inspired by our culture of maximalism. As you travel around the interior of Mexico, away from the resort glitz, the gentle pull of the country's atmosphere and heritage begins to seep into your very being.

The *Pueblos Mágicos* represent the very best of this subtle beauty. They don't necessarily jump right out at you. First and foremost, they are real communities, where people pass their normal quotidian lives. I come into towns and try to let the spirit of the place seep into me. Some places call out strongly and begin to resonate almost immediately; others take a while to grow on me, and a few leave me flat. They all have something special to offer, as otherwise they would not be in the program, but that special vibe is always going to be individual.

I did not see Zacatlán coming; in fact, it was not even on my initial itinerary. But from the moment I climbed down from the bus and walked a few blocks into the central streets, I already knew that I was someplace special.

After the bus ride from Huachinango, which featured a hilarious panhandler dressed and miming as a clown, I entered the Centro from the bus station on a broad, car-free lane bursting with life and color. Zacatlán specializes in all kinds of artisanal products, like big, juicy apples, jams, wines, and an array of homemade salsas. The place is also a mecca for craftspeople, so there are plenty of other goodies all over town. That first feeling of utter spaciousness and ease persisted in the main plaza, with its large apple monument and one of the few flower clocks in the world. The architecture in the Centro is strikingly beautiful, and the interconnected plazas are perfect spots to while away a warm afternoon.

Two blocks away, I easily found my reserved hotel—pretty, clean, comfortable, and as always, a bargain at 400 pesos or $20. The owner, Gonzalo, and I immediately took a shine to each other. He was delighted to meet a gringo who could speak his language well.

A festive display of locally made products

Zacatlán is also a town that draws plenty of upscale domestic tourism, even though the rest of the world has pretty much never heard of it. As such, there is a bounty of delicious cuisine. Traditional Restaurante La Chichipinga was one of the most appealing, with its aesthetic decor and no-nonsense menu. And maybe the high degree of domestic tourism is because, unlike many of my Top Ten *pueblos*, this town is an easy place to get to. The state capitals of Puebla and Tlaxcala are only a short drive away, and even Mexico City is just over three hours by car.

I hope I have already piqued your interest. Because I haven't even gotten to the best parts. Zacatlán is built along the side of the enormous *barranca* (canyon), called Barranca de los Jilgueros. From the edge of this fissure, you can look down to profound depths of over 400 meters (1300 feet), and all the way across over the canyon's impressive breadth. This enormous ditch is filled with the usual lush foliage of Gulf Coast Mexico and boasts numerous cascades and streamlets. This is the type of place that I would never get tired of hiking. The spacious avenue on the south side of town has an equally wide *malecón* (boardwalk), which runs along the north rim of the canyon. It is a perfect venue for a scenic and relaxing stroll of any length. There is even a vintage Mexican Air Force plane from WWII along the wayside.

A tiny section of the tiled art that extends along the boardwalk

On the opposite side of this same avenue is a gorgeous wall of tile art with primarily indigenous themes that extends hundreds of meters. You could easily spend hours examining the individual panels if so inclined. Farther down is one of the prettier cemeteries you are likely to encounter anywhere.

As I mentioned, Zacatlán was not even on my original agenda. Since it was only twenty minutes short of another *Pueblo Mágico*, Chignahuapan, I changed my mind after spending less time than expected in two more in northern Puebla; I had only booked one night in Zacatlán, but I swiftly added two more. Who knows? I might have stayed even longer if a severe storm had not been headed in. This first trip was meant as a survey. Although I prefer to have my wanderings free of time constraints, I did have a flight booked from Guadalajara to Seattle, which limited my stay length in each selected place. If I ever return, it will be more open-ended.

The morning after my arrival, Gonzalo walked me down the street to meet his tiny *madre* (mother), who ran a tamale shop. She wrapped her wares in gigantic green leaves. From there, we trekked out of town and then down a trail that descended into the canyon, where he located and cut some of the same impressive leaves. We were gone for almost three hours, during which we managed to solve some of the world's most intractable problems during our conversations.

Getting there: Pretty easy. Buses leave Mexico City constantly for Puebla and Tlaxcala (another of my Hidden Gems). Change at either for Chignahuapan, which is then a short combi hop from Zacatlán. If you are continuing north toward Huachinango or Pahuatlán (or coming down from there as I did), it is on one of the main state highways.

CHAPTER 3:
The Honorable Mentions

10) Bernal, Querétaro
9) Capulálpam de Méndez, Oaxaca (Hidden Gem)
8) Twin Towns
Mineral del Monte, Hidalgo
Mineral del Chico, Hidalgo
7) Pahuatlán, Puebla (Hidden Gem)
6) Cuatrociénegas, Coahuila
Poza Azul, Coahuila
5) Calvillo, Aguascalientes
4) Malinalco, México
3) Valley de Bravo, México
2) Tepoztlán, Morelos
1) Tzintzuntzan, Michoacán
Isla de Janitzio, Michoacán
Pátzcuaro, Michoacán (Bonus Town)

The Honorable Mentions

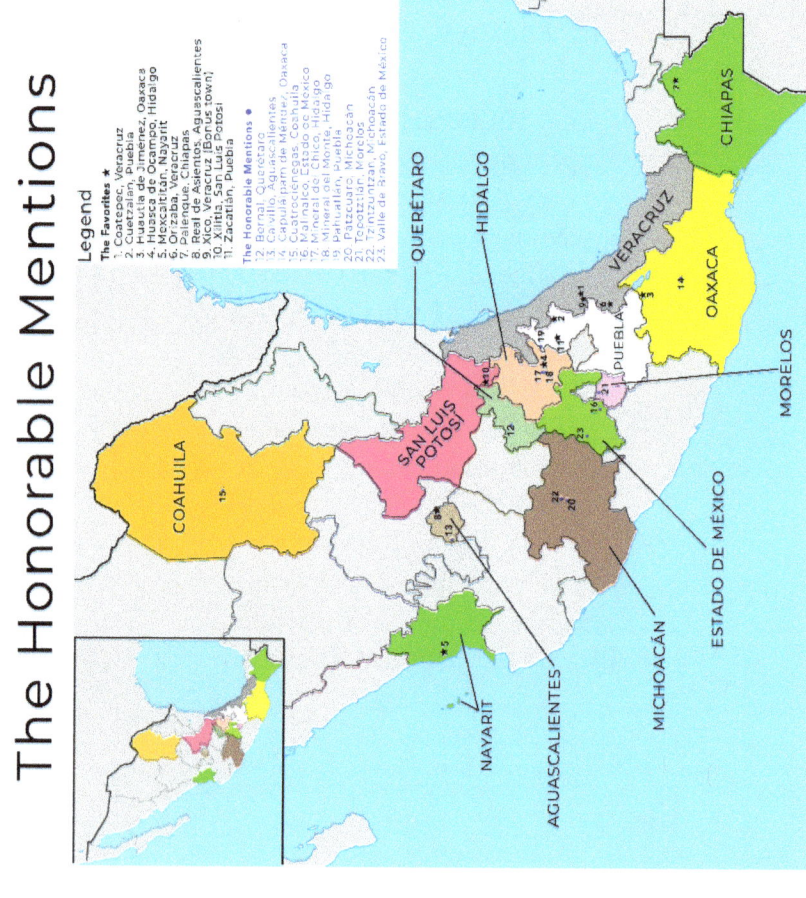

Now that I have chosen my (certainly subjective) ten favorites, it is time to move on to another group of lovely *pueblos*. None of these towns is necessarily less delightful than those in the Top Ten. In many ways, this list simply exists because I ran out of space in the Top Ten. So, I give you my blessing to enjoy them all as much as I did!

10) *Bernal, Querétaro*

Another upscale weekend destination for well-heeled Mexican families, Bernal is an easy 58 kilometers (36 miles) from the beautiful city of Querétaro. Bernal is mostly known for its massive monolith, the third largest in the world after the Rock of Gibraltar and the Pan de Azúcar in Rio de Janeiro. There is practically no spot in Bernal where this behemoth does not dominate your view. North of the town center, you can easily reach the path that ascends most of the way to the top. From the last level spot, though, you need serious climbing gear and a permit to go farther. Most folks stop at the first plateau viewpoint, where the going starts to get tough. When I arrived at the final trailhead, there was a booth requesting 30 pesos entry. I seldom carry my Senior card around and certainly had no reason to do so on a hike. But the girl was content to accept the photo of it on my phone, so I did get in for free. Feel free to call me a cheapskate. As a fairly well-off foreigner, am I gaming the system? Let's not go there, but I really do enjoy making use of the few advantages I get for enduring the outrageous slings and arrows of old age! And anyway, it is all good, clean fun.

This is a bit of a party *pueblo*. It is more than pleasant to walk up and down the streets, with their wealth of boutiques, art stores, souvenirs, bars, nightclubs, stylish restaurants, and hotels. An old mining town founded in 1642, Bernal has definitely come a long way. As a bit of a playground, small-town authenticity is not its main selling point. On weekends, the town has a lively fiesta mood, with the patrons of the cafes and bars spilling out onto the sidewalks late into the night. I even saw some foreigners there, and I met and climbed with a German girl on the hike.

The massive rock of Bernal

I particularly enjoyed the fabulous mask museum (not as extensive as the one in the city of San Luis Potosí, but still with plenty to see). Such mask collections provide deep insights into pre-Colombian indigenous culture. A lot of these intricate, splashy disguises are eminently jaw-dropping.

At just over 2,000 meters (6,600 feet), Bernal has a comfortable, spring-like climate. It would be an easy place to hang out for a while, particularly on weekdays when lodging prices go down and the crowds melt away. Unlike most other *Pueblos Mágicos*, I did spot a few foreign visitors here, as there also are in the nearby and under-appreciated city of Querétaro.

Getting there: You don't need my help getting to Bernal from Querétaro. It is also easily accessible from Mexico City. Take any non-direct bus heading toward Querétaro and get off in the city of San Juan del Rio. From that smallish city, there are buses that head straight north to Bernal, avoiding a time-consuming detour getting in and out of Querétaro. As a bonus, many of these buses pass through or near to two other *Pueblos Mágicos*, Cadereyta de Montes and Tequisquiapan.

9) *Capulálpam de Méndez, Oaxaca* (Hidden Gem)

As I observed in my introduction, Oaxaca is possibly the number one destination in Mexico for those who can drag themselves away from their coastal comfort zones. Its joys are legion, including the grandeur of the ruins at Monte Alban, and the impressive El Tule, a staggeringly large and old tree with the greatest circumference of any in the world. The city is also surrounded by numerous indigenous towns, each one offering its own crafts and a weekly market. Some of the native cuisine is unique to the region. The Museum of Cultures housed in the Temple of Santo Domingo is one of the finest in Mexico. Every evening, the shaded Zocalo is filled with music and street artists. There is no doubt about it—Oaxaca is a top destination.

Now, if I told you that there was a lovely and interesting *Pueblo Mágico* only 74 kilometers (42 miles) away, you might guess that it would draw at least some small percentage of the hordes who descend upon Oaxaca. But that's not so. This fact only fuels my suspicions that the powers that be are not putting a great deal of effort into promoting the *Pueblos Mágicos* program to foreigners.

When I visited the State Tourist Office trying to find out how to get to Huautla, I asked about Capulálpam. But they had no brochures and surprisingly little to say. That can be excused, of course, what with the wealth of information available on *Pueblos Mágicos* websites and YouTube, even if they are almost all in Spanish. But it is pretty hard to find something if you have not heard of it in the first place (a bit of a shameless plug for this book, perhaps?). Anyway, it turned out not to be a big deal to arrange a day trip. And I am glad I did.

Capulálpam is not hard to get to, with the proviso that you understand the system. A cross between a bus and a collective van left the Oaxaca bus terminal at 9 AM. It wasn't crowded, and I could sit back and take in the pretty scenery in comfort. The only minor wrinkle occurred when I got down along the main road in a community called Ixtlán de Juárez. The bus station clerk told me I needed to walk up the hill into the town center and ask for the shared taxis for the last nine kilometers. I soon found myself in one along with three others and paid the 25 pesos. I was also gratified that my chauffeur was a young woman. The fair sex keeps making great strides here (witness our new Presidenta Claudia Sheinbaum), but they are still a rare sight in traditionally male jobs. It is encouraging that, even in rural Mexico, the times are a-changin'.

Sign in three languages (and Spanish is not first)

There is nothing truly spectacular about this *pueblo*. But the one thing I can say is that they try harder. Every old building is graced with a handsome wood marker explaining its history in three languages. Capulálpam has clearly made good use of its government spruce-up money. And all the old architecture is graceful and aesthetic, taking advantage of and complementing the beautiful natural setting. The whole town is neat as a pin, with vines and flowers all about. And beyond the settlement, the views over the rolling green hills go on forever. There were few people walking about in the narrow streets, but virtually everybody I came across greeted me warmly. In this way, it was as if I had walked back sixty years into Mexico's past. This has to be one of the friendliest towns anywhere.

As is my custom, I spent a couple of hours hiking up and through the countryside to a Christ statue on top of the hill, meeting a number of friendly people along the way. Afterwards, I had a relaxing and delicious meal at one of the tidy restaurants in the central market. I ducked inside a genuinely delightful hotel and discovered that a room was 425 pesos ($22). Anyone wishing to spend a couple of days taking refuge from the hustle and bustle of the modern world could do a lot worse than spending them in Capulálpam de Mendes.

Getting there: A few mini-buses leave the Oaxaca Bus terminal throughout the day. For a day trip, I recommend the 9 AM. Get off in Ixtlán de Juárez and walk up the hill on your right to the center of town, where you can inquire about a share taxi the rest of the way into Capulálpam.

8) *Twin Towns*

The next two towns are in a way a matched pair (actually, as I mentioned in the Top Ten section, they're part of a set of three, the other being Huasca de Ocampo). A stone's throw from Mexico City and grouped closely around Pachuca, the three offer one of the most convenient portals into the joys of the *Pueblos Mágicos*. But if you are attracted to Mexico for its hot, sunny days, stay away from these in the winter. In my first major tour in 2021, I dropped down into Hidalgo from the adjoining state of San Luis Potosí, planning to visit these two, along with Huasca, their proximity to each other being one of the primary lures. I had arrived in Mexico in mid-September, and the only high-altitude place I had so far visited was the beautiful city of Zacatecas, which had been warm enough. The main reason I chose the months of October and November to travel in the Mexican Sierra is that that's the season when my summer home in the Pacific Northwest starts to get uncomfortably cold and grey, while my primary residence in Mazatlán is still hot, wet, and muggy. And until I arrived in Mineral del Monte, interchangeably known as Real de Monte, the climate had not been an issue. In fact, in the uplands, October tends to be one of the finest weather months.

Mineral del Monte (Real de Monte), Hidalgo
The town personifies the fascinating and byzantine tapestry of contemporary Mexican history. Its primary settlers were English miners from Cornwall who, among other things, imported their number one favorite food, the hearty Cornish pasty, which is particularly pleasing in a cold climate. These savory and filling treats are now endemic to the state of Hidalgo, though seldom seen in any other part of Mexico. Many of the monuments to mining culture are scattered about town, and the old English cemetery is a must-visit.

The combi ride from Pachuca was quick and easy. I disembarked in the historic center of Mineral del Monte, the loveliest town I had yet visited, surrounded by beautiful classical architecture and multiple picturesque *plazuelas* (miniature plazas) with stunning mountain vistas. I most often prefer to stay in the *Centro* of a town for reasons of ease and comfort, along with quick access to most places of interest. This can be a problem in cities due to noise pollution at night, but the majority of *Pueblos Mágicos* have only moderate traffic, and people go to bed early. Often, there is an old colonial hotel or two on the main plaza, which is my favorite kind of lodging. In Mineral del Monte, I chose a typically handsome old building. First thing, I checked the WiFi signal in the lobby, which was fine. The room seemed okay, if a bit austere. The rate was a lofty 600 pesos, which stood in stark contrast to the 250 or so pesos

I had been paying per night for the first weeks of the trip. However, in the affluence of my old age, I have been battling with the inherent stinginess of my upbringing and the financial challenges of my child-rearing years, and I refused to let the price ruffle or dissuade me.

Miners' Monument in Mineral del Monte

In my travels between 1972 and my marriage in 1979, I slept rough or crashed with friends considerably more often than paying for lodging. In 1972, I was pleased to be paying $10 a month for a cottage on top of the hill on the Greek Island of Karpathos. The only amenities were a rude outhouse and a mattress I dragged up onto the roof. I spent many memorable nights up there in the summer after consuming immoderate amounts of ouzo and retsina, while the August meteor showers glittered all around, falling down on my spinning head. But my ego was put back into place by an English couple who were inhabiting a spacious five-chamber beach cave, a twenty-minute walk out of the capital town of Pigadia. They had spear guns, traded fish for other supplies, and claimed to have spent a total of five dollars in the two months they stayed there!

I offer that aside to emphasize that plunking down thirty dollars for a bed was far from a routine occurrence in that first tour year. And it turned out to be the worst mistake of the trip. Before venturing out, I spent a few minutes researching the town's attractions, but the internet signal quickly disappeared. Undeterred, I trudged out to the office. The girl took my report, fiddled around, and rebooted, all to no avail. The signal was gone, never to return. In any case, it was time to venture out. The day was gorgeous and there were plenty of impromptu celebrations in the plazas. It turned out the town was hosting a Halloween-style horror festival three weeks before the *Día de Muertos*, with street parades, booths, and colorful decorations. After enjoying all of this and checking out the historical monuments, I had a delicious meal at a very nice restaurant. Then I departed on a long and hilly hike above town, with one beautiful panorama after another. As dusk hit and the temperatures began to drop, I had a bowl of wild mushroom soup, sometimes available in these mountains if I get lucky, and a quesadilla at the fancy hotel just up the street.

When darkness fell, I was in my room as usual. After such a pleasant day, who would expect that a hellish night awaited me?

Lack of online access was not the most urgent problem, just a bit of a nuisance. I had my library book and my music. But it was cold. Very cold. That night it got down to 4°C (40°F), which is no joke in mountain hotels that have no heat and paltry insulation. My two blankets were thin. I stayed in my warm clothes and pulled them around me. But the worst villains were the thin window slats that would not close properly. Directly outside my room was a brilliant streetlamp. The useless slats failed to block any of the glare. Cold, shivering, and spotlit, I tossed and turned for most of the night.

Hanging out with locals in Mineral del Monte

In the morning, grumpy from lack of sleep, I huddled in my blankets, forestalling the moment when I would have to brave the frigid air of the room and bathroom. A little after eight, I ventured out in search of coffee, although in Mexico, there often isn't anything open at that hour. Anything was better than staying in my refrigerator of a room. The nearby fancy hotel was open, but at the door, I was told that the restaurant would not begin service until 9. I wandered around Centro, peering inside some other restaurants. Nothing. Surely the Municipal Market would offer something, I reassured myself. But when I walked the few blocks to reach it, the place was just beginning to stir. Cooks in all the small family fondas were just beginning to set up for the day, and in a manner far too desultory to help me. It was now just past 8:30. Walking out of the market, I noticed some activity in an adjacent plaza, a wrinkled old señora with a cart. She had a large metal bucket, a ladle, and some styrofoam cups. "Praise the Lord," I whispered to myself. This angel of an *indigena* was serving *atole*, a traditional thick and sweetened beverage made from cornmeal. I ordered a cup, trying to mask my eagerness.

"Where are you from, *joven*?" she inquired. *Joven* is one of those peculiar Mexican words. Its literal meaning is young man, but in fact, it is usually what a proprietor or vendor will call any male customer. Even in my mid-seventies, I continue to be addressed as "joven." I answered that I was from Mazatlán, as good a response as any. In spite of Mineral del Monte's English roots, few foreigners pass this way. In any case it was clear that she had no idea what I was talking about. Another patron clarified by saying "Sinaloa," our state name, but she continued to be mystified. For a few seconds, I pondered the huge chasm between our respective realities. Then she gingerly handed over a large cup, warning me that it was hot. "*Ojala*," I responded. I hope so. The price was 12 pesos (60 cents). I chugged it down as quickly as the temperature allowed, then ordered another.

Somewhat fortified, I walked out of town in search of the old English cemetery. As usual, Apple Maps made a total mess of the directions, but I was able to catch a glimpse of the site, dug into a hillside off to the west, and managed to find it despite my duplicitous phone. The grassy field was very rustic, with fine views. Yet it was a curious feeling to read all those English homilies and odes to fair young men far out in rural

Mexico. Returning to town, I had a proper breakfast at the fancy hotel. Then I packed up and got out of Dodge. My next planned stop had been Mineral del Chico, which lies at the same elevation, but I just couldn't stomach the idea of another freezing night. Instead, I made the short hop east to Huasca de Ocampo, a happy visit related in the previous section. By this juncture, you probably think I am some kind of cold-weather wimp. You would be correct. Growing up in California spoiled me, and in the years following my graduation from university, I even tended to flee south from the Golden State at the first sign of grey and bluster. I know many people who extol the four seasons, but I will happily enjoy warm sunny days as long as I live.

Mineral del Chico, Hidalgo

National Park El Chico is one of the oldest and most ecologically protected sites in Mexico, and for that matter, in all of Latin America. It is a center for all types of mountain sports and activities, including camping. All of this natural splendor is anchored by the hamlet of Mineral del Chico. In 2021, following my harrowing night in its neighbor Mineral del Monte, I gave it a pass. An easy rationalization at the time was that I could go back anytime, given how easy it is to get there from Mexico City.

So, in early October, the town was my first designated stop following three nights in the big city. The weather in Mexico City, about 500 meters (1,600 feet) lower in elevation than Mineral del Chico, was perfect. For once trying to be well-prepared, I was equipped with a wool hat and gloves, along with a light rain jacket, all of which I had lacked in 2021. I was quite eager to spend two or three nights in this purported paradise and add it to my *Pueblos Mágicos* collection. Then, the morning I was leaving Mexico City, a strong tropical disturbance began to blow through southern Mexico from the Gulf. By the time I rode the two hours into Pachuca, the entire region was grey, chilly, and drizzly. And the forecast for the next two days was even worse. I checked into a pleasant hotel and walked the streets of the capital, glad that I was dressed for the conditions. I suffer from a mild version of Seasonal Affective Disorder, which is why I like to spend as much if my life as possible in the sunshine (not to mention my aforementioned antipathy to cold). Still, I try not to let the grey days mess with my mood.

Reading the forecast in bed the next morning, the prediction was that Mineral del Chico would be chilly but fairly dry until a steady drizzle was predicted to set in beginning in the early afternoon. Clearly, a visit of two or three nights was not in the offing. Still, I might as well take a look. After a hot and hearty breakfast of eggs, chilaquiles, and coffee, I grabbed a combi. The distance up to Chico is only 26 kilometers (16 miles), but the road is twisty, narrow, and under constant maintenance. The combi was full, hot, and stuffy. It was hard enough to see the scenery at first, then halfway up, the fog set in. And ten minutes before arrival, the driver was using the windshield wipers. The entire uncomfortable slog took an hour and a half. As for the predicted afternoon rainfall, it had already arrived. At least I was reasonably well equipped.

It was a Saturday, and the town was bustling with Mexican families making the best of the foul conditions, as the Mexicans always do. The center of town was lovely and charming with plenty of attractive eateries and refreshment stands, and it was bursting with vibrant colors—when I got close enough to make them out through the gloom. There was enough evocative old architecture to please a connoisseur. As for all the heralded vistas and hiking trails featured in YouTube videos, forget it. Everything was a soppy mess. After a long hour of slogging around the town and its outskirts, I decided to retreat to Pachuca. Perhaps I will be able to make it back someday during better conditions. They say that the third time is the charm. I'm looking forward to it.

Getting there: No challenge here. There are buses from

Mexico City to Pachuca, leaving the Northern Bus Terminal on the Metro line every few minutes. From the Pachuca bus station, just cross the street and grab a taxi or combi to the nearby Historic Center. This is not a large area, and most anybody should be able to direct you to the correct combi departure point. Cabs are also reasonably priced.

7) *Pahuatlán, Puebla (Hidden Gem)*

With this *pueblo*, we're still in the hill country northeast of Mexico City, and with good reason. The region is brimming with clusters of easily accessible, verdant *Pueblos Mágicos* rich in indigenous culture and cuisine, along with a wealth of history. Of course, some are more accessible than others.

Pahuatlán does not fit easily into the normal *Pueblos Mágicos* categories. It boasts no spectacular architecture or distinctive historical background. In fact, it presents only one notable and unusual attraction, which is well out of town and takes some effort to find. (That effort was well rewarded as you will soon read.)

I arrived in Pahuatlán from Huasca de Ocampo, which is only 68 kilometers (42 miles) away by the most direct route (if you don't mind cramped, small-town buses). The first bus took me from Huasca to Tulancingo, the second largest city in the state of Hidalgo. Based on information on the internet, this city of 150,000 seemed to have little to offer. Trying to use my schedule judiciously, I did not tarry in order to see whether that was truly the case.

My little bus disappointed me by terminating in the general area of Centro, instead of the bus station, which, like most of its city cousins, was located somewhere on the outskirts. This is still another reason that I prefer small towns, where there is no need to scramble around trying to figure out where to go and how to get there. (Today, virtually every Mexican city has a Central Terminal. Fifty years ago, every individual company had its own separate office, causing you to have to wander around for hours, plaintively asking for directions in order to find the next office in hopes of continuing your journey. Needless to say, it was a real mess, made even worse by my terrible Spanish.) It was still very early, with few people on the streets, but after bumbling about and asking around, I did eventually get to the terminal. And, characteristically, there was a bus leaving right away for Pahuatlán. Should I eat or wait an hour for the next? I suppose I like waiting in bus stations less than being hungry. So, I boarded.

This bus was another creaky, old-fashioned conveyance, reminiscent of my earlier days in Mexico, and it remained fairly empty as we passed through a typically dreary cityscape before moving into the surrounding high desert. But soon enough, we were picking up frequent newcomers on every other corner, the vehicle squealing and groaning as we pulled off the narrow byways. In a while, we passed through the nearby *pueblo* of Honey (pronounced "oh-nay"). I have no idea of the reason for this name since honey has no meaning in Spanish. Progress was very slow, which was not helped at all by a large series of brutal *topes* (speed bumps). Without warning, the route suddenly transitioned, bumping its way onto a sinuous country road that ran downhill into a mountainous landscape thick with foliage. And forty minutes later, we had fallen off the edge of the known world into a very different kind of place.

There was no terminal here, just a stop on a narrow and busy street, which turned out to be one of two parallel avenues in town. It was the type of street where all the traffic waits while larger vehicles weave around obstacles. I was very fortunate to arrive on Sunday morning, the town's major market day. I walked toward the church and plaza a couple of blocks up a slope. Pretty much everything in Pahautlán is up or down a slope. As is my usual habit, I wanted to lodge in some old and atmospheric relic on the main square. To get there involved pushing through the *Zocalo*, which was crammed with stalls, vendors, and crowds of customers—an experience I love and one which never fails to fill my heart with the joy of travel and adventure.

At the summit, I saw a sign for a hotel that boasted a view. Perfect! The boy at the desk seemed nonplussed to see me. Good rooms would not be available for a few hours, he said, until the heavy weekend traffic checked out. He showed me one for temporary use for 450 pesos. It was dark and depressing, with tired, peeling wallpaper and a bed that was more like a cot. By this time, I had grown accustomed to much nicer rooms for lower prices. But I was tired and didn't want to fight. Still, I asked to check the internet. He gave me the password, but neither of my devices would connect—definitely a dealbreaker. So, I picked up my backpack and headed back down to the bus stop, where I had seen a couple of other lodging establishments. On a side lane, I noticed a sign for the Hotel Jardin, and I headed for it. As soon as I walked up the driveway, I could see its charm, and the mountain vistas visible from its windows. A very friendly man sat in front of the office. On the wall was a list of prices, including a single for only 250 pesos ($12.50). Single rooms are a bit of a rarity in Mexico, but they do exist. That can't be right, I thought. What would the room be like? The answer: large and airy, with old-but-serviceable furniture, a television, internet, and hot water. I could hardly believe it. Up to that point, my cheapest rooms had cost around 300 pesos and were essentially boxes—most of them in towns which offered few lodging options.

After all this, I was starving. Not bothering to unpack, I dropped my bag and headed back to the market. I looked around for a nice restaurant. But in those early days of the pandemic, it was hard to find one that was open. There were all kinds of interesting items in the stalls, but I was mainly fixated on obtaining sustenance. A man was selling something called *tepache*, a cold and slightly fermented mixture of pineapple and sugar cane. A big, delicious glass set me back ten pesos. My stomach stopped growling. Farther along, I passed an old indigenous woman, probably not the sister of the one in Mineral del Monte; the region is crawling with them. And thank goodness. These ladies know how to cook! She was cooking blue corn gorditas filled with a spicy bean mixture, and the whole thing was smothered in cheese, lettuce, and salsa. I still wanted to find a restaurant, but decided to have one of these inviting snacks to take the edge off. I asked how much it was for one gordita. But she replied that she didn't sell just one; they were three for ten pesos. Fifty cents? I felt like I had entered some kind of Twilight Zone, the realm of Mexico from decades in the past.

After that full plate, I wasn't going to need any more food until evening, so I continued to wander around the fascinating market. Many of the streets ended in precipitous drops. The colorfully decorated Municipal Market building was beautiful, even if the entranceway was clogged by a gaggle of indigenous girls vending horrible, gaudy, plastic kitchenware. Soon, I passed a modern young couple bargaining for crafts. Fashionably dressed, everything about them screamed *Chilango* (people from Mexico City). They were hip and sophisticated, and we chatted for a while. The man talked about motorcycling from Mexico to Argentina, just like Che Guevara. They said that this town was not very well known in Mexico City, although it was just a few hours away, but that some friends had recommended it for its market. For them, this was just a day trip (with six hours total travel time). Ah, youth.

I spent the afternoon lazing about in the peaceful Hotel Jardin. Late in the day, I walked around some more, still not finding a real restaurant. Near the bus stop, there was a modest hole-in-the-wall called Comedor Vicky. I walked in and the Señora greeted me ecstatically, in good English. She and her husband had lived for many years in North Carolina, working in the restaurant industry. Their grown children, born in the US, still lived there. But as it is for most Mexicans, there is no place like home, and the parents had returned to the place of their birth to live out their lives. Not wishing to speak English, I soon switched to Spanish. Vicky was amazed. The concept of a gringo who spoke good Spanish was beyond her experience, and she complimented me over and over again. Unfortunately, I know plenty of people who are unhappy when they hear people speaking Spanish in the USA but expect the natives in Mexico to know English. What a world. The delicious meal of hot vegetable soup, chicken breast in sauce, tortillas, and a fruit drink was 50 pesos.

In the morning, I came out into a different world, with very few people about. Pahautlán is lively on Sundays, but on other days it is peaceful and silent, feeling almost like a forgotten town. No foreigners here; it is off the map and close to completely unknown. I set off to visit the hanging bridge, the Puente Colgante Miguel Hidalgo y Costilla. My host told me to take the combi heading toward the nearby village of Xolotla. The combi snaked down a steep hill to the river for about ten or fifteen minutes. I was looking for a turnoff or a sign that might indicate my intended destination, but I didn't see any. Of course, I could have asked the driver, but "real men" don't ask directions…or so I have heard. Then, before I knew it, we had crossed a bridge and were starting to ascend, leaving me none the wiser about where I should be getting off. But I had seen Xolotla from the terrace of my lodging and was curious. Had any foreigners ever visited the village? It didn't seem so far away, so I stayed in the van, and ten minutes later we arrived. I was glad I had come. The village was even slower and sleepier than Pahuatlán, and the views were utterly magnificent. The people looked at me curiously, but they were friendly enough. I continued to doubt if they had ever seen any foreigners here. And the simple old church was beautiful.

Hanging bridge to nowhere

After walking around and drinking a glass of fresh-squeezed orange juice for ten whole pesos, I made the fairly short hike back down to the river. I came to the bridge at the bottom but still saw no sign directing me to the old, hanging one I was seeking. Some people were picnicking, and they pointed out a nearly hidden path that wound uphill beside a creek. After another fifteen minutes of meandering, I at last came to the ancient suspension bridge. Certainly, a very interesting sight, and fun to walk and sway back and forth across on. Oddly, it seemed to have neither a starting nor an ending point at all, just the slight dirt path leading from one jungly patch of hillside to another, seemingly miles from any human habitation. Why was it here? I never found out. Afterwards, I left the trail and traced the stream downward. I came across a lovely dark pool, stripped down, and luxuriated in the clear, cold water. Butterflies flitted about, and there were many unusual semi-tropical trees and flowers. An Edenic spot.

Back in Pahuatlán, I walked around the marketplace again. There was a group of old indigenous women in native garb, chattering away in their native language. I paused and listened in fascination. Around the corner from my lodging stood the town's swanky hotel, complete with its own *temescal* (steam bath). A double was all of 700 pesos. Inside, I finally found the real restaurant I had been looking for and enjoyed a delicious meal—not as cheap as the others, but still a bargain. Pahuatlán is definitely a magical place. Insanely inexpensive, too.

I have noted that my first large *pueblo* circuit in 2021 was strongly influenced by the pandemic. Many places of interest were shut down, and mask use was in force almost everywhere, though some places were a great deal more fastidious than others. After having difficulty finding a standard restaurant in Pahuatlán, with the belated exception of the fancy Villas de Cortez, I surmised that they were also victims of the plague. Then I realized that they were simply closed from lack of business, a side effect rather than a proximate cause. It is a real measure of Pahautlán's isolation, along with its startlingly low prices, that in terms of COVID, the town was a total anomaly. Very few people were wearing masks, and there were no signs restricting entry to stores and other public places. I can't explain it.

Getting there: Like Cuetzalán, Pahuatlán is at the end of a paved road with nothing else beyond it (save the tiny village of Xolotla). The only way to get there is to take a bus from the city of Tulancingo, making a connection to it from either Mexico City, Pachuca, or Puebla.

6) *Cuatrociénegas, Coahuila*

In all my years of travel, I have spent very little time visiting the northern deserts of Mexico, including Baja California. These areas are culturally intertwined with the U.S. Southwest, which was once part of the Mexican Republic. The cuisine runs heavily to meat instead of fresh produce, and the region is the origin of Tex-Mex cuisine, which is what most people north of the border have traditionally thought of as "Mexican food." There is a lot of spectacular scenery in this vast, mountainous desert-scape, but it's mostly long stretches of dreary flatlands that bring little pleasure to the eye of the traveler. But Monterrey (along with Veracruz, which I had planned but failed to visit in 2022 and which is now on an upcoming itinerary) was pretty much the only major city I had never visited. I endeavored to change that.

In the fall of 2023, I flew from Seattle to San Antonio to see the Alamo, then took a Greyhound and crossed into Mexico from Eagle Pass to Piedras Negras. From there, I took a long bus ride to the unremarkable town of Monclova, where I overnighted, then continued westward to the first *Pueblo Mágico* of this northern tour, Cuatrociénegas (Four Marshes). I have driven down to Mazatlán through northern Mexico many times, passing mostly dusty and unattractive cities along Highway 15. Cuatrociénegas was very different. In fact, it is open, clean, and handsome. There are a number of attractive historical buildings surrounding the plaza. The other points of interest inside the town limits are two vineyards, with their accompanying wineries.

Mostly, though, I came to Cuatrociénegas for its natural wonders, none of which are particularly close to town. Lacking a car, I have missed a number of these kinds of attractions in other *Pueblos Mágicos*. And as I've related more than once here, my natural stinginess and my desire to live like locals have kept me out of taxis whenever possible for my entire traveling life. (I am slowly coming to grips with this tendency and continue to plod along the road to recovery!) And after all, it's considerably cheaper to pay for some taxis than to drive a private automobile. I visited the friendly tourist office in the Municipal Palace, and they called a local guide who met me out front ten minutes later. There are three main attractions in the area: a disused marble mine, the Dunas de Yeso (Yeso Dunes), and the Poza Azul (Blue Well). This area is blessed with a large number of such pools, most of which connect to underground irrigation channels dating to pre-Columbian times. He agreed to take me on a tour to all these the next morning. He wanted $80. I gulped. Well, there is a first time for everything.

For breakfast, I picked the most unassuming eatery I could find in the town center. It held the expected minimalist decor and one typical *abuela* (grandmother), who served as chef, waitress, and bottle-washer. This unpretentious eatery was much the same as anywhere in Mexico, except for the prices, which were almost twice as much as I had been used to paying.

Back at the plaza, I was a bit disappointed to find the son of my guide rather than the father. He said that the "old man" was taking a bus tour group around. Anyway, off we went. The boy was friendly and knowledgeable enough, but as the morning progressed, his impatience became obvious. Clearly, he wanted to be doing something more entertaining than carting around an old gringo fogey like me. At each locale of the tour, I wanted to loiter and stroll around as always. His body language clearly communicated his desire to do quite the opposite.

Our first stop was the old marble mine. We ambled around as he filled me in on the basics, some of which were quite interesting and a bit surprising, most especially how long and tedious the whole process of creating marble is. The weirdest aspect of the site was the colorful, but discordant dinosaur sculptures strewn about, reminding me a bit of the Carnival statues in Mazatlán that dot the boardwalk every February. Another point of interest is that this old mining pit is transformed into a disco with light and sound shows in the evening. No doubt it was a lot more boring out there a hundred years ago.

Next up were the famous Dunas de Yeso. This area, which was once a small part of an enormous inland sea, is gleamingly white due to its calcium sulfate sand. It was quite windy and a bit cold there in the morning. The parking lot was full of tour buses, and crowds of people were milling about. We walked among fascinating rock formations scattered with oddly shaped cacti. I wanted to take a longer stroll and get away from the mob, but clearly the boy didn't share this desire, subtly steering me to any points of scripted interest and arcing back in the direction of his car. Well, as I said, it was pretty cold and windy.

Poza Azul

Finally, we drove back toward town, stopping at the Poza Azul, which was gorgeous. The water was a deep turquoise, reflecting in its depths the soaring sky and the surrounding craggy rocks. Birds chirped all around. There were far fewer people and buses here than at the dunes, but still more than I usually like. Poza Azul is the largest and deepest of the numerous pools in the vicinity. I was allowed to dawdle there for a while, then my guide rather unilaterally declared that the tour was over.

Back in town, we said a brief goodbye. I was annoyed, and my tip was about half of what I had planned when we set out. He was a smart enough boy, and it felt like he just didn't care. Was it all worth it? There was no other real purpose to coming to Cuatrociénegas than to view the natural wonders. I could certainly afford it. The continuing lesson is to prioritize my choices as I age. And the answer is that I did get good value for the money and experienced a lot. This was the only place I could have seen these particular awe-inspiring sights.

Poza Azul (Blue Well)

This visit certainly confirmed my general expectations regarding the northern desert areas of Mexico. There is a dearth of municipal markets and very little local fresh produce—which is only available, at a steep premium, in the supermarkets. There seems to be little in the way of color, festivities, or indigenous culture. The place is *pocho*—Americanized. There were none of my normal lodging choices. The most economical was an Airbnb for almost $80 a night, which was pretty much double any amount I had ever paid in Mexico. The old mansion was graceful, peaceful, and full of flowers. The internet was mediocre; I had to go out in the hall for a decent signal. The housekeeper was very friendly. It was fine, but nothing I would want to repeat on a regular basis. The year before, I had stayed in a much nicer, more comfortable Airbnb near the center of Cuernavaca and paid only $25 a night.

I visited only two other *Pueblos Mágicos* in the region that fall, before having to run back to Mazatlán due to a medical emergency. I know there are others certainly worth seeing if I ever return to this region. Whether I get back is an open question. At my age, I am definitely not into making any very long-term plans.

Getting there: From Eagle Pass/Piedras Negras or Monterrey, take a bus to Monclova, where you can connect. There are regular buses for the 79-kilometer (50-mile) trip to Cuatrociénegas. From Monclova, there are two other *Pueblos Mágicos* located due east—the first, 97 kilometers away, is Candela, which I hope to visit sometime. Curiously, there was no bus service at all from Monclova to Candela, only a 1,000-peso taxi ride. This is an anomaly for Mexico. Maybe it is a pretty bad road, or perhaps northern Mexico has its own rhythms. If I ever want to visit the adjacent *Pueblos Mágicos* of Candela and Bustamante, I will have to come south from Laredo or north from Monterrey.

5) *Calvillo, Aguascalientes*

Calvillo was the second *Pueblo Mágico* I visited during my initial tour in the fall of 2021. The first, Nochistlán, was locked down, including the gardens and the churchyard. Lots of yellow tape everywhere. In Aguascalientes city, the National Museum of Death sounded fascinating (to me at least). What a disappointment to find it was also shut down. I was beginning to think that this project was premature, with so many pandemic-induced limitations. Fortunately, my concerns were not always warranted. In Calvillo, unlike Pahuatlán (which evidently stands alone), everyone was wearing masks inside, mostly, but on the streets, life felt pretty ordinary.

I left Aguascalientes (the state is named for its many *balnearios* or hot water springs) after spending a couple of pleasant days there. Like many of its colonial counterparts, it has plenty of charm and character and virtually zero foreign tourists. I had checked onward connections upon my arrival at the bus terminal. There were frequent departures to Calvillo, a popular Mexican weekend getaway. They even had their own bus company for the short hop. The supremely comfortable coach put Greyhound to shame, as did my minimal half-price fare.

My Airbnb was spacious, comfortable, and cheap. It was also devoid of other guests. I phoned my landlady when I arrived. She let me in, showed me around, and gave me the keys. I never saw her or anyone else again, so my time on the premises was very quiet and stress-free. After checking in, I was hungry and ready to see what made Calvillo magical. Despite the fact that there is an open vista of the older neighborhoods clinging to the nearby western hills, along with plenty of pretty colonial architecture, central Calvillo has quite a modern feel to it. After a seven-minute walk, I found a marketplace that felt more like a mini-mall, bright and impeccably clean. I was immediately drawn to a counter-style seafood eatery with a colorful menu. I ordered a garlic fish plate, which came with rice, salad, and tortillas. I was practically starving and greedily asked for some beans on the side (five pesos!) I also treated myself to a cold Negra Modelo. Once they discovered I could speak Spanish, the couple running the place couldn't have been friendlier. The bill for this delicious and filling meal was 125 pesos, or just over six dollars.

After eating, I continued my meandering. It was a cool, late-summer day, the sky a bright blue and fluffy white cumulus clouds drifting above the old buildings.

Soon, I saw an elegant staircase leading straight up a hill—always an irresistible draw for me. At the top were some older and more austere church buildings, along with an impressive view of the now-darkening sky. I also bumped into a couple of young Mormon missionaries. There may not be tourists in these towns, but it is never much of a shock to run into these guys. One was Mexican, the other from Illinois. He insisted on pronouncing the silent "s" for Illinois, even after ascertaining that I was a fellow gringo. I would like to say that there are no silent letters in Spanish, but there is one—the "H," although it is challenging to get North American tourists not to voice it anyway. We chatted for a few minutes. As always, I kept the conversation on travel, not religion. It always amuses me when these callow youths try to explain the world to a man in his seventies. Soon, I got bored with their attempts to proselytize and continued my walk.

As evening approached, I bought a corn on the cob with all the local trimmings from a vendor in the plaza. This hot snack of *elote* comes smothered with mayo, cream, cheese, and hot red pepper flakes. The once unthreatening clouds were now turning even darker. A couple of hours later, back at my nest, my reading was interrupted by one of the loudest explosions I had ever heard. Alarmed at first, I soon heard the pounding of rain on the roof and realized it was just nearby thunder and lightning.

In the morning, I found some car-free streets with boutique shops—confirmation that I was indeed in a tourist town. I had a delicious and economical breakfast in a pleasant nook with only three tables, joined by a man who had spent fifteen years in Los Angeles and Chicago. Like the restauranteur in Pahuatlán, he was incredulous that I spoke fluent Spanish. What does that say about us Americans?

After eating, I visited the tourist office for suggestions. In rapid-fire Spanish, the girl gave me information about enough sites to fill three days of touring. I had to ask her to slow down. These days it's hard enough for my old ears to understand English spoken through masks, let alone machine-gun Mexican Spanish. But enough about language issues.

One of the main attractions of Calvillo was a *presa* (dam) and its accompanying artificial lake. I tend to have little interest in Mexico's large number of manmade lakes, as they're usually full of families being expensively rowed around and pricey fish restaurants designed for vacationers. But the countryside was beautiful, so I decided to venture out to the dam. The combi station held a bewildering assortment of vehicles heading for all the surrounding villages, but I finally found the right one. However, when I arrived in the cute adjacent village, I discovered that the lake was still a good 45 minutes away, at least by foot. No problem, of course. I enjoyed my stroll as always. Then, halfway there, a pickup truck driven by a local pulled over and drove me the rest of the way.

The lake and dam were pretty much what I expected, with plenty of well-off families enjoying a Sunday outing away from the city. The water was full of rowboats lazing along. Out of curiosity, I checked out a couple of menus and saw the expected high prices. A meal like the one I had enjoyed the previous afternoon was more than twice as much here.

The dam complex held all kinds of old equipment, which was fun to explore. And where the water fell off the edge to form the stream that ran toward town, there was a small craggy gorge where cascades coursed down the rocks, rainbows glimmering in the spray. What a treat! I tarried for ten minutes, entranced by the impromptu prismatic light shows above the water, then started back to the village. Emboldened by my easy trip out, I stuck out my thumb and scored a ride in no time. This one was not only going to the neighboring settlement, but all the way back to Calvillo.

There was one other attraction in town which, for my purposes, was amusing: a *Pueblos Mágicos* museum. The focus was mainly on the three towns in Aguascalientes state, with a few snippets of information about some other places and the program in general. I didn't learn much that I hadn't already known. But one exhibit was very helpful—an elaborate oversized wall map showing the location of all the 132 participants circa 2020. Paper maps which show perspective and the spatial relationship of geographical entities to each other are not very common these days, so I was pleased to see the towns' distribution graphically depicted, which gave me a much better sense of prospective routes and itineraries.

All in all, Calvillo is another one of those towns which just feels good. Like a few others, it's an easy place to hang around as long as you feel like it.

Getting there: Not a challenge. The city of Aguascalientes is situated on the main highway between Guadalajara and Zacatecas. There are regular departures to Calvillo from the central bus terminal.

4) *Malinalco, México*

A small disclaimer: We have now reached the point where these rankings are more or less random. All the remaining towns merit a visit or even a stay and would have been included in my Top Ten if there had been space.

In the days of yore, rich Mexico City residents liked to escape its cold mountain winters, establishing personal winter homes in Cuernavaca, about 700 meters (2,300 feet) lower. Just for fun, I'll tell you that Cuernavaca translates literally as the "cow's horn," but in reality, it is a thinly-veiled reference to adultery. I'll leave the true historical ambience of the city to your imagination. This region, with its mild climate, holds a number of attractive areas where the privileged enjoy having vacation homes. The towns tend to be artier and more intellectual than *campesino* (peasant) Mexico. What I can promise is that Malinalco, along with its sister town Tepoztlán (chronicled later in this chapter), is one of the loveliest communities in these parts, and perhaps in all of Mexico. I have been in Malinalco twice, neither time very recently. Though I want to provide as current information as possible, I would feel derelict in my duty to you, dear reader, if I left it off my list. I did watch a recent YouTube video about the town, and it looks nicer than ever.

Nestled in an alpine valley, Malinalco is a true hiker's paradise, and home to all kinds of exotic sub-tropical flora and fauna. Everything here, both manmade and natural, exudes beauty and charm. There are many boutique lodgings and upscale restaurants, and a never-ending artisans' market spills out into the quiet lanes of this 700-year-old community. It is reputed to have been the early home of witches and sorcerers, courtesy of the goddess Malinalxochitl (whew, these indigenous names can be a mouthful). This powerful sorceress is the ruler of snakes, scorpions, and desert insects. I'm not sure how this translates to green and gentle Malinalco, but she is certainly nobody to mess with.

The Aztecs chose a steep escarpment on one side of this valley on which to erect one of their most sacred shrines. This monolithic rock temple built into the side of a cliff is one of the largest of its kind in the world, and not to be missed. It's accompanied by a small but fine museum. The other historical attraction is the beautiful ex-convent founded by Augustinian monks in 1540. But Malinalco would feel magical even without these sites. It is simply a joy to stroll around town or hike into the surrounding valley. The streets are narrow and cobblestoned, with sparse traffic. Houses of all sizes sport bright red tile roofs, and fruit trees abound. The climate is perfect, rarely too hot or too cold. On the other hand, real estate here, which can be dirt cheap in many of the lesser-known *pueblos*, is at a premium. As I pointed out, this is an artistic/intellectual community in easy proximity to a great metropolis, and there are undoubtedly a number of affluent foreigners discreetly enjoying its enchantments.

If all this were not enough, the two-hour bus ride from Mexico City ends seven kilometers (four miles) above Malinalco in the temple town of Chalma, home to the most prominent sacred grotto in the country, which is visited by more pilgrims than any shrine except for that devoted to the sainted Guadelupe. The self-styled "Lourdes of Mexico," Chalma is a sanctuary that came to renown following the purported apparition of a crucified black Christ. Whether you are arriving by combi or bus, you emerge in a flat area along the main road, looking down on the rest of the village. From there, the carnival-like atmosphere takes over as you descend the maze of tiny alleys that lead down to the grotto and temple. Amid all the food and drink, there are all kinds of touristy souvenir shops. And, like its bigger and more famous French cousin, the most popular purchase is a plastic flask of holy water guaranteed to bring you long life and vitality — I should have grabbed a case, but sadly it wouldn't fit in my backpack. Malinalco's boutique markets feature a plenitude of fresh-baked bread and tasty fruit. The gastronomic specialty of the region is mouth-watering fresh mountain trout.

In 1990, my ex and I were parked in the campground just outside the ruins, in our Toyota van with our five-year-old daughter. It was Saturday, and we were waiting for the next day, when entrance to Mexico's myriad museums and archeological treasures is free to the public. Across the clearing was a converted school bus. Outside it were three dark-skinned indigenous girls and a blond hippie type with long scraggly hair. After a while he walked over and engaged me in conversation. It turned out that he was not a fellow foreigner, but a full-fledged Mexican son of a very prominent family. As a typical black sheep, his family had farmed him out with an ultra-generous allowance in exchange for his promising never to show his face in the city again.

Chalma Sacred Grotto

In the afternoon, a very expensive touring car showed up. From it emerged a well-scrubbed mom and dad with two little girls in tow, all dressed casually, but with everything about them screaming money. They were friendly enough and suggested that we might join them with our own precious one in visiting the temple and museum. I mumbled something about waiting until Sunday when it would be free entry. That was the end of that. From that moment we may as well have been invisible.

In today's world, such overt classism seldom shows its face. Malinalco is a peaceful and tranquil refuge where artists and nobility can and do rub elbows without strain, give or take a few haughty weekend visitors. Along with a few other *Pueblos Mágicos*, it would be an easy place to hang out for a few weeks or months. So, have I piqued your interest enough? After writing this section, I have penciled this town in for my next circuit in the fall of 2025. I haven't been there for some time and am looking forward to seeing it without the limitations of the penury of my earlier days.

As a brief aside, here are a couple of juicy personal anecdotes involving Mexico's lingering class and gender issues:

1) In 1973, my parents were touring Mexico in a Volkswagen Bus. They were camped in a fairly ritzy trailer park inhabited mainly by the Airstream contingent. Although not wealthy, my parents were neither young nor long-haired, and as such they were tolerated right up to the day of the following incident. My father (a retired advertising executive) was innocently washing the dishes outside the van when he was approached by a concerned group of men who requested that he refrain from such duties, or at the least move to a spot not so easily observable by their wives. Dad, who was not known for either his sobriety or his ability to suffer fools, told them to "stick it where the sun never shines."

2) Despite their dabbling with a faux-hippie image, my folks were cultured people with good manners and clothes, and my mother spoke decent Spanish. One day they were invited

to a Mexican potluck in an affluent home, the only foreigners attending. Everyone was sitting at a large table conversing, when there was a bell that the food was ready. All the wives stood up, picked up a plate, and walked over to the buffet table, as did my mom. They all loaded the plates and returned to the table. My mother started to sit down with her food, then noticed that every other woman had given the plate to her husband. Proof positive that sexism has no national boundaries.

Getting there: Malinalco is easily reachable by bus from Mexico City, Cuernavaca (the state capital of Toluca), and the famous adjoining *Pueblo Mágico* of Taxco. Depending on which of these you are departing from, you may need to ride the last stretch from Chalma in a combi or taxi.

3) *Valley de Bravo, México*

When I describe the *Pueblos Mágicos* program to people who have never heard of it, one question comes up again and again: What makes a town "magic"? No doubt when the concept was in its infancy, someone came up with the slogan. Looking back, it feels like a very adroit word choice, evoking a sense of beauty, adventure, and perhaps even mysticism. So, what is the first thing that comes to my mind when I hear the title? Certainly not reputation or things to see and do. Those are unarguably important, but as I look at my travels, "magic" is mostly just about how a place feels—its ambience, its aura. And that is one attribute that pretty much all of my favorite *Pueblo Mágico*s have in common. From the beginning, you just *feel glad to be there*. And I now realize, from the lessons of a lifetime of travel, what I think I always knew: If there is some kind of secret sauce, it becomes evident in the overall feeling, the atmosphere, the subtle spirit of a place. It can't be described in words, really. Only felt.

A Mexican friend had recommended Valle de Bravo. He said it was one of his favorite places, so I was predisposed to like it from the beginning. Riding the bus downhill to the town, snaking through the bright green scenery replete with flowers and with occasional glimpses of a sapphire-blue lake on the horizon, magic was certainly already in the air. Valle de Bravo is about two and a half hours from Mexico City (obviously less in a private car). It has long been a weekend and holiday resort for the *Chilangos*—the hip, the artistic, and the revelers. As a note, the term Chilango for a resident of Mexico City has a checkered history in the same way the term gringo does. Though it is not inherently pejorative, some people do take it negatively. But my online research shows that there really are no appropriate alternative choices, so I am stuck with it. (By the way, if you wish to appear to be in the know, you can learn the nicknames for the denizens of the other large Mexican cities: Guadalajara—*Tapatios;* Veracruz—*Jarochos;* Puebla—*Poblanos;* Mazatlán—*Patas Saladas;* and Monterey—*Regios* or *Norteños.*) In Valle, there is not a whole lot in the way of history and architecture. The game here is adventure sports, boat rides, markets, and open plazas full of people in their finery. A kaleidoscope of light and color.

There are a variety of high-class restaurants, but also common eateries offering basic and delicious meals at rock-bottom prices. Walking from the bus station to my hotel, I passed a sign that promised a full *comida* (meal) with a fruit drink and a choice of entree for only four dollars. Though it was just past noon, the place was already filling up with locals. Checking in, I dropped my bags and returned to the restaurant. That first meal after arriving in a new destination can be problematic. Generally, when you arrive in a new place and haven't had a chance to look around, the tendency is to gravitate to the first visible establishment in order to appease your growling stomach. In this case, that first meal was quite good, which had seemed likely when I first walked past the place. But by the following afternoon, I had been gallivanting around enough to locate a meal I could definitely savor. Near the lake, I found a fancy Middle Eastern place. There I had a filling falafel plate with mezzes, salad, and a dark beer, all for $10. These are the types of elevated establishments you can find in the more touristy *pueblos*.

Strolling around Valle de Bravo

Since I had arrived on a Saturday, the town was full of party-going weekenders. Yet I did not notice a single obvious foreigner the whole time. How can a place so pleasant, interesting, and easily accessible from Mexico City be so totally devoid of international travelers? It simply astounds me. I have spent a lot of time in Europe and Southeast Asia, where the young backpacking crowd is omnipresent. But Mexico may as well be terra incognito, in spite of the fact that it offers almost anything that these backpackers would desire, and, to ice the cake, all at cut-rate prices. All I can say so far is my gain, their loss!

As I mentioned, there are few special sights in Valle. It is mainly a "walking around" sort of place. The lakeside in front of the town is jammed with boats of all sizes catering to tourists. But the rest of the waterfront is more or less empty and ruggedly scenic. Well-off Mexicans are typically similar to their brethren worldwide—they don't care to walk or, even more likely, never even consider doing so to be a possibility. That happy fact left me alone to roam the undeveloped shoreline, surrounded by natural beauty.

Another colorful promenade led me away from the busy Centro through affluent neighborhoods, the avenues lined with one beautiful vacation home after another. I walked for forty-five minutes out to La Peña ("The Rock"), a community built on a peninsula jutting into the lake, with its enormous eponymous natural formation towering above. At times, I stopped and chatted with locals immersed in their gardening chores.

Another slightly longer trek (combi available) took me to Avándaro and its waterfall. This place is noted for having hosted a sprawling Woodstock-style rock festival in 1971. The village is pretty enough, but there is nothing left of its earlier vibes. Sunday was the best day for walking, as the central part of town transformed itself into one giant covered market. Even if you are not into consumerism, as I am not, it is still a lot of fun to window-shop.

Some of the *Pueblos Mágicos* abound in special attractions.

And some, like Valle de Bravo, are perfect just for leaving the stress and anxiety of the modern world far behind.

Getting there: There are regular direct-route departures from Mexico City and Toluca.

2) *Tepoztlán, Morelos*

Is Tepoztlán a well-known town? Or completely obscure? It's one of the silly questions I ask myself. Ironically, it is possibly the very first town I ever heard of in Mexico. I was a sociology major at the University of California and recall reading a book called *Life in a Mexican Village* by Oscar Lewis, written in the 1950s, which was about the cycle of poverty in the Mexican peasant class. This village is where he lived and did his research. These days, one thing you certainly cannot claim about contemporary Tepoztlán is that it has any connection to poverty or peasantry. Like Malinalco and Valle de Bravo, it is a lovely and thoroughly upscale refuge from Mexico City, and it's hopping on the weekends.

At a fairly low 1,710 meters (5,300 feet), Tepoztlán is another resort-style town where you can escape the winter chills of the national capital. The town is situated in a valley. Whether walking in the central lanes or hiking in the surrounding emerald countryside, you'll see endless jagged and towering rock formations soaring high above.

I am tempted to call it the Bali of Mexico. Both are steeped in their respective country's identities and cultures, but not fully "of" them. They are replete with artists, hippies, and new-agers, eccentric international wanderers, and ex-pats. There are plenty of North Americans living here, both short- and long-term. Unlike their more staid and affluent cousins in Malinalco, some of these Americans are more than happy to let their freak flag fly. You can't walk around central Tepoztlán without tripping over spas, temescals, native steam baths, massage parlors, tarot card readers, and a full gauntlet of vegetarian and vegan restaurants. The sidewalks and markets are bursting with every kind of art under the sun, and the vibrant colors are delightful.

Lodging prices are at a premium, as are the dishes at fancy restaurants. But I stayed at a reasonably priced Airbnb straight (and a bit arduously) uphill from the Centro, with a woman originally from New York City who arrived here forty-one years ago. She ekes out a living with rents and a remote therapy practice. Her house is gorgeously decorated and surrounded by exuberant foliage and flowers. Just don't expect the relatively low cost to include up-to-date infrastructure. The narrow streets and hilly terrain do not encourage easy renovations. In this case, both the plumbing and cooking facilities seriously needed some updating, which under the circumstances seemed very unlikely to ever materialize.

In addition to its festive atmosphere, the town offers a number of attractions. The church and ex-convent are decorative examples of their epochs, and sitting around the shaded plazas taking in the historic vibes is a delight. The town's main claim to fame is the ancient Aztec Tepozteco Pyramid, high on a hill looking down upon the entire valley. Leaving the crowds behind at the end of the main street, it's a serious hike to get to the top, and quite steep. The trek is beautiful, though, and you're surrounded by plenty of water running alongside you as you pass on your way.

My experience of this hike was typically Mexican. I set out intrepidly—as you already know I do—and fed my vanity by passing crowds of young people who were huffing and puffing and taking frequent breaks. After thirty minutes of fairly strenuous effort, I reached the gate to the pyramid. It was locked, another casualty of the pandemic. Not one person, vendor, or posted sign had given warning of this tiny inconvenience in any language. In normal Mexican cultural fashion, why would they give any advanced thought to a problem that is not personal? I was not too disappointed, though. It was a splendid hike and workout.

Street art

On the second day, I took a long and meandering walk into the countryside, turning onto any lane that looked interesting, then returning to the road with the help of my phone map. It was a joy. Besides the constant views of the rock formations, there were gorgeous villas everywhere.

On my walk I was treated to plenty of classical music filling the air. I came to a sign advertising a small Indian restaurant. It wasn't open yet at this early hour, but I walked up the driveway and pushed the bell on a gate. A handsome young East Indian emerged and greeted me. He had come to Tepoztlán a couple of years earlier and married a Mexican girl. I wondered to myself how he could possibly be earning a living. Only an odd duck like me who delights in random walks out to the middle of nowhere would be likely to chance upon his restaurant. But Tepoztlán is a very eclectic place, and no doubt some clients would seek out his form of cuisine—but only if they had some way of knowing about it. I gently suggested that some kind of advertising might be helpful.

The town has one quirk which is highly amusing. There is almost no available parking amidst the narrow and winding lanes of the Centro. But problem created, problem solved: Where there are paying customers, there are entrepreneurs. Walk these side lanes away from the concentrations of shops and restaurants and look down the driveways that lead off to homes. You will see large open spaces full of graceful old trees, flowers, bushes…and cars. People have converted their garden spaces into cash. And that is pretty much the story of Tepoztlán: beauty at a price.

Getting there: There is regular bus service to Tepoztlán from both Mexico City and Cuernavaca.

1) *Tzintzuntzan, Michoacán*

The town of Tzintzuntzan is still relatively unknown today. Its name comes from the melodic Purépecha word for hummingbird ("colibri" in Spanish). Tucked into a remote section of a lakeshore where fisherman ply their trade in solemn solitude, it is a tranquil spot. However, it has not completely escaped mass tourism. In the middle of the day, buses full of domestic visitors roll in, and it seems like most of the villagers now earn their cash selling snacks and tacky crafts. Still, if you walk away from the pleasant (if not particularly authentic) market, the town has more than enough other sites of interest. There is a truly magnificent ex-convent and museum, along with some impressive pre-Columbian ruins.

I am not a big fan of the large and flashy cathedrals of Mexico and Spain, which are generally considered to be the highlights of any large city. The conquistadores exploited slave labor to plunder the earth of huge quantities of gold, silver, and other gems, then had those same abused peons construct enormous monuments to greed and excess. In the process, they more or less destroyed the economy of their Spanish homeland through uncontrolled inflation. Of course, it is undeniable that these works are incredible repositories of beautiful and exquisitely crafted art. But I personally have trouble looking past their sordid and bloody origins.

I far prefer the simplicity and austerity of small-town churches and chapels and, on a larger scale, the ex-convents, where for the most part the monks' spiritual philosophy ran toward asceticism. In any case, the ex-convent in this *pueblo* is a fine example. The rooms devoted to museum exhibits did a better job of recreating the history of this rich region than many much larger museums elsewhere, and the art was a joy to view.

My favorite part of the complex lies in the entrance walk, which runs through a large plaza and extensive gardens. The whole area is filled with copses of gnarled and ancient olive trees. I love trees, especially very old ones, so it was thrilling to walk around and check them out. I enjoy sitting in mediation in front of and under magnificent trees. I sometimes wonder if they pity us for our rushed and pressured lives. What tales could these old olive trees relate to us if only we could listen to them?

Through the market to the entrance of the ex-convent

After visiting the ex-convent, I walked back out through the open market, crossed the road, and headed up the stairs that passed through the village toward the old ruins that dominated the skyline. Arriving at the parking lot, I ran into some of the first foreigners I had seen in quite a while. One very brightly colored and oversized van held a young Argentine couple with a baby, who had been driving through Latin America while supporting themselves by selling crafts. We had a delightful conversation. Further up the lot was a dingy old white van without windows. I was surprised to find that its occupant was a middle-aged Englishwoman on her own for the first time in her life. She had been traveling around Mexico on the cheap for almost two years. Naturally, we had a lot to talk about and later became email friends.

It was pleasant enough walking through the piles of rocks, and there were fine views of the lake, but, as per normal there was nothing that filled me with awe. Clearly, I value the vibrations emanating from trees over those coming from rocks!

Isla de Janitzio

Isla de Janitzio is a beautiful place. It always has been. But it was once the humble home of fishermen, netmakers, and peasants living lives of self-sustenance. Nowadays, almost everyone has eschewed that heritage of simplicity for a life of catering to tourism. And much of the authenticity that gave the island its fundamental charm has evaporated. And yet, its ethereal beauty continues to mandate a visit.

To get to the lakeshore, you drive or ride a bus from downtown Pátzcuaro and walk to the boat slips. You are greeted with a panoramic view of the isle, crowned by the huge statue of Jose Maria Morelos y Pavon, a charter member of the pantheon of national heroes. Morelos was a Catholic priest, statesman, and military leader who led the Mexican War of Independence movement from 1811. His absolutely gargantuan statue stands nearly 48 meters (156 feet high) ascending from Janitzio's peak and dominating the skyline.

You'll likely settle in with a crowd of Mexican families for the pleasant boat ride across the placid surface of Lake Pátzcuaro. Then the trouble starts. Usually at least a couple of fishermen are trolling for the tiny whitefish with their famous butterfly nets. If you are like half the passengers, you whip out your phone and start taking pictures or a video. In response the men leave off their activity and paddle next to the boat, now trolling for tips, hat in hand.

Alas, arriving at the island pier, the sense of tourism-induced disconnection picks up pace. Whereas in the past everyone would have been engaged in their traditional daily routines, now they are almost all selling something to the visitors (at least in this section of the community. If you want to spend quality time on the island, just walk away from the prescribed visitor route. There is plenty of authenticity to be had once you do so). I cannot deny that Janitzio is still a very scenic place, with lots of fascinating nooks and crannies and plenty of the typical life that I just noted, but most visitors confine their visit to walking up the main narrow arteries and staircases to the top, ignoring anything else that the place has to offer. One of the main cultural events that previously garnered Pátzcuaro fame was the Dance of the Little Old Men. And when I first visited back in the 70s, this performance could only be found in one hotel, once daily. Today there are troupes all over the island plaza doing ersatz versions throughout the day.

After arriving at Janitzio's crowning plaza and catching your breath, you can wander around marveling at all the touristy glitz that has inundated a place once subdued and reverential. Then it is time to pay a visit to Señor Morelos y Pavon. Unfortunately, when you enter the base of this colossus, the staircase to the top is jammed, making it hard to breathe. What has happened here is a prime example of the Disney-fication of the world.

It was pretty. It was fun. The island's specialty food is a snack of the delicious white fish, toasted and served like miniature french fries in a little white bag. You crunch them down head, tail, and all, then chase it with a michelada. Who am I to complain? I wouldn't miss a trip to Janitzio, but I really long for the time when it had its own distinct atmosphere. It is still captivating and beautiful, even carrying an aura of mysticism.

But it is also very sad to see that its lovely culture has been all but destroyed by tourism.

Pátzcuaro, Michoacán (Bonus Town)

Pátzcuaro has long been known on the intrepid traveler circuit. It was on my itinerary in the 1970s, when I spoke hardly any Spanish and knew very little about Mexico.

Without doubt, Pátzcuaro is one of the prettiest towns in Mexico. It is also high up in the mountains and can be quite cold and damp, so plan your dress accordingly. Only an hour from the state capital in Morelia, it is easy to reach, whether for a stay or a day trip. Like San Miguel de Allende and Tepoztlán, the heart of the town is heavily controlled. Signs must be made in a certain style, with the same black and red motifs. Any work on a building must be approved. I would like to think that all this is in the service of preserving heritage. But I fear that its main incentive is the aforementioned Disney-fication of the town. The venial God of Tourism runs the place.

Authenticity aside, it is a joy to stroll around the Centro. Old architecture, plazas, and markets appear around every bend. I was in Pátzcuaro just days before the Day of the Dead, and that holiday's vivid accoutrements were everywhere, all bright colors and exotic forms. I met a woman who said that there were about 250 North Americans living in town—far fewer than places like Chapala and Ajijic or San Miguel. I can certainly see the attraction. But it is way too cold and damp for me.

Getting there: There are constant departures from Mexico City and Guadalajara to Morelia, where you can switch buses for the short hop to Pátzcuaro.

CHAPTER 4:
And All of the Rest (Northern)

Background
Todos Santos, Baja California Sur
Barranca del Cobre
Batopilas, Chihuahua
Creel, Chihuahua
Parras, Coahuila
Santiago, Nuevo León
El Rosario, Sinaloa
Magdalena de Kino, Sonora
Jerez de García Salinas, Zacatecas
Nochistlán, Zacatecas

All of the Rest (Northern)

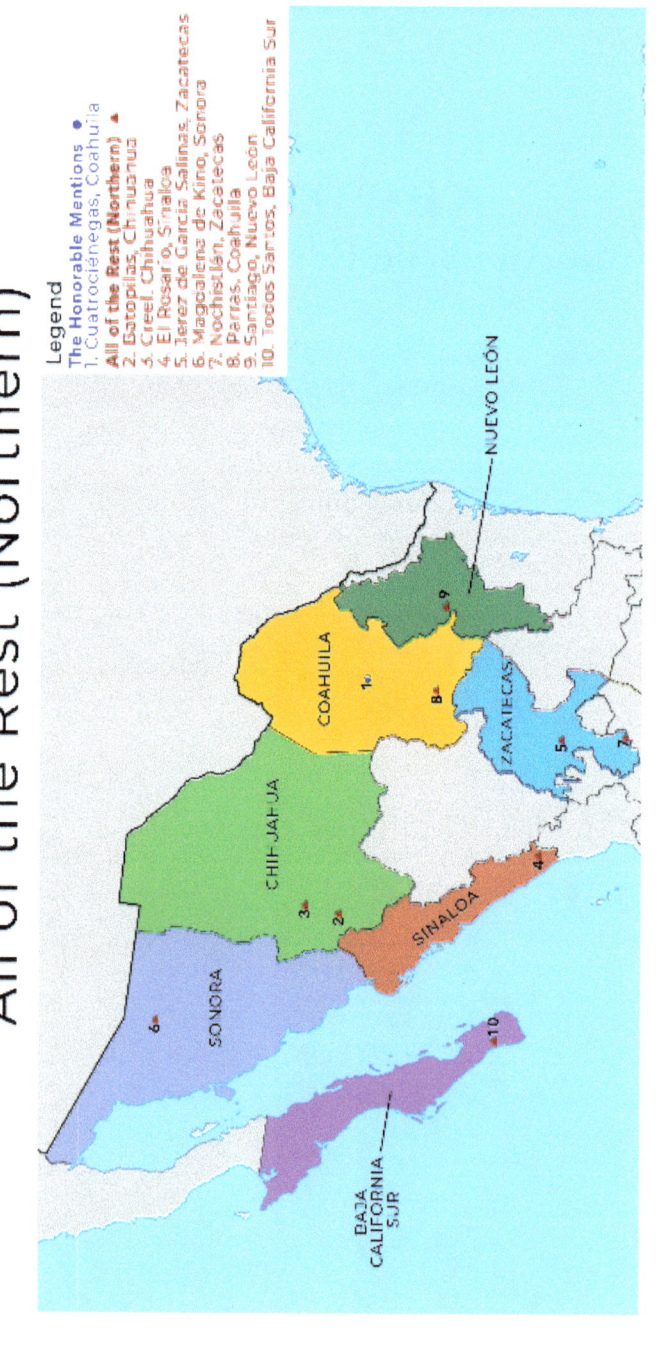

Legend
The Honorable Mentions ●
1. Cuatrociénegas, Coahuila
All of the Rest (Northern) ▲
2. Batopilas, Chihuahua
3. Creel, Chihuahua
4. El Rosario, Sinaloa
5. Jerez de García Salinas, Zacatecas
6. Magdalena de Kino, Sonora
7. Nochistlán, Zacatecas
8. Parras, Coahuila
9. Santiago, Nuevo León
10. Todos Santos, Baja California Sur

Background

I have visited 79 of the *Pueblos Mágicos* so far, mostly in the last four years, but some of them only in the bygone days of my youth. I hesitate to write in depth about these older trips, simply because I don't remember much, or perhaps because the towns might have changed too much. For example, when my ex and I slept on the beach in Sayulita in 1979, it was nothing but a tiny fishing village with frighteningly high waves braved only by the most valiant - or reckless - of surfers. Now it is apparently an upscale North American resort town and *Pueblo Mágico*. I'll need to revisit it before giving any opinions. Still, a couple of other places from those early visits are included in the upcoming section because I want to be sure that nobody will miss them on my account. And I will note a few more in the Appendix.

As of this writing, the government has recently added 45 new towns to the *Pueblos Mágicos* program, almost all of which I hadn't heard of. A few of the others are so well known that I have little to add in terms of travel guidance, such as places like Taxco, San Cristobal, Tulum, and Isla Mujeres. So, this next section, with its large grouping of brief town descriptions, does not include every single town that I have ever been in, nor does it represent a comprehensive listing of all the remaining *Pueblos Mágicos*.

Mostly, this part of the book describes some towns that might have been included in the top twenty, and others that I took pleasure in visiting but that did not really rock my world. And a very small number really did not appeal to me at all. Since you already have a good sense of my tastes, you can adjust for your own interests. To help with itineraries, the towns have been grouped more or less into four geographical areas. Please look to the end of each description for a numerical grade. And a note that I alluded to earlier: A number of towns had little to offer me within their municipal limits. They have made it into the program for natural attractions, some of which are difficult or time-consuming to get to without a car. My travels have not included many such jaunts, perhaps due to a lack of time or maybe because getting out by taxi does not guarantee getting back easily, short of paying the driver generously to hang around. And with that one exception in Cuatrociénegas, I do not do tours. Consider it a personal quirk.

Todos Santos, Baja California Sur

Most of the Baja Peninsula consists of sparsely populated desert. In the south, the main attractions are the state capital La Paz and the resort meccas of Los Cabos, San José del Cabo, and the Magic Town of Todos Santos. There is also a *Pueblo Mágico*, Loreto, up the coast from La Paz, which I have not yet visited. I have never been much of a Baja person. As I noted in the description of my abbreviated visit to northern Mexico, these vast desert lands lack color, vibrancy, markets, indigenous cultures, and festivity—all the qualities I cherish about Mexico. I watched a YouTube video about Loreto, and it does appear to be quite attractive. I have, however, been to Mulejé, the next town to the north, which is a ruggedly scenic, but as of yet not a *Pueblo Mágico*. Interestingly enough, the entire Baja Peninsula can be visited without an automobile permit. However, unlike the border towns, tourist entry papers are required.

The town of Todos Santos ("All Saints") has always held appeal to the hippie and surfer sets. Almost completely isolated on the rugged Pacific coast, it is best known as the home of the real Hotel California, memorialized by the Eagles.

With my daughter in front of the real Hotel California

In the northern Thai hippie haven of Pai stands a Hotel Pailifornia, so I suppose it is a "thing." This hotel is nothing special, but it draws plenty of people (like me) for photo ops.

Todos Santos is a bright, cheerful, and colorful town that draws plenty of tourist buses and day-trippers on tours from Los Cabos. There are street markets and more than sufficient fancy dining options. Some old mission-style architecture can be found here and there. Outside of town, on the open beach you'll see the surfers with their vans. For this writer, the name of the town is probably the most magical and evocative thing about the place. It's a pleasant enough destination, particularly if you are set up to camp. It goes without saying that it is clean, casual, and friendly.

Overall rating: 7 (But I'm a big Eagles fan.)

Getting there: Halfway between La Paz and Los Cabos. There is plenty of bus access.

Barranca del Cobre, Chihuahua

The Barranca del Cobre, or Copper Canyon, named for the metallic green tinge of the native rock, is actually a series of six deep canyons which rival the Grand Canyon for breadth and depth, if not grandeur. Recently, the region has joined Oaxaca as one of the most fashionable tourist destinations in Mexico, though few see much of the region other than the upscale attractions along the railway. Creel is accessible by road from the state capital of Chihuahua, but almost everybody comes in on the tourist train that runs between it and Los Mochis near the Pacific Coast.

Mexico once had an extensive passenger railway system, which was very cheap (and very slow), but it was shut down in the nineties. Now there are just freight trains, except for those going into Copper Canyon. (Actually, as of this writing, there is a new Maya Train that rapidly connects tourist sites in the Yucatán, but I have not yet been down that way.) The Copper Canyon railroad is a stupendous project that took sixty years to build. A marvel of engineering, it has numerous bridges and tunnels and offers one of the most exciting and beautiful rail journeys in the world.

I rode these rails in 1977 and 1997, so my information is naturally out of date, but I have felt compelled to make an exception and write about it. With the current level of interest, I just did not want to leave these towns off my list. Particularly Batopilas, discussed later, which is still remote and little visited. Back in the day, there were two trains, El Chepe, the expensive tourist version, and the old local. All of us hippie types took the local, which was a much better deal in every way. It was a good deal slower, but who wants to speed through this spectacular terrain? The windows opened, unlike its far more expensive cousin, where a dirty film on the glass obscured the views. Today there is only the tourist option remaining, and it has to be booked far ahead. The locals are exempt from any restrictions and get discounted fares.

Before leaving the subject of the train and moving into Creel, I want to tell you about something special I saw along the line fifty years ago. Coming out of a tunnel, we passed through a wide, flat area with an old siding full of abandoned freight cars. But they were not truly abandoned. They were all inhabited by poor families, and each had a windowsill with a flower pot, the blossoms radiantly colorful above the hordes of ragged children playing out front.

Batopilas, Chihuahua

Batopilas feels like the proverbial end of the world. I'm sure it was completely unknown when I visited in 1977 at the urging of a fellow hitchhiker who knew a lot about Mexico. I don't know how good the road from Creel is today, but Google Maps says that the 136-kilometer (85 mile) trip takes about three and a half hours. Besides the option of hiring a private driver, there appears to be a shuttle, but I believe it only runs three times a week and returns on alternate days. If you go, make sure to research the latest transportation information, as the situation may have changed.

In my day, the only transport was riding on the back of the mail truck atop bags and parcels. My companions were a group of Tarahumaras drinking aguardiente, the local rotgut, which I managed to avoid as much as possible—although I took a few sips so as not to be rude. My primary strategy was to take small swigs and surreptitiously spit a bit of it over the side of the truck when I thought no one was looking. I had been unprepared for the climate in Creel, and for the first stretch until we had descended enough in altitude for the chill air to warm up, I was freezing my butt off. The gang was laughing and calling out like feral birds, delighted to tease the neophyte gringo. But soon enough, they were snoring away. The first unplanned stop was La Bufa, a tiny hamlet, which would eventually require a couple of hours of hiking down the rest of the grade to reach Batopilas, situated at the true bottom of the Urique Canyon.

I eagerly got down to stretch my legs and was astounded to be greeted by a Scotsman, who it turned out owned a traveler's inn (which saw little patronage). I spent a week with him and his stolid and mute Tarahumara wife, soaking up local lore. (If you are interested in this story and accounts of traveling in back-country Mexico circa 1968, you can read about them in my novel *The Gold Star*. There is also a wonderful and enchanting book on the folkloric history of the entire region titled *Rain of Gold*, by Victor Villaseñor.)

After tarrying for a week, I descended the rest of the way on foot to Batopilas, which was about 16 kilometers (10 miles) away. The town was reputed to be the second place in Mexico to have been electrified, courtesy of the American mine owners who had generators hauled down on the backs of donkeys. These tycoons departed after winding up on the wrong side of the Mexican Revolution, and in 1915 Batopilas descended once more into darkness. Real electricity only returned to the town in the late twentieth century. During my 1997 visit to the area, I stayed in a cute hotel in Urique, upriver from Batopilas. There was a lamp in the bedroom and another in the bathroom. But there was no way to turn either of them on or off. The mystery was solved at dusk when the town generator groaned into action and the room filled with light. Then at 10 PM it grumbled again, and the dark returned. Fortunately, I only had to wait 20 hours for it to restart, instead of 70 years!

I had been told that Batopilas was a populous town, so my first view of this purported metropolis took me aback. The walls of the canyon had been edging ever closer together as I hiked down to the river. Up ahead all I could see were a couple of buildings. Where was the town? It turns out that Batopilas has basically one street, bordered by the river and a steep cliff on one side, and with a single row of buildings backed by the opposing steep cliffs on the other. So, you only come across a few structures at a time, yet the town goes on for five kilometers. There are a few broader, more open spots that are graced by a community park and a school. The main interest in Batopilas is its mining heritage. Remember that this account is from nearly fifty-year-old memories, so I can't vouch for its complete accuracy. And I don't know what there is there now, although I hope to visit again. But I am confident that it remains a fascinating and completely distinct place to experience and that its basic contours have not altered.

Overall rating: 8

Getting there: If you are staying in Creel, it should be simple enough to explore your options. Unless you have your own wheels, don't count on getting back the same day, but I can't imagine why you would want to.

Creel, Chihuahua

Creel is the name for a basket that carries fish, but it is not a Spanish word. Spanish, as far as I know, has no words with the doubled weak vowel of e. Thus, the town's name is pronounced as it would be in English. The settlement was named after Enrique Creel, the Mexican-born son of a United States delegate to Mexico, who subsequently became the governor of the state of Chihuahua. It was originally a logging town surrounded by pine forests. It gets cold and snowy in the winter, in sharp contrast to the torrid climates of the communities many thousands of feet below along the rivers. Today Creel is mainly a tourist town, with plenty of expensive lodges in the area catering to foreigners, and a mix of traditional tours along with more "modern" options such as ziplines, bungee jumping, and the like.

In terms of the more old-fashioned attractions, a nearby possibility is one of the nation's most scenic waterfalls, Basaseachi. There is also the pretty Areko Lake, a few miles out of town, where a Rod Steiger B-movie called *Wolf Lake* was being filmed during my first visit. The scenery of the Copper Canyon(s) and the mountains of the state of Durango are spectacular, and the cost for set labor and extras was far lower than they were north of the border. That is the main reason why many Hollywood Westerns were once filmed in Mexico. I happened to be passing through during this particular filming, and one day hiked out to the set. On the way back, I was passed by an entourage of cars, which included a limo transporting the famous actor and the unheralded supporting actor, with whom I had actually chatted in town. They stopped and picked me up, though neither spoke to me the rest of the way back! Not surprisingly, there is more to this story, but you'll have to wait for the release of my yet-unwritten account of free love in the 70s in order to discover all the weird details.

This region is the home of the Tarahumaras, a shy and mysterious tribe known for their indefatigable long-distance running. They have been known to run up to 200 miles in a few days, wearing only huaraches (Mexican-style leather sandals). Their crafts are featured in the town's market.

Creel is a pretty and pleasant town steeped in history, with plenty of old buildings to enjoy. There are modern lodgings, and restaurants with fare designed to please tourists. Whether these upscale amenities add to or detract from the town's ambience is an open question. There are sufficient points of interest for the casual visitor here, but I would definitely recommend "shoulder season" rather than the cold winter.

Overall rating: 7

Getting there: There are inexpensive buses available from Chihuahua city. But pretty much everybody rides El Chepe. I recommend starting the train trip in the beautiful *Pueblo Mágico* of El Fuerte, 85 kilometers (53 miles) outside of Los Mochis. I unfortunately will not cover El Fuerte in this guide, having spent only an afternoon and a night there in 1997 before catching the train, but I recall it being a very attractive stopover.

Parras, Coahuila

Parras is a pleasant oasis town whose main claim to fame is that it is the home of Mexico's very first vineyard, founded in 1498. In between the cities of Monterey and Torreon, the town is surrounded by huge swaths of open desert. I am not an oenophile, so I didn't visit the winery, but there was enough in town to keep me going for a day and a half. The official town name is Parras de la Fuente, the last word meaning fountain, so as one might expect there is a large quantity of deep spring-driven water here and a very nice municipal swimming complex.

The town is clean, attractive, and definitely laid back, as most of these small country places are. The old architecture of the cathedral, municipal palace, and plaza is easy on the eyes. One of my favorite activities is hiking, so I set out early on my first morning to visit the canyon lands to the south. As always, I thoroughly enjoyed the rugged scenery and the way the vivid greenery of the town transformed into high, craggy desert canyons.

The other, much shorter walk I enjoyed was up the hill to the Temple of San Ignacio de Loyola, which took a brisk thirty minutes. The structure itself is modern and of no particular interest to me, but the 360-degree view from it was magnificent. Is Parras a magical place? Certainly, in contrast to the unforgiving desert that surrounds it, especially in the fantastical way that the town unexpectedly appears from that dry and bleak vastness. Would you regret spending a couple of days here? Certainly not. It is a very nice and peaceful town. And I would definitely recommend passing through the state of Coahuila and visiting Parras if you are interested in wine and history.

Overall rating: 6

Getting there: Buses and colectivos ply the highways to and from the nearby large cities of Saltillo and Torreon.

Santiago, Nuevo León

This is a historical weekend getaway town, only 37 kilometers (23 miles) from Monterrey. It is known for its tidy and lovely old town center, its large lake with accompanying recreational opportunities, and a *malecón* (boardwalk) teeming with popular restaurants.

Walking around the charming center of town is reminiscent of exploring a fairy tale village, with all the buildings painted in cheerful hues of pink and white. There is not a hair out of place; everything is orderly, clean, and pretty. The lanes are winding and cobblestoned, with only light traffic.

This is clearly a well-off community, with the poorer face of Mexico banished from the district. (While enjoying this sanitized beauty, I also like to be aware that the majority of Mexicans lack the ability to live in it. That is why I also visit poorer districts with a mind to witnessing the more typical hardscrabble life of Mexicans. I suppose that this is my biggest objection to upscale tourism: 100% pretty, 0% reality. To me, the essence of slow travel is gaining an appreciation for all the facets of a society, warts and all. When I left Santiago to hike to the waterfall I will describe in a bit, I also passed through the nearby village of Cercado. After all, Mexico is not all "magical towns." (And by the way, my experience is that the Mexican people are just as friendly and generous in these more modest places, maybe more so.)

Town view

Back to Santiago: There are a couple of small museums in the center. People flock to the famous Casa de las Abuelas, though there are a number of other fine restaurants around. At the top of a hill is a small amphitheater with excellent views of the whole area.

That is the good. Now for the not-so-good. Santiago is

noted for its lakefront, but unfortunately, this region of Mexico has been hit hard by a disastrous drought. It's easy to see the extent of the drought's effects; there are wide, brown mud flats in places that were once covered by water. If the shoreline was once alongside the edge of the malecón, it has now receded dramatically. I walked along this stretch a couple of different times, and there were never any tourist boats operating. The restaurants were mainly empty. Of course, this was not the weekend, so it might be different on those days.

The other dissonant note is that the town and the lake are cleaved by a wide, busy, loud highway coming from the city and linking all the towns in the region. There are no traffic lights, and only a couple of underpasses, so you may have to take a significant detour in order to get across the road. This roaring modern nuisance definitely detracts from the ethereal ambience that Santiago likely once boasted.

My main entertainment was a long hike (surprise, surprise) to the Cola de Caballo (Horse Tail) Waterfall. Despite the lack of water in the lake, there seemed to be enough coming from the mountains to keep the falls pounding down on the distant rocks beneath it. But I was there at the end of the rainy season, such that it was.

A very nice town, which was undoubtedly once a lot nicer. Overall rating: 7

Getting there: Frequent bus service from the Monterrey bus terminal will get you there quickly—much more quickly once you clear the city limits. There is no clearly marked arrival point. You might have to tell the driver that you want off at the Centro. Returning to Monterrey, you will need to find the bus stop on the opposite side of the highway. It's very close to the pedestrian overpass.

El Rosario, Sinaloa

El Rosario is the closest *Pueblo Mágico* to my hometown of Mazatlán, just an hour's drive south on the expensive toll road, or an hour and a half on the Libre (free highway). I have driven or ridden through the town numerous times over the past decades without realizing that it was anything special. It achieved *Pueblo Mágico* status in 2019, barely in time for me to become aware of it for my travel project. So, there is definitely value in the *Pueblo Mágico* mission, and perhaps also in this written attempt to increase awareness of it.

Our friend Nancy, Kathy, and I drove to Mexcaltitán a couple of years ago, stopping for a night in the cozy beach town of Teacapán. The next day, we headed home and stopped in El Rosario for the first time ever. We walked around a bit in the morning, but in May it soon got too hot for the ladies, so we wound up only spending a couple of hours there. I do need to go back some other time, but I suppose I'm in no hurry. When I am not traveling madly, I am often actually quite lazy about leaving the peaceful and lovely beach that lies just steps away from our home.

El Rosario is a history-steeped town. Founded in 1655, it reached the height of its political influence in the eighteenth century. It has all of the requisite architectural gems, which I mainly saw from the car as we were beating a hasty retreat from the heat, my companions having outvoted me two to one over loitering in the Centro. Is this why I have spent so much of my life as a solo traveler?

The earlier morning hours were certainly delightful. Following Siri or whatever alias she is currently using, we spent some time looking for a recommended restaurant in the narrow back lanes, which are of course all one-way. Apple Maps did its usual face-plant, making things harder than if we hadn't used it at all. But eventually we found the place, and the breakfast there turned out to be excellent. Nearby was a park spanned by a charming old wooden bridge, which I navigated on my own as my companions sat on a bench in the shade.

The highlight of the morning was a visit to the Lola Beltran Museum. Lola Beltran (1932-1996) was a singer/actress known as the Queen of Rancho Music. I had previously heard her name because there is a prominent monument to her along the Mazatlán boardwalk. She was born, however, in Rosario. I spent little time in the section of the museum devoted to her life and career. As I have mentioned a couple of times already, this type of museum minutiae tends to narcotize me unless I have a special interest in the subject. But there were a couple of rooms devoted to some excellent contemporary art and paintings that did resonate with me. So, I would happily return to the park and museum and take more time to relax into them. And I'd certainly also return to the architectural heart of the town. Considering that I haven't had an opportunity recently to make a full, rigorous assessment, I will give the town a judicious rating of 6 or 7.

Getting there: Rosario is south of Mazatlán along the free highway to Tepic, otherwise off on an exit from the toll road. A second-class bus from either city will get you to the terminal in town.

Magdalena de Kino, Sonora

I have driven up and down Mexico Highway from the border crossing in Nogales about ten times in my life. Magdalena lies some 90 kilometers (50 miles) into Mexico. The entirety of the highway down to Mazatlán is not a particularly scenic drive, passing as it does through wide swathes of barren Sonoran Desert. The greenery does increase a bit when you enter the state of Sinaloa.

Most of the cities on the route have little to recommend them (as far as my tastes go); they're modern, dusty, and have little history. An exception is San Carlos Bay, a new *Pueblo Mágico* (since 2023) just north of Guaymas, which features attractive beaches, majestic rock formations, and is a bit of haven for trailer park gringos. If like most you are in a hurry to speed by, the main highway bypasses it and also Guaymas, an old-fashioned fishing city and the only port between the border and Mazatlán. I slept on the San Carlos beach on my first Mexican foray back in the seventies. The stretch was called Catch-22 Beach back then, as that movie was filmed there and there still remained an airstrip and some artificially aged wooden buildings. But all that is long forgotten, and I can't really knowledgeably comment on the contemporary scene following a fifty-year absence.

Magdalena is an eye-pleasing anomaly tucked away in the monotonous desert, anchoring a sudden and surprising oasis of lush greenery. On a small scale, it reminds me of the Atacama Desert in northern Chile. That region is among the driest spots in the world, and in the early twentieth century it went over thirty years without a single drop of measurable precipitation. My ex and I rode a luxury bus over that moonscape in 1980. At two points, melting glaciers flow west from the high Andes and create thin strips of brilliant green which house the towns of Arica and Antofagasta.

Magdalena is not close to matching that dramatic contrast, but it does offer a bit of relief as you pass through the otherwise arid landscape. The Spanish Padre Kino must have thought the same thing when he established a mission there. I imagine his entourage wandering through this wasteland wondering if they were going to die of thirst. Then out of nowhere, a cry of "Agua, agua!" Kathy and I have stayed there a couple of times. It seemed like the perfect pretty, sleepy, and peaceful venue to spend the night. But the last time we stopped there, at 8 PM our seemingly empty hotel was suddenly invaded by a convention of dune buggies whose music pounded until the early morning hours. The horror! And we are still annoyed at the girl at reception, who didn't see fit to give us a word of warning so that we might have relocated. Afterwards I recalled her giving me a funny look when I checked in, though.

But I am forgetting myself. I am supposed to tell you why to visit, not why not. The settlement has all the fine architecture that you would expect: plazas, temples, convents, a municipal palace—all of it quite handsome in the mission style. And as I have intimated, simply driving out of the vast desert into such an oasis is certainly very striking. There is also a nice trail along the riverbank and some pleasant parkland. The town is surrounded by rich farmland and has plenty of decent restaurants.

The curious thing is that Magdalena de Kino was awarded *Pueblo Mágico* status way back in 2012, when I wasn't even aware of the program. And in the beginning of my circuit, when I was concentrating on Central Mexico, I was still unaware of its status. So, I was quite surprised in 2022 when we got off the highway exit and saw our first sign with the familiar *Pueblos Mágicos* logo. In celebration, we had a very pleasant meander around the parts of town we had previously neglected. We enjoyed a good supper. Then back to the hotel to read and flip through the television stations in the forlorn hope of finding something in English (for Kathy). And then, alas, the dreaded Invasion of the Dune Buggies.

Overall rating: 6

Getting there: Driving south from Nogales or north back to it, Magdalena is impossible to miss.

Jerez de García Salinas, Zacatecas

For seven years now, I have been a moderator of a Facebook group once called Earth Vagabonds (now named Budget Slow Travelers in Retirement). I saw that another member was driving around Mexico and would be in Zacatecas about the same time as I, so we decided to meet up and take a daytrip together. Jerez de García Salinas is only 54 kilometers (34 miles) out from the city. It was a luxury for me to get a ride in a private vehicle. Still, we got all turned around in the confusing web of roads surrounding Zacatecas. He also told me that locating his Airbnb and finding parking nearby had been a Herculean task. (Some of the many reasons why I still prefer taking the bus.) These old towns were not designed in the linear fashion demanded by the passenger automobile.

From Wikipedia: "Jerez was designated a *Pueblo Mágico* to promote tourism, as it is close to the state capital and offers tradition, handicap access, and architecture." This seems like putting the cart before the horse to me. Every *Pueblo Mágico* tends to have all these elements, along with numerous unrecognized others. The point of the program is to find and protect something distinctive about a community. As far as I am concerned, Jerez does not make the grade. But there were indeed a lot of attractive old buildings about. Maybe I am getting too picky.

The most enjoyable part of the morning was an eight-block-long open market with a colorful assortment of goods and refreshments. I have noted that I tend to blend in and am rarely addressed on the streets in my travels. Stuart, on the other hand, is quite pale in complexion and has long and wild snowy white hair. Walking with someone like that, I discovered how many Mexican men had spent time in the USA and wanted to trot out their English with him. By the way, my companion grew up in El Paso, Texas and Juarez, Mexico and is fluent in Spanish. Our most interesting conversation was with the proprietor of a Stetson hat store.

All in all, we spent an enjoyable half day in Jerez. Simpatico company will do that for you. The town itself, alas, was a bit forgettable.

Overall rating: 3

Nochistlán, Zacatecas

Back in 2021, Nochistlán was the very first *Pueblo Mágico* that I visited for that specific purpose. I got off the red-eye from Seattle to Guadalajara, and just after dawn, in a drizzle, I took a cab to the bus terminal and hopped a bus north. The state lines twist around in this region, much like the convoluted congressional districts in the USA. I started in Jalisco, visited Nochistlán in Zacatecas, then continued north into Aguascalientes before returning once again to Zacatecas. In this kind of rugged terrain, which is mainly wilderness, state lines are of no real importance anyway.

Despite winding along a backcountry road, I found myself on what is called a first-class bus. Why do they always advertise their onboard Wi-Fi? It almost never works. Still, the presence of a toilet was a godsend to a 71-year-old man with an enlarged prostate. The drive was two and a half hours, all through exuberant green hills. I had never before been in Mexico at the height of the rainy season (September), but putting up with water and mud was well worth it. Everything sparkles after the rain, and plant, bird, and animal life abound.

We arrived in Nochistlán at a tiny terminal. I approached the counter to ask about departure times to Aguascalientes and directions to my hotel. In typical small-town Mexico fashion, the man was exceedingly courteous, friendly, and helpful. It was a fifteen-minute walk to my lodging. The girl at the check-in desk there was confused at seeing a reservation with an Anglo name, but her mother, probably the hotel owner, soon arrived and got everything in order. In Mazatlán, the locals often fall over in amazement when I speak good Spanish, but here in the hinterlands it does not occasion any comment at all, as they are not used to foreigners.

Strolling about town I was delighted not to see a McDonald's, Starbucks, or any of the other foreign invaders that now infest Mexican cities. There were mostly mom-and-pop stores, markets, and *tortillerías*, along with myriad stands offering delectable treats. Prices were also dirt-cheap compared to what I am used to in the city where I reside, where they are heavily inflated by the presence of tourists.

On the bus ride to town, I had pondered the question of what makes a *Pueblo Mágico* "magical." Perhaps I was about to find out, but I had a suspicion that the question might continue to come up again and again during my travels. Likely, the rationale for Nochistlán was historical, as it was one of the earliest settlements in the area. The presence of abundant water always matters. It was founded by the conquistador Nuño de Guzman in 1531, and he named it Guadalajara in honor of his birthplace in Spain. So, this little town was the first Guadalajara in Mexico. Later he went on to found the "real" Guadalajara on a much more open and advantageous site. For such a small town, there were a great many old colonial buildings. Unfortunately, a lot of them were closed due to the pandemic. Also, the town garden was locked and inaccessible. Nochistlán was my introduction to travel in the age of COVID.

The next morning, I walked to an outlying chapel and well-preserved aqueduct before venturing into the open countryside. The land was very beautiful, full of cornfields, the stalks tall and waving in the breeze, along with fruit trees, livestock, wildflowers, songbirds, modest cottages, and grand country homes. The nopal cactus bushes were in bloom, adorned with a profusion of bright red fruit called *tuna* (not to be confused with the fish, which is *atun*). I followed a narrow dirt road up into the hills. At one point it dead-ended, so I asked some kids playing nearby for directions. They peppered me with questions, asking how to say such and such in English. They didn't seem particularly interested in the answers, just the game of asking. They didn't help much with the directions, either.

Soon enough, I passed an elderly couple sitting in front of their home. Often, people in the countryside are a bit shy of outsiders, but Rafael and Maria brightened right up as soon as I addressed them in their mother tongue. I immediately learned that they had sons in Texas.

I asked how long they had lived in this small house. He replied Seventy-two years, his entire life. What different existences we all lead. At least they had once visited Fort Worth and knew a little bit about the outside world. They thought it was marvelous. Who am I to disagree? Even though they are far out of town, Maria sells soft drinks, cans of heavily sweetened Jumex-brand juice, and snacks in order to make a little cash. She insisted on gifting me a small can and resisted all my efforts to pay her. So kind and typical of the generosity one finds in Mexico among the poor.

In some ways, Nochistlán was an excellent if impromptu choice for my first official *pueblo*, as it had a little bit of everything. The natural location is very lovely, at least in the right season, and its historical aspects are fascinating. If I ever get back, I look forward to seeing everything that was closed at the time. From a little table on the sidewalk at the edge of the Zocalo, a man was selling homemade artisanal chocolate. I was so impressed by the label he designed that I bought a bar for 50 pesos. Sadly, despite the simple aesthetic of the wrapper, the product inside was the same old Mexican crumbly chocolate, mainly suitable for making a cup of cocoa.

Overall rating: 7

Getting there: Nochistlán is on one of the main bus lines between Guadalajara and Aguascalientes.

CHAPTER 5:
And All of the Rest (North Central States)

Salvatierra, Guanajuato
Yuriria, Guanajuato
Ajijic, Jalisco
Mazamitla, Jalisco
Tlaquepaque, Jalisco
Cadereyta de Montes, Querétaro (Bonus Town)
Jalpan de Serra, Querétaro
Tequisquiapan, Querétaro
Aquismón, San Luis Potosí
Pinos, San Luis Potosí

All of the Rest (North Central)

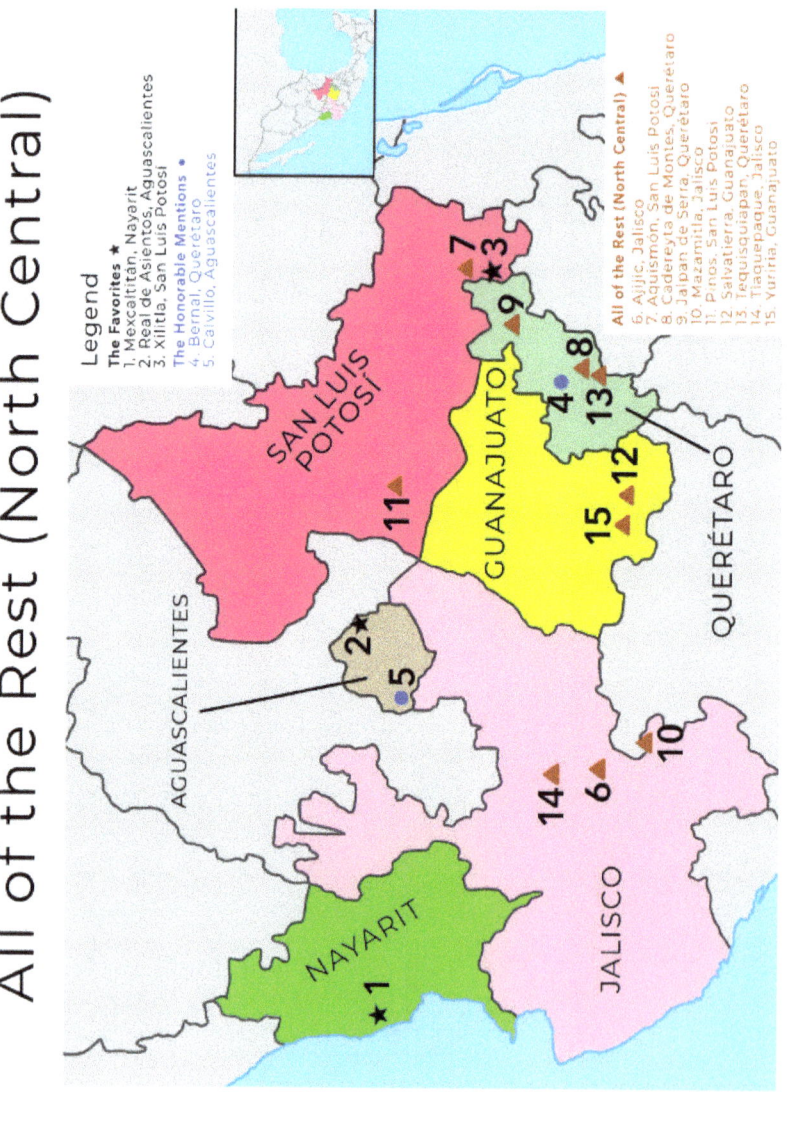

Twin Towns: Salvatierra, Guanajuato, and Yuriria, Guanajuato

These two towns are only 28 kilometers (17.5 miles apart), so it feels reasonable to pair them.

Salvatierra, Guanajuato

This is one of the towns where I had to ask myself, "Why is this a *Pueblo Mágico*?" Don't get me wrong, Salvatierra is a very nice town. It is attractive and very clean. The main plaza and gardens are relaxing places to sit and hang out, and the churches and temples are fine examples of historic architecture. I took a hike out to a large park alongside a river and enjoyed all of it. But one can find these sorts of things in countless other towns around the country—they're certainly not unique to the *Pueblos Mágicos*. This speaks well of Mexico as a general travel destination, but it makes it difficult to see anything "extra special" about Salvatierra. If I haven't convinced you by now of the beauty and grace of Mexico, I never will. So, by all means, come to Salvatierra. I liked being there. I had a good time and nothing about my stay there grated on me. I guess I just love the leisurely pace and visual delights of Mexico, period. But is Salvatierra noticeably magical? Sorry, I just didn't see it. My most entertaining experience was dining in a mom-and-pop restaurant where I was treated practically like family and enjoyed a delicious meal for pennies.

When rating these towns, one of the most important criteria I consider is if there's some aspect of a town that makes it truly special. And for Salvatierra I can't answer that question in the affirmative, so I've rated it low. (Although it really does feel a bit cruel to rate poorly what is essentially just a nice, sweet *pueblo*.)

Overall rating: 3

Yuriria, Guanajuato

Just down the road from Salvatierra is Yuriria, another lovely town, and one which definitely delivers the "magic." It's honestly too bad that I spent two nights in Salvatierra with just a day trip to Yuriria, instead of the other way around. But hindsight is everything. Sometimes there is no way of knowing these things in advance. (Nudge, nudge, that's why you are reading this book.) The town's name translates to Lake of Blood, which refers to the interaction of the sun with the waters of the deep Crater Lake some distance out of town, which reflects visual tones of pink, orange, and scarlet. There is also a large lagoon right on the edge of town, filled with lilies and small islands, so Yuriria is a good spot for casual nature hiking.

Ex-convent of Yuriria

The gems of the place are its fort, museum, and another Augustinian ex-convent, which was built in the sixteenth century and which now ranks high on my list of Mexico's architectural treasures. There are more than enough visual sights here to fill a couple of hours, and just walking around Centro, one can profitably gape at the ex-convent from any angle. My verdict for the whole town? To me, it feels archetypically Mexican, and it is no doubt rarely visited by foreigners. Definitely a fine hangout and well worth a visit. You can even take a pleasant day trip to Salvatierra if you're inclined to investigate the accuracy of my perspective.

Overall rating: 7

Getting there: These towns are nearer to the state capitals of Morelia and Querétaro than they are to Guanajuato city, but you can stage from any of them. The nearest city is Celaya, where you may have to change buses if you are coming from Querétaro.

There are 12 *Pueblos Mágicos* each in the states of Jalisco and Puebla, making those states the richest in the country in that attribute. I go to Guadalajara frequently and have been lazy about visiting the state's far-flung Magic Towns. I keep telling myself that I can visit them anytime, as Guadalajara is the closest major air hub to Mazatlán. A taxi for the ride from my home to our local airport costs 500 pesos, and 55 more if you want to save half an hour by taking the toll road. Yet a comfortable first-class bus costs only 450 pesos for the seven-hour ride to Guadalajara (at the Senior rate). And there is public transportation to the airport. So, it costs me more to get to the Mazatlán airport than to Guadalajara's. Go figure.

Ajijic, Jalisco

This is definitely not the easiest place to pronounce. Remember that the J (or jota) is somewhat equivalent to the German sound "ch," like when you say "Ich spreche." It comes from deep in your throat. Phonetically, the name that comes out is ah-chi-chic, cha-lees-co, which is quite a mouthful in any language.

I posted a blog about Ajijic on my Facebook travel group, where I included one mildly critical comment in my general assessment. Actually, "critical" is a bit of an overstatement. It was really just one observation that lacked praise, in which I pointed out a slightly below-average level of friendliness from the locals compared to any other *Pueblo Mágico* I had visited. This rather benign observation drew a scathing riposte from an angry lady who said I didn't know what I was talking about, and I knew nothing about Mexico. (The fact that she happened to be a local gringa real estate agent probably had nothing to do with her displeasure…) There are a lot of things you can say about me, but knowing nothing about Mexico is not one of them!

Located on the north shore of Lake Chapala, an hour south of Guadalajara, Ajijic is the artsier cousin of its much larger near neighbor, the town of Chapala. The population on this shoreline enjoys one of the most pleasant climates in the world, often compared to the San Francisco Bay Area.

A few decades ago, the lake was reputed to be the most polluted body of water in Mexico. There have been energetic and somewhat successful attempts to clean it up since, but walking along its edge, I still was not inclined to jump in.

Ajijic and its neighboring communities are Grand Central for retired North Americans, with the attendant traffic congestion. In fact, this area hosts possibly the largest concentration of expatriates in the world. In places like Puerto Vallarta, which was once a tiny fishing village, most of the Mexican people living there were first drawn by work opportunities in the tourist industry. This is not true in an old traditional town like Ajijic, where the native residents are well aware of their tranquil past and perhaps cannot help feeling invaded. This invasion does come with some benefits, like added prosperity and business opportunities, but it inevitably creates tension between two such disparate populations.

I would like to believe that most of the North American residents are busy learning Spanish and involving themselves in local activities. Certainly, many do study Spanish, but from my time in town talking to everyone, far more do not. I suppose that's understandable, though—I earlier spoke about the difficulties that older people have in learning a foreign language. I have been working on it for fifty years and still get discouraged by my lapses.

What clearly upset the aforementioned realtor was that I wrote that Ajijic was the "least friendly" of any *Pueblo Mágico* I had visited. But this needs some context. Mexicans can be a bit reserved, but once you draw them into conversation, they are among the friendliest and most helpful people in the world. But in Ajijic, I felt some palpable distancing more than once. And buying a ticket back to Guadalajara at the bus station, the girl was positively sullen, ignoring my greeting and barely speaking to me. I understand that she gets tired of dealing with people who insist that she understand English. But still. I was speaking to her in more or less perfect and fluent Spanish, and she still could not bother to hide her disdain. Or I might be overreacting, and she was just having a bad day. I only mention this because it virtually <u>never</u> happens in Mexico. I drew my conclusions, and you can draw yours.

Preamble aside, Ajijic is a very pretty town with lots to see and do and a surfeit of art, along with a diverse number of street markets. Carefree walks along the water are always calming to the soul, and Ajijic boasts a lengthy pathway along the lakeshore, perfect for a springtime promenade. I wouldn't suggest taking a dip, however. The government has done a good job of lessening Lake Chapala's pollution, but it is still a long way from being safely clean. I also took a more strenuous hike into the steep hills that surround the lake. The natural beauty is easily accessible and lovely.

Getting from Ajijic to Guadalajara is a slow but reasonably painless public bus trip, giving residents an easy entrée to all of the city's stunning colonial beauty and its cosmopolitan shopping. This proximity is also a big plus. Back in town, there is an enormous North American cultural complex located in a hidden walled garden in the center of town, with a library and an array of interesting cultural activities. It serves as a refuge and haven for homesick expats. For good or bad, you can live here comfortably without speaking Spanish.

There are the same old plazas and historic buildings that you find in any prominent colonial town. An eclectic cross-cultural life is the rule, rather than the exception.

One thing is sure: If you enjoy the street art of Mexico—and who wouldn't?—this is the town to come to. One of the most striking sights, and not to be missed, is the Wall of the Dead, an impressive artistic creation with a thousand clay skulls and philosophical poetry.

In summary, Ajijic is a hybrid experience. It is a visual feast with a great climate and enough going on to please almost anyone. You could choose a far worse place to live, as attested to by its thousands of foreign residents. With apologies to the realtor on Facebook, I doubt that my obscure post has hurt her business. Ajijic continues to draw significant numbers of retired North Americans.

Overall rating: 7+

Getting there: There are hourly departures from the Viejo (old) bus terminal in Guadalajara, with stops at the airport, Chapala, and finally Ajijic. The slow and jumbled traffic on this route can be frustrating. I always like to suggest people-watching over annoyance. As always in Mexico, try to arrange your life to be less hurried. Referring back to the old terminal, which isn't far from Centro (a short Uber ride), it can be confusing. The building is dark with crowded aisles. It is also poorly marked compared to the spacious new terminal that handles long-distance travel. The best bet is to keep saying

Chapala with a questioning lift of your eyebrows, and someone is bound to point you to the correct window.

Mazamitla, Jalisco

Mazamitla is the type of place that I would normally consider spending a couple of days in. Located 133 kilometers (83 miles) up in the hills from Guadalajara, this *pueblo* is a long way to go for just a day trip. But that is what I decided to do. My annual *pueblo* trek had extended well into November, and the higher altitudes were chilling rapidly. I thought about spending the night, but I read reviews of a number of reasonably priced lodging choices, and they all said more or less the same thing: It could be very cold, there were not always enough blankets, and Wi-Fi signals were erratic or worse. You probably know me well enough by now to understand that such reviews discouraged an overnight visit.

Here are the results of my day trip: Mazamitla is a very pretty town, surrounded by forests and natural scenery. It is a weekend haven for campers, fishermen, mountain hikers, and more. The area is full of upscale lodging and activities, including horseback riding, ziplines, and wine-tasting. In town, there is some history, some classic architecture, a small "museum of magic," and a handsome plaza. The museum contained a number of exhibits pertaining to various forms of the black arts. But Mazamitla itself felt less "magical" than other hill retreats, such as Mineral del Monte or Tlalpujahua (coming soon), at least to me.

The roads were winding and not great. The cramped country bus ride took almost seven hours round-trip. I walked around town for two hours and had a decent meal. I am absolutely not trying to disrespect this very nice place, but I won't be coming back anytime soon.

Overall rating: 5

Getting there: A tiring and not very comfortable bus ride from Guadalajara will get you to Mazamitla.

Tlaquepaque, Jalisco

In a sense, this *Pueblo Mágico* is an anomaly, as it is entirely surrounded by the city of Guadalajara and thus not truly its own discrete entity. Tourists might not even realize that they are visiting anywhere other than an outlying urban district. You could justifiably call Tlaquepaque a "*Pueblo Mágico* which isn't really a *pueblo*." But, however you categorize it, you don't want to miss this place when you come to Guadalajara. The central core of Tlaquepaque is rife with art, architecture, color, entertainment, museums, history, and fine dining—almost a complete microcosm of Mexico itself.

You can simply wander the streets and still have a great time. I never like to pass through Guadalajara without spending at least a couple of hours here. The "town" has an interesting history. At one time, it was a populous separate entity, even though now it sits only a handful of kilometers from the center of Guadalajara. In 1821, it was the cradle of the proclamation of independence for the state of Jalisco.

The part of Tlaquepaque that you want to visit occupies a very small area. The rest of its boundaries are indistinguishable from those of any big city. You hardly need me to find all the churches nestled close to each other. And the old buildings and mansions on every avenue are just as pretty to look at. It's all anchored by the Jardin Hidalgo (Hidalgo Garden), which is full of mariachis, street artists, and crafts. There is art and sculpture all about. As I said, just walking around the area is enjoyable enough. Additionally, there are many fine restaurants and cantinas—something for everyone. If you are interested in authentic and traditional Mexican food, this is the place to come. I particularly recommend the retro feeling of the Rincon de la Abuela (Grandmother's Corner), located right on the plaza.

Tlaquepaque Plaza

Flying north to our summer home after completing this book, I took Kathy to Guadalajara, where she had never been. Doing so was an option this year owing to being able to ride the bus, which had been impossible previously due to the presence of our feline companion Samantha, recently deceased. Tlaquepaque has one long street brimming with decidedly upscale arts and crafts, which Kathy thinks is one of the best she has ever visited anywhere. So, I am happy to pass her review on to you shoppers. Undoubtedly, you know who you are. For you non-shoppers, like yours truly, the stores that are filling bygone mansions are a visual treat all on their own.

Overall rating: 9

Getting there: Grab a taxi or Uber from the Centro Historico (historic city center). Or, if you don't mind a short walk, ride the attractive city Metro (10 pesos) on the line toward the Central Bus Terminal. Tlaquepaque is the penultimate stop.

Cadereyta de Montes, Querétaro (Bonus Town)

If you are going to Bernal and have some spare time, there is little reason not to take a short detour to this tidy and quiet town. For those seeking hiking and camping far from the madding crowd, it's a gateway to the beautiful and still-wild Sierra Gorda ("fat highlands") of Querétaro state. Few mountainous regions in North America and Europe are so unspoiled.

Cadereyta itself is notable as one of the earliest Spanish settlements in the region, with the architecture to match. Its location was almost certainly chosen due to a complex of gushing springs near the Centro, which makes for a striking sight.

The main attraction for me was an extensive cactus garden and park, located a thirty-minute walk from town. COVID was still a major issue at the time of my visit, and a young, uniformed woman sat just inside a locked gate. She seemed a bit surprised to see me, but she recovered enough to inquire if I wanted to enter. I responded, "Si, por favor," and she asked if I had an appointment. This was a new wrinkle. After I answered in the negative, she said that there was no problem. Indicating a phone number on a small sign, she directed me to call it. I asked if someone would really answer and if there would be any other obstacles. In bureaucratic Mexico, labyrinthine barriers of rules and regulations can be a matter of routine.

Having received an encouraging response, I dug my cell out of my pocket, but she told me to wait a minute. Then she walked away and disappeared into a small office building. I called, she answered, and a minute later she returned and let me in, appointment in hand. Ah, Mexico. A more or less twin version of her then joined us, waiting to guide me. We began the tour wearing masks, but to my relief, she soon removed hers. It was necessary to have this guide in order to visit the garden and greenhouse area. That accomplished, she wanted to sell me some small potted cacti. I explained my inability to transport much of anything, especially something spiny. So, she had to settle for a tip.

After that, I hiked the area trails unmolested. There were good markers (in Spanish only), and a multitude of flora, some unique to this region, which the town officials were trying to protect and help flourish. All in all, it was my type of good time, with a wonderful little anecdote acquired to boot.

My room was comfy, and the landlady extremely friendly. I had a passable meal at a pizza, sandwich, and burger type of place.

Overall rating: 5-6, depending on your interest in cacti.

Getting there: An easy bus ride from Querétaro. If you are arriving from Mexico City, be sure to get off early in San Juan del Rio and take a local bus north. From Tequisquiapan, there are buses to Cadereyta. If you want to continue to Bernal, it gets a bit tricky. To avoid a lengthy roundabout, you ride the bus from Cadereyta to a nearby crossroads, then take a share taxi across to another crossroads that meets the direct Bernal route. It sounds complicated, but a glance at Google Maps should make it clear.

Jalpan de Serra, Querétaro

I took a fairly significant detour between San Luis Potosí and Xilitla for the purpose of adding Jalpan to my bag. I hoped the town would justify the added hours of not-so-comfortable bus travel, but I'm afraid it didn't. This is another *pueblo* where much of the "magic" lies in natural attractions rather far out of the way.

Jalpan sports the usual lovely religious architecture. There is a nice statue of the itinerant Franciscan priest Junípero Serra, which was meaningful to me, having grown up on the San Francisco mission trail of El Camino Real, which was mainly his handiwork. The missions are certainly beautiful, and full of deep history, but it's also true that the Spanish holy men who "built them" inflicted untold suffering among the native peoples who did all the unpaid toil. Of course, I never thought about any of this growing up, but standing before a historical monument can focus one's mind.

Outside of the typical core, there was little of interest in town. The municipal market was small and shabby. I asked for my usual *jugo verde*, green drink, at an orange juice stall. I always feel rather nutritionally virtuous downing this OJ-based beverage that's blended with whatever greens may be on hand. It can be a touch bitter, but it is certainly an inexpensive source of fresh vitamins. I was surprised that the proprietor didn't have this fairly common drink on her "menu." But she clearly knew what I wanted and asked me to wait a few minutes. Soon enough, she returned with a handful of greens to mix in, a very kind gesture.

My hotel was a fifteen-minute walk from the center. The people were friendly, and the lodging decently appointed, but the Wi-Fi was erratic. Then a strong rainstorm blew in early in the evening, as is common in these parts, and wiped out the internet connection completely.

I took a bracing and scenic hike to a lake and dam early in the morning, fighting off the chilly fog and some not-so-welcoming

country dogs. After a good breakfast at the hotel's restaurant, I walked back to the bus and moved on to Xilitla.
Overall rating: 4

Getting there: A little bit of a challenge. You can take a bus from San Luis Potosí to Ciudad Valles and change buses midway in Rio Verde. There is also a direct bus to Xilitla, but it is on a slow and tortuous road through the Sierra Gorda. If you have time on your hands, though, the scenery on that route is gorgeous.

Tequisquiapan, Querétaro

Like so many other towns near state capitals, this attractive *Pueblo Mágico* is best known as a weekend spa getaway. It's located an easy 63 kilometers (40 miles) from Querétaro and is serviced by a good road.

Tequisquiapan felt special because for me it emanated the warm and cozy feeling you get when you walk into a room, a house, or, in this case, a town where you feel completely at home and at ease.

Tequisquiapan is an open and airy place, with enough old Spanish architecture along the cobblestoned streets to hold your attention throughout a walking tour. I was there on a weekday, so traffic was quiet and almost nonexistent in the back lanes. The town is best known for its *balneario*, but it also has a fine crafts market. The main plaza is an attractive and tranquil place for some late-afternoon reading and people-watching.

This is a domestic tourism haven. There are city tram tours and balloon rides, and the prices are geared to the relatively small Mexican upper middle class. It is also located in wine country, and you can sample the local vintages. One thing distinctive to Tequisquiapan is its large number of artisanal cheese shops, all carrying a colorful round logo with a picture of a contented cow at the center. Free samples! You could walk around town and have a light meal of wine and cheese completely gratis if you wished. Add some sourdough bread, and it could hold you until dinner.

It's a very nice place, if not particularly fascinating. Definitely a possibility for a chill hangout.

Overall rating: 7

Aquismón, San Luis Potosí

I set off from Xilitla on a day trip to Aquismón, in the wild heart of the Huasteca region, which stretches across three states. This enormous untamed area is full of canyons, gorges, riotous subtropical jungles, caves, grottoes, and rushing streams—a nature-lover's dream. But it's not an easy region to navigate solo. There are plenty of pricey tours running out of Xilitla and the cities. I wanted to avoid an expensive group excursion, but I was very interested in seeing the Cueva de Golondrinas (The Cave of Swallows), along with some other sites. I figured someone local would be my best and cheapest option. There's always a taxi driver around happy to pick up some extra cash. Unfortunately, I miscalculated and made a rookie error. It was Monday and everything was closed, even the cave and grotto.

I had sampled some local passion fruit sorbet outside the realm of the Mad King of Xilitla (see the write-up of the artist Edward James earlier). On the bus ride to Aquismón, we passed through a tiny village where both sides of the road were lined with stalls selling—you guessed it—sorbet. I continue to wonder how any individual vendor can begin to make a living under such competitive circumstances, much less why every person in a village would want to pursue an identical trade. And on a bus, I couldn't buy it anyway. Such quirks of local Mexican economies can boggle the mind.

Not yet realizing that everything would be closed, I got off at an intersection where there were share taxis into the town. It was only a few kilometers walk, so I hoofed it. The bus itself continued on the main road to Ciudad Valles. When I reached the Centro, all the tourist stuff was closed, and I gave myself a well-deserved forehead slap for ignoring the implications of Monday in Mexico.

The area is heavily indigenous. Decades ago, I spent a night here. Walking on a random path into the woods, I encountered many friendly men in native garb and was invited to a piñata party in a village. When I got there, I discovered that none of the women or children spoke Spanish, not that mine was very good at the time.

Back in the present, I strolled around the pretty town and saw what there was to see. I came to an indigenous market full of local crafts. There were only three women in colorful native garb about, with many of the stalls closed. Definitely the wrong day of the week. Back in the city center, I had a pleasant early lunch at a modern cafe. In Mexico, it is common to find groups of mongrels lying in the sun on the sidewalks or edges of lanes, seemingly dead to the world. All I can say is that Aquismón must be the national center for this type of (in) activity. They were everywhere.

It was still quite early, and there was not much left for me to do back in Xilitla. On the map, I noticed a nearby village with the typically tongue-twisting name of Tancanhuitz de Santos. I wouldn't want to try to learn any of these indigenous languages. On a whim, I decided to go there. It was a total of only 16 kilometers (10 miles) from Aquismón, but it wasn't a fast trip. I started with an easy share-taxi to the main road, then took another taxi south to the next crossroads. From there, it was a tediously slow grind on a narrow, twisty road where we got stuck behind a creeping concrete truck belching diesel. For me, that evoked unpleasant memories of driving on more major highways in bygone Mexico. When I arrived, I soon became aware that I was in authentic, rural small-town Mexico. I doubted if any gringo had ever trodden these streets, but maybe I was flattering myself. But I am very fortunate. Nobody even seemed to notice me. Many decades ago, in places like Morocco or India, a foreign visitor would be assailed by every child in a village, along with plenty of their parents. But in Mexico, I am unremarkable, just a little, brown man of possibly dubious lineage. The town municipal market was a treat, with many fruits and vegetables that I couldn't identify. As in Pahautlán, I felt as if I had ridden a time machine back into a much simpler world.

It is not easy to rate Aquismón. Some of the towns I visited in 2021 suffered from pandemic-associated limitations. With plazas, gardens, and museums shut down or locked, there was no way for them to "strut their stuff." Something akin to this happened to me in Aquismón, but this time due to my own foolishness in coming on the wrong day of the week. Apart from that self-inflicted issue, I have consistently shown bias against towns being given "magic" status owing to external sites like rivers, canyons, and ruins. However, there is good reason to make an exception for this one, as it anchors some truly wild terrain and sites that cannot be found elsewhere. Some of the towns I have rated poorly are near lakes or are jumping-off places for adventure sports or camping—attributes which are certainly pluses, but which are in no way special or magical. In this aspect, Aquismón is distinct. Sites outside of the town, such as the Cave of the Swallows, are unique. As for the town itself, it is a more than pleasant place, even though it lacks a lot of obvious attractions. Just walking around seeing the numerous old women in festive indigenous dress was a treat. And when the native market is open, those same women vend art that is characteristic of their local culture and also can't be found elsewhere.

So as long as you don't visit on Monday, I can confidently rate the town as a 7 or even perhaps 8.

Getting there: Regular buses from Xilitla, Tamazunchale and Ciudad Valles. Get off at the crossroads along the main highway and grab a share-taxi into the Centro.

Pinos, San Luis Potosí

The bus ride from Zacatecas to Pinos was a bit slow and uninteresting. We soon left the direct highway to San Luis Potosí (S.L.P.) and began passing through dusty semi-desert on a pitted road. The villages by the roadside looked very impoverished. The only sight of interest happened when we passed through a tiny village with a roadside sign extolling Tony's Fried Chicken. I didn't see that one coming.

By the time we pulled into Pinos, the surrounding landscape hadn't improved all that much, and my first impression was tepid at best. Before I left the bus station, I tried without success to check the connections to my next stop, the capital city of S.L.P. It turned out that those buses departed from a different station. I passed a fancy hotel and went in to inquire about a room. This was very early in my first 2021 tour, and 800 pesos a night, the rate they quoted me, seemed very high. Anyway, I usually prefer the hotels on the Zocalo, and I knew that plaza was just a few blocks away.

Surprisingly, there was only one, with the rather obvious name of Hotel Plaza. I walked in and found the reception desk, which was connected to a loud gymnasium. But the receptionist promised that the gym would close at 9 PM, which at least sounded plausible, so that was no problem (and it actually did close at that time!). The room was basic, but inexpensive at 300 pesos. She promised reliable internet and hot water. In the evening, I ran the C, (for *caliente*, hot) tap for five minutes. Nothing. An element in the hot water tank was broken, but the proprietors hadn't known it yet as there were no other guests. Oh well, the Wi-Fi was decent and one out of two is not so bad.

I strolled around the Centro, which was typically attractive but nothing special. The Municipal Palace and tourist office were closed, with paper signs announcing a sympathy strike for some municipal workers. Pinos did not seem very magical, but it was to grow on me somewhat. One of the positive elements was handsome bilingual signs at every point of interest, along with civic maps. In fact, all four plaza corners had arcane historical information posted. At least the town was trying. But it was still hard to imagine many, or even any, foreigners coming here to read the English.

I paused to eat at a colorful modern restaurant with good contemporary music playing. A very sweet dog sat beneath my table, soliciting affection if not more material goodies. The waiter/cook was equally friendly. I ordered a chicken burger, a large tropical house salad, and a Negra Modelo, all for a quite reasonable 170 pesos. After devouring all of that, I greedily tried for the vegan brownie touted on a sign above the counter. Alas, there were no brownies to be had on that day. (Fifty years ago, Mexican menus frequently represented the proprietor's aspirations, rather than what she actually had on hand. This often led to a battle of wits where I would order something and she would sadly shrug and say "*No hay.*" There isn't any. Once I asked at some place if there was chicken. The Señora beamed and said of course. I was not sure what I felt five minutes later upon hearing some aggravated squawking emanating from the back yard. In these more modern times, menus generally reflect what they really have to offer.)

After lunch, the tourist office had reopened, and the girls proved to be very friendly and helpful. They marked up a map, showing me in detail how to find everything. Too bad there wasn't that much to see. But they were trying hard, and the walks I took to the sites were pleasant. The museums were closed, and the main garden was locked due to COVID. Still, the ancient aqueduct was fascinating and well preserved.

In the early evening, I was back hanging out in the plaza. I noticed a crowd of about thirty people gathered around a speaker in front of the Municipal Palace. Facing them on the plaza proper were four cops, heavily weaponized and armored, watching them. Was this some kind of protest associated with the strike earlier in the day? No, they were just unveiling a commemorative plaque. The cops, including one young woman, were chatting and smiling. I wasn't sure why they were there. Bored? Or maybe they check out any kind of crowd.

The distinguished speaker was discussing contemporary history, beginning with the Spanish Flu, so I imagined that his theme tied into the current pandemic. My grandfather died of the flu in 1918 when my father was a baby. Then the speaker moved forward to the Holocaust. My mother was born in Berlin and managed to escape to New York in 1939 when she was 12. Almost the entirety of their extended family disappeared in the camps. So, the speech hit me on a deep, emotional level.

When he was finished and the congratulatory thanks began to ebb, I approached and mentioned the personal connections he had touched upon. Another man joined in, and we chatted for a few minutes. Fun.

In the morning, I grabbed an early bus and headed for S.L.P. No magic here in Pinos, but an enjoyable visit.
Overall rating: 6

CHAPTER 6:
And All of the Rest (South Central States)

Huichapan, Hidalgo
Tecozautla, Hidalgo
Zimapán, Hidalgo
El Oro de Hidalgo, México
Ixtapan de la Sal, México
Tepotzotlán, México
Angangueo, Michoacán (Hidden Gem)
Cuitzeo del Porvenir, Michoacán
Tacámbaro, Michoacán
Tlalpujahua, Michoacán

All of the Rest (South Central)

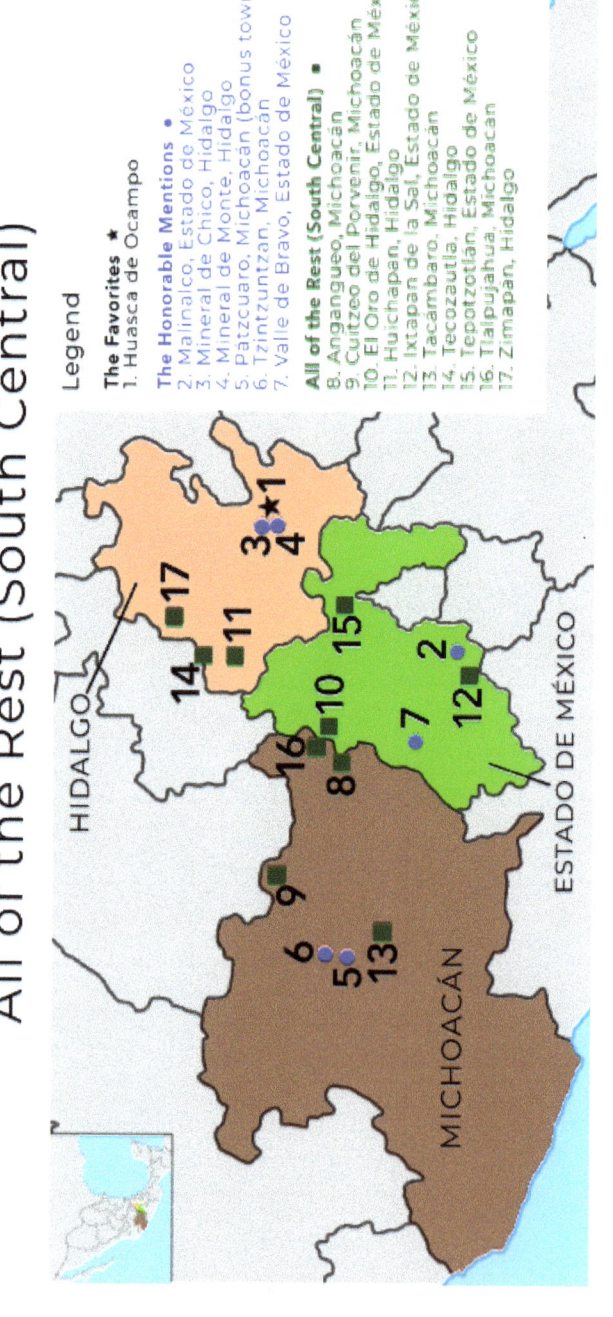

Legend

The Favorites ★
1. Huasca de Ocampo

The Honorable Mentions •
2. Malinalco, Estado de México
3. Mineral de Chico, Hidalgo
4. Mineral de Monte, Hidalgo
5. Patzcuaro, Michoacán (bonus town)
6. Tzintzuntzan, Michoacán
7. Valle de Bravo, Estado de México

All of the Rest (South Central) ■
8. Angangueo, Michoacán
9. Cuitzeo del Porvenir, Michoacán
10. El Oro de Hidalgo, Estado de México
11. Huichapan, Hidalgo
12. Ixtapan de la Sal, Estado de México
13. Tacámbaro, Michoacán
14. Tecozautla, Hidalgo
15. Tepotzotlán, Estado de México
16. Tlalpujahua, Michoacán
17. Zimapan, Hidalgo

Huichapan, Hidalgo

Another pair of "twin towns," and only 19 kilometers (12 miles) apart, Huichapan and Tecozautla are nice, but alas, unable to compete with the trio in south central Hidalgo around Pachuca, which I have already written about. However, if you are a hot spring lover, you should definitely include the Balneario El Geiser on your itinerary—it's just a short drive from Tecozautla. The pools and springs are major draws for Mexican families, so this area fills up on weekends. But when I came to Huichapan on a Wednesday, none of the restaurants mentioned in Tripadvisor were even open. Still, you are never going to starve to death in Mexico. It was easy to find a modest place in Centro with pizza, hamburgers, salads, and more.

It seems that Huichapan shares some history with Dolores Hidalgo, another *Pueblo Mágico* in Guanajuato state, where the priest Miguel Hidalgo first gave out "the cry of independence" in 1812. Thus, the town is known as Mexico's second "cradle of independence." Forgive me if I am vague about which particular independence they are talking about. Mexico seems to have so many independence days (with their corresponding holidays) that I struggle to distinguish one from another. All I know is that the banks are closed surprisingly often on Mondays! Along with this claim to fame, Huichapan Centro contains plenty of grand architecture to match, pretty much like almost every town in these listings. There is also an ex-convent with relics of religious significance, but this one is small and cramped compared to most.

My hotelier asked me if I was going to visit one of the *balnearios*, or hot springs. But in this town, they were more like warm-water pool complexes and playgrounds. I said that I planned to visit the "real" thing in Tecozautla.

It's common when visiting *Pueblos Mágicos* to discover that some attractions are well out of town, and Huichapan is one of those towns. There is often public transportation, though you may have to be insistent if you want to get the tourist kiosk girls to let you in on the secret. After all, what foreigner ever wants to use it? Failing that, there are taxis or even small tours on offer. (I should do more of that, as I am aware that I have missed things I would have enjoyed seeing.) There are two such major attractions in the area. One is a large and well-preserved section of an aqueduct, Los Arcos de Saucillo, which I glimpsed twenty minutes before coming into Huichapan on the bus. The other is the grottos and falls of Tolantongo, which are said to be spectacular. They are actually nearer to Zimapán, my next entry in this guide. However, I did find one site much closer, which was very worthwhile and was what I like to call an accidental find (my favorite kind!).

In going over possibilities of things to see near Huichapan, I noticed a listing for a Parque Ecológico Los Sabinos in the adjacent village of Atlán. Just for form's sake, I asked at the tourist kiosk about transportation options. And just like usual, the girl said there were only taxis. Sigh. In any case, I was already planning on walking the five kilometers there, and, yes, on the walk I became aware that there are colectivos which pass every twenty minutes. I rode one back.

Atlán, Náhuatl for "Place of the Waters," is a modest village which outperforms its diminutiveness. The so-called Ecological Park is very rundown and ill-kept, but I soon found out that its seediness was irrelevant. After paying 10 pesos to the old guardian at the entrance, I walked in and had the whole place to myself. The sign markers were mainly rusted out and difficult to read. On the plus side, there were little streams all throughout, teeming with carousing *mariposas* (butterflies). Lazing in the warm air, I was filled with a feeling of enchantment. And then there were the *ahuehetes*, huge old Montezuma Cypress trees, which were absolutely magnificent. This is the kind of thing that thrills me to the core. I spent a long time basking in their aura.

Afterward, I walked out to the village plaza, where it was market day. I sat at a bench for a while and noticed a young matron studying me curiously and smiling. So, I called out a greeting to her and the kids. We chatted for a few minutes. She was clearly modern and sophisticated, and she told me that she had never before seen a foreigner in Atlán. After that encounter I walked around the market and had a refreshing mixed fruit juice. The people were exceedingly friendly and welcoming, and it warmed my heart. This type of experience is one of the greatest joys of slow traveling around Mexico.

Another lovely moment occurred later in the day back in Huichapan. I was sitting in the plaza reading when kindergarten let out. All the parents were outside waiting. The teacher let the children out one by one, calling their names out clearly as they ran to meet their families. Such touching moments speak to the ways of a bygone age.

It is difficult to separate these small happy incidents from one's overall impressions when rating a town. If you include Huichapan's outlying natural wonders, the town's rating could be quite high. But my tendency is to discount towns whose inclusion in the program relies on natural wonders in the area, which are at times very far afield (for example. the spectacular falls of Tolantongo), while offering little inside the town limits. Mind you, there is nothing wrong with the town of Huichapan. It is a nice place. But my best moments occurred in the nearby village of Atlán, to which I walked on a whim. For me, the town proper of Huichapan was middling.

Overall rating: 5

Tecozautla, Hidalgo

For most, the main draw of Tecozautla is the hot spring of Balneario El Geiser. The town is otherwise ordinary (but quite pleasant). The only other thing I might point out as special here is the clock tower, an excellent piece of architecture that's even more alluring when it is lit up pink and purple after dark—a sight both evocative and somehow spooky. And the spectral sensations are only enhanced by the shrill cries of the thousands of starlings who arrive to roost in the surrounding trees at dusk.

Clock tower at night

Once more I was fortunate to be there on Thursday, the market day. The whole plaza was filled with stalls, local produce, and crafts. It was fun to walk around and look, but as already related too many times, with my small backpack, I am not much of a buyer. Wednesday night would be a good time to arrive in order to profit from the Thursday pageantry and hit up El Geiser ahead of the madness of the weekend.

I had a good first impression of Tecozautla. By 11 AM I had arrived at the terminal in Tecozautla and was quite hungry. I had enjoyed a dinner in a small family place the previous evening in Huichapan, enlivened by a pleasant chat with the Señora. Her breakfast menu was enticing, and she told me that she would open at 10 in the morning (I have discussed Mexico's odd breakfast hours earlier). She probably should have said that she would open at the appointed hour only if she felt like it. At 10:17 I cut my losses and grabbed a bus. Ahh, the joys of Mexican mañana!

Walking toward Tecozautla's Centro, I passed a typical small eatery and glanced inside. I saw tablecloths, flower vases, and, behind the counter, a tiny old indigenous woman. There were no other patrons. Just my cup of tea! The *abuelita*, literally "little grandmother," appeared to be a bit unsettled at the odd and completely unexpected sight of a foreigner. But as I spoke to her in her own tongue, one of them anyway, she relaxed. I ordered some *huevos a la mexicana* and some coffee, which is one of my favorite breakfast choices, with the added virtue of being meatless, Mexican style eggs are scrambled with onions, tomatoes, and pretty spicy jalapeño peppers. If you lack my cast-iron taste buds, be careful with those little guys.

Reassured that I posed no threat, she started to cook. As she worked, she prattled on in a singsong, birdlike manner; I was sure that she was inserting some, or many, non-Spanish words into her discourse. As she also spoke very fast. I understood almost nothing she said, but smiles and nods work well in these situations.

After a few minutes I was served a large plate of eggs, beans, and tortillas, along with a steaming cup of coffee. One of my biggest complaints in Mexico is that food, soup, and coffee are frequently served not hot enough for my tastes. But there was no problem here. The eggs were absolutely delicious; this lady knew how to cook. Then came the moment of truth. There was no menu or visible prices. Long and hard experience, particularly in dog-eat-dog cultures like India, has taught me to habitually ask first and pay later to avoid unpleasant altercations. But I had no suspicion that my present proprietor might try to take advantage of an unusual outsider client. In fact, the thought would not likely occur to her. And I was right, more than I could have ever imagined. I was stunned when she asked me for only 45 pesos, or just over two dollars. Of course I returned the following morning.

The hot springs were 9 kilometers (5.5 miles) out of town. The countryside was pretty, with farmland, marigold fields, and quite a few prominent rock formations. I was content to enjoy a good hike, planning to return to town on a colectivo. And it worked out well. I passed a large crew working some tomato fields and walked off the narrow road to say hello. I was welcomed with laughter and some of the men who had picked crops in the north practiced their broken English with, or I should say on, me.

A little later I passed a miniature house with a pretty garden and heard some festive and stereotypical country *corridos*. Generally, these are non-melodic wails of lost love, which tend to grate on my ears. But each to his own. I glanced in the direction of the cottage and saw an old man reposing in a threadbare chair at the edge of an arbor, a well-shaded garden facing the house. He showed little surprise at my presence, and we began chatting. Soon he offered me a twin of his chair. It looked fragile, but fortunately was adequate to support my small frame. Probably my visit was a welcome break for him in an otherwise unchanging daily routine. While we talked, his very shy wife bustled around preparing the midday meal, never approaching us. The man was 80 years old and a retired farm laborer. He said that I was the first foreigner he had ever met in his life.

An hour later, I reached Balneario El Geiser. It is a special place indeed. Many Mexican businesses promote themselves as hot water bathing establishments, but they deliver a tepid substitute at best. El Geiser is the real thing. The source water is piped in from the spring above and later mixed below to achieve a perfect temperature. It is more than toasty, coming in at a quite perilous 82°C (180°F). The pools themselves start at a minimum of 39°C (102°F). The complex is located in a bowl surrounded by eye-catching rock towers. Walking around the pools and footbridges, you are frequently engulfed in clouds of steam, a bit of a scalding contrast to the cool mountain air.

For over forty years I have frequented Breitenbush Hot Springs in Oregon, a fabulously rustic, hip, and new-age retreat center, with clothing optional and a totally chill vibe. On Friday, El Geiser was a mass of families and their squalling kids. There was unfortunately nothing laid back about it and very little elbow room. The crowds definitely detracted from the experience, but the area itself is truly breathtaking. Photos don't do it justice. (To get the full flavor of the place, I recommend that you watch the YouTube video titled "Tecozautla Costo X Destino," where your gorgeous hostess Alejandra Toledano, the Queen of *Pueblo Mágico* YouTube videos, will deliver the visual goods that this attraction merits. More on Alejandra later.)

A relaxing dinner in my hotel on the plaza just after sunset capped an enjoyable day in authentic Mexico at its best.
Overall rating: 7

Getting there: There is regular bus service to Huichapan between Pachuca and Querétaro. You need to change there for the Tecozautla bus. Across the main street there, I noticed a bus going directly to Tequisquiapan, a neighboring *Pueblo Mágico* just across the Querétaro state line. In fact, in less than an 80- kilometer (50-mile) area, you can visit five *pueblos*, two in Hidalgo and three in Querétaro.

Zimapán, Hidalgo

Zimapán is another scenic old mining town with a delightful ambience. The long ride here from Xilitla through the wild mountains of the Huasteca felt like a real adventure. The narrow highway followed a deep river gorge before ascending high into the clouds and fog. I was more than happy to have a warm hat and jacket during our snack break in one of the only towns en route. Leaving this alpine enclave, we soon headed back down into some more temperate valleys, one magnificent vista after another.

Zimapán boasts a wealth of sixteenth-century architecture. The cathedral is especially worth a look. It's constructed in an unusual Baroque style, and its size is imposing, especially for a small town. The center of town is full of pleasant gardens, and there is one enormous *ahuehuete* (Montezuma Cypress) tree.

Meanwhile, far out of town are imposing *cañones* (canyons). Also worth noting is the Caracol de Carrizal, a serpentine highway that runs through stunning mountain scenery. Even farther out is the Tolantongo Waterfall. Unfortunately, no public transportation runs to these gorgeous sites. This is one of those towns where personal transportation would be a plus. You might also consider hiring a driver.

Zimapán is an aesthetically pleasing town to walk around. In particular, the market goods and art are local and not imported, a big plus in today's plastic world. I contentedly spent a couple of days there, and, although not blown away, I was certainly not in any way displeased.

Overall rating: 6

Getting there: From the north, buses from Tamazunchale, near Xilitla, will take you to Zimapán via a beautiful (but long) ride. Coming in from the south, there are frequent buses originating in Pachuca.

Twin Towns: El Oro de Hidalgo, México, and Tlalpujahua, Michoacán

These are "twin" *Pueblos Mágicos* that lie only 8 kilometers apart, although in different states. Naturally, in visiting both, I walked one way and took a share-taxi back for the requisite ten pesos. The pronunciation of the first town is fairly obvious, but just try saying the latter! Tlalpujahua is covered below later in this chapter.

El Oro de Hidalgo, México

Gold was discovered here a few centuries ago. First came the Spanish, then in the early nineteenth century the English and French shouldered their way in. They built the Juarez Theatre and Municipal Palace along Neo-classic and Art Nouveau lines. Supply was always a difficulty through the mountains and rocky terrain. Eventually electrical transmission lines and a railway were built. But by 1926 the gold and silver were mostly tapped out and the town reverted to the sleepy and bucolic place it is today.

I actually found the railway station (completed in 1860) to be the most interesting structure in town. One of the old cars has been lovingly restored and now houses an upscale restaurant. Quite a contrast to the ramshackle freight cars I once passed on the train to Creel, now used as single-family residences. Outside of this relic, there were a number of architectural treasures scattered about, courtesy of rich mine owners from bygone times. I skipped the Mining Museum since I had learned more than enough about that industry and epoch in Mineral del Monte.

The town is mainly agricultural, with some crafts and light industry, although tourism is creeping in. This was another place that was cold at night and in the early morning, so be advised. I enjoyed walking around and seeing the neat fields and gardens.

Overall rating: 5

Ixtapan de la Sal, México

Another town with a springlike climate that draws well-heeled families and winter refugees from chilly Mexico City, Ixtapan de la Sal is said to have the largest aquatic park in Latin America. Enough said. (Only joking. Well, sort of. Read on.)

The water park here is a weekenders' destination, with many swimming pools and all sorts of kids' entertainment, along with spas, massage parlors, and holistic medicine practitioners. But none of that was open during the week when I was there (not that I would have gone even if it was). Ixtapan is famous as a spa destination, but the facilities don't hold a candle to a marvel like El Geiser. The town itself was pleasant enough to walk around, with ample history, monuments, small and tidy parks, and street art—all the hallmarks of a prosperous Mexican tourist resort. I am probably sounding monotonous now, as this could be a rewrite of a number of the previous summaries. So is Ixtapan boring, or am I becoming jaded about how nice *Pueblos Mágicos* generally are?

The overall verdict is that I was rather bored, so I grabbed a bus out to the Grutas de la Estrella (Estrella Caves). This was too far to hike, as it took me almost half an hour to get just from the main road to the park after getting off the bus. I am not particularly a cave person, but this one was worthwhile. A guide was required, and I enjoyed the company of an affable and knowledgeable middle-aged man who clearly enjoyed his job.

Getting back to town was not so easy. Once I had hoofed it back to the intersection along the narrow dirt road, there was no convenient place or even shoulder for buses to stop at the tiny intersection, and I rather doubted that they would. Earlier, I noted that buses will stop for prospective passengers almost anywhere. You have to trust me that this was an exception to the rule. I wound up paying a taxi driver 200 pesos for the return trip, which included an entertaining detour to pick up his daughter from school and deliver her to their village. I have to say that this diversion was more interesting to me than Ixtapan. And yet another confirmation that Mexico is no place to be in a hurry.

If you want to spend a weekend surrounded by innumerable shrieking children in swimming pools, this town is your ticket. Forgive my sarcasm.

Overall rating: 3

Getting there: Ixtapan de la Sal is midway between Toluca and Taxco.

Tepotzotlán, México

This *Pueblo Mágico*, only 45 minutes north of the Northern Bus Terminal in Mexico City, makes for a fun and interesting daytrip. It's a very tranquil place and is surrounded by attractive hill scenery. In fact, the Náhuatl name, which translates to "humpbacks," is indeed quite descriptive of the shapes of the hills around the town. For those who might wish to spend many days touring the big city, but are put off by the traffic, smog, and hustle and bustle, this town could well serve as a pleasant base (if you don't mind a commute).

Tepotzotlán offers plenty of history, and the soaring architecture beside the tree-shaded central plaza is quite spectacular. The garden-like plaza is an excellent place to kick back and let the hours roll by. Outside of that truly magical city core, I found the town to be a bit on the kitschy side, heavily trading on its *Pueblos Mágicos* status. The recognizable logo is featured everywhere in the central part of town, just in case visitors might forget.

The pretty Municipal Market is unlike any of its counterparts in other towns. Instead of stalls selling produce, meats, and household goods, which is the norm, the space is filled with colorful *fondas* (breakfast and lunch counters). In short, it is more like a food court than a market. The street market, which spreads out between the cathedral gardens and the town's commercial district, is great fun to walk around.

Street art

One of the quirkiest aspects of Tepotzotlán is the back-and-forth transportation from the city, which threw me for a loop

(more on that below). Though there isn't a lot here, the main attractions are enchanting.
Overall rating: 7

Getting there: Tepotzotlán is divided by a major four-lane highway leading to Querétaro. There is only a road or two crossing over the highway, as well as a pedestrian walkway from the bus station. Getting here was a breeze. First, take the metro to the Northern Bus Terminal, where there are departures every few minutes from multiple companies. From the Tepotzotlán station, cross the highway, then take a taxi or walk a mile to the center.

(Normally, I check on return transportation before leaving the station, but at the time of my visit, I oddly forgot to. After all, how difficult could it be to return to one of the largest cities in the world, a stone's throw away? Oops. After lunch, I walked back to the station. I was then summarily told that you could not get back to Mexico City from the side of the road I was on; only northbound buses stopped on my side. They told me to go back to the other side. After crossing the bridge, I stood at the edge of the road, frustrated as a number of buses sped by, ignoring my waving arm. There was nobody else around, and I finally concluded that I was in the wrong place. Was I going to make it back at all? Looking around, I glimpsed some people by the side of the road a few hundred meters to the north. I trudged up there. It was the municipal bus stop. A couple of minutes later I was headed back to Mexico City. Whew! Just another Mexican adventure.)

Angangueo, Michoacán (Hidden Gem)

Since I decided to write this "Best of the Rest" section by state alphabetical order, it's now time to segue back into the state of Michoacán. Continuing west from Tlalpujahua on the Mexico City-Morelia highway, the biggest town you pass through is Zitácuaro, population 145,000. From there, Angangueo, a short detour to the north, is one of the monarch butterfly sanctuary towns. Since I was unfortunately pre-season for that amazing event, there seemed to be little urgent reason to visit. Still, the detour was only 32 kilometers (20 miles) from Zitácuaro. Needing to transit the city anyway, I decided to check out Angangueo. One day in my always fluid schedule is usually not a big deal.

Arriving at Zitácuaro, I walked out of the terminal and saw a hotel sign on a reasonably quiet side lane a couple of blocks away. Inside the Hotel Janny, I was checked in by the friendliest man in Mexico, which is saying a lot. He seemed absolutely delighted to have a foreign visitor, and we chatted for a while. The room was very basic, but it had a comfy bed, a reliable hot shower, and strong WiFi. Did I mention the price? 200 pesos ($10), easily the cheapest in all my recent circuits.

After dropping off my bag, I returned to the terminal. Soon enough, I was on a small bus to Angangueo. It was supposed to be just an hour trip. It wasn't. The culprits were the sinister speed bumps, which seemed to be everywhere. Each time the vehicle began to gain decent speed, it braked hard. The trip was an agonizing and bumpy ride, and I started to question the wisdom of this side trip made on a whim. But when I finally arrived in Angangueo, I quickly began to sing a different tune. It is one of the prettiest towns in Mexico. And pre-butterfly season, there was almost nobody on the street, so I practically had the whole place to myself.

In terms of the churches, the plaza, the old houses—the only descriptor I can come up with is "exquisite." The town is hilly, and everywhere I turned, the views were stunning. I walked about in bliss for a couple of hours, sitting here and there in tranquility and reveling in the beauty. The highlight of the fairly short circuit was a pair of alleys whose walls were covered by vibrant and colorful art detailing the history of the region. An absolute treat.

Angangueo Pastoral Beauty

When I was ready for lunch, there was not a lot to choose from. There are no hotels in the center, and only a few dinky local snack-type eateries. I found one proper restaurant, but it lacked a menu. The Señora offered me chicken cooked in three possible ways. I settled for a vegetarian burrito. I would imagine that Angangueo gets few solo visitors. Most people likely arrive as part of a group tour, then stay and eat at the fancy lodge some ways out from the center.

Whew! To think that I came close to skipping this place. If you are in the area, butterfly season or not, don't make that mistake. There is one mid-priced lodge a little bit less than a mile from the center, the Hotel La Margarita. Someday I may come back and hang out for a couple of days, terrible bus ride and all.

Overall rating: 9

Getting there: There are frequent arrivals in Zitácuaro from both Mexico City and Morelia. Transfer to the small Angangueo bus and be sure to prepare yourself for a less than comfortable bus ride. Just consider the trial by speed bumps to be part of the admission price to this wonderful town.

Cuitzeo del Porvenir, Michoacán

This decidedly "un-magical town" could be considered the inverse of Angangueo. Only 34 kilometers (21 miles) from Morelia, and on a good road, it is an easy day trip. As Cuitzeo is practically devoid of attractions, hotels, and restaurants, a quick daytrip is certainly my recommendation. There's no purpose in spending a night.

There is only one reason I can find to come here: The town boasts a cathedral, ex-convent, and associated buildings which are stunning examples of their kind. (Of course, this kind of thing is not that hard to come by in Mexico, but Cuitzeo's really are especially beautiful.) Otherwise, there is little here. I did find a nice urban trail above Centro that led to decent views of the lake and town. The Centro itself is unfortunately rather bleak. I found only one old hotel, and it had been shut down. In all the streets I walked down, I came upon only one real restaurant, and it was so jammed full that I ended up just getting some tacos elsewhere in a basic-but-friendly hole-in-the-wall. There are two lakeshores, but they are pretty much polluted wastelands. I assume that Cuitzeo received infrastructure improvement funds like all of the *Pueblo Mágicos*, but the only use of such funds that I saw was an arched concrete sign that you drive beneath when entering town. If you are in Morelia and have time on your hands, come out and take a look. I would give it a higher rating for architecture aficionados, but to me the only non-grubby aspect was that small section of past grandeur.

Overall rating: 3

Getting there: Cuitzeo is a hop, skip, and a jump from Morelia. (It is actually closer to the *Pueblo Mágico* of Yuriria in neighboring Guanajuato.) If you are traveling from there to Morelia, you might consider jumping off a bus in Cuitzeo for an hour, then continuing on another one into Morelia.

Tacámbaro, Michoacán

I took a bus from Pátzcuaro through some attractive mountain scenery to the *Pueblo Mágico* of Tacámbaro. There is a lake and balneario somewhere in the area. Reading the government tourist website, there is also some "important" history and some old buildings in the town. If so, I wandered around for about ninety minutes but didn't find anything (or anything else of particular interest). A pleasant town isolated in the mountains, but there is not much else to recommend it.

Overall rating: 2

Getting there: Take the bus from Morelia or Pátzcuaro.

Tlalpujahua, Michoacán

This is another old mining town, smaller than El Oro but carrying a far more intriguing historical aura. The absurdly complicated Náhuatl name means "spongy earth," but Tlalpujahua is also known as the Town of the Eternal Christmas. I have never tried hard to pronounce the name, but Wikipedia says tlahl-poo-ha-wa, with the third syllable of *jota* complicating things.

This lonely tower survived the landslide

Tlalpujahua was a major gold mining site until 1937, when it was severely damaged by a major earthquake and landslide. Hundreds of people died in the disaster. The mines never quite recovered, then were nationalized, and finally had all operations halted in 1959, more or less crippling the local economy.

At that moment, one enterprising citizen got a lightbulb

over his head and started to make Christmas ornaments. The idea clearly caught on and is now the town's main economy, hence the nickname. It is difficult to fathom how an entire community manages to sustain itself from what appears to be a cottage industry. But perhaps Tlalpujahua has more solid economic footing than the village where the entire citizenry is trying to sell artisan fruit sorbet to all the passing vehicles.

The most interesting sight in town is the Iglesia Enterrada de Carmen, the buried church, which is a short hike from the Centro. All that remains is the upper part of the old structure. It reminded me of another place in Michoacán, Angahuan, which I visited long ago. The nearby volcano, Paracutin, erupted in 1943, leaving a long and wide swath of jagged black lava along its slopes. Hiking through that moonscape is quite eerie, especially when you come to the buried village where nothing is left but the top of the church steeple.

Tlalpujahua reminded me of some small, old European village, with its narrow and winding stone streets bordered by ancient buildings with red roof tiles. There is also a broad plaza with great views of the surrounding green hills, a typically pretty cathedral, and an ex-convent. All of this stands on an extensive plateau, and the entire area is a visual treat. As with Salvatierra and Yuriria, I wished I had stayed here and made my day trip to Oro, instead of the other way around. This town is a much more enjoyable hangout. Live and learn. I was also fortunate to eat at the Cocina de Jenny, where I had a full meal with drink for 85 pesos and enjoyed one of the most delicious *chile rellenos* (stuffed pepper) I have ever eaten.

Never forget that good country cooking in old Mexico leaves the average U.S. Tex-Mex restaurant in the dust!
Overall rating: 7

Getting there: Both towns are just off the main highway that runs between Mexico City and Morelia.

CHAPTER 7:
And All of the Rest (Southern)

Tlayacapan, Morelos
Mitla, Oaxaca
Atlixco, Puebla
Chignahuapan, Puebla
Cholula, Puebla
Huachinango, Puebla
Tetela de Ocampo, Puebla
Tlatlauquitepec, Puebla (Hidden Gem)
Xicotepec, Puebla
Coscomatepec, Veracruz
Author's Note

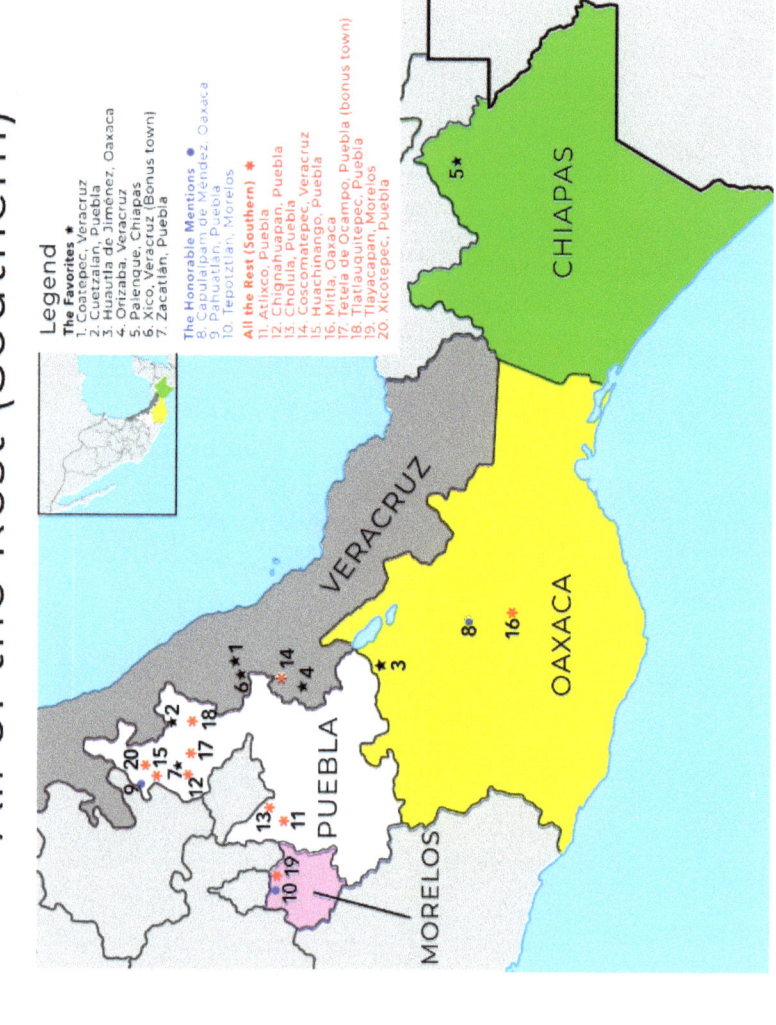

Tlayacapan, Morelos

With all the tourists flocking to nearby Tepoztlán, this *pueblo* is a bit like that town's overlooked sibling. I definitely didn't see any other foreigners there. Tlayacapan checks all the usual boxes for a reasonably prosperous, historical Mexican town. You can walk around and enjoy all the predictable sights. But there is one standout here. I mentioned the craggy stone hills that dominate the skyline above Tepoztlán. Tlayacapan has them in spades. Anywhere you go, you'll have a 360° view of them, and they're truly impressive. I ate lunch on the roof of a fancy hotel just out of town and was able to get a great video of the landscape.

On my one full day there, I took a lengthy hike, an enjoyably challenging up-and-down through wild and colorful vegetation. There are also a few cows here and there. Passing a couple of nights in the town was certainly no chore. Alas, I don't have a single photo that does the beautiful hills justice, but trust me, they're special.

I stayed in an antiquated mini-manse Airbnb with a delightfully eccentric and equally antiquated Spanish Señora. The place was rustic, bucolic, romantic, and very peaceful. Some of the infrastructure needed an update, but you take what you get. The town market that filled the Centro on the day after my hike had a genuine *campesino* (peasant) feel to it. I saw some sandals right up my alley, even if they were a touch "girly." But there were none in my size, even though I have small feet. Maybe the sandals were for children. Certainly, nobody here is catering to outside tourists.

If you are a nature-lover like me, this is a fine town in which to spend a couple of days. Likewise, if you are a seeker of the kind of authenticity not offered by touristy venues like Tepoztlán.

Overall rating: 6 (Higher, really, if you love trail hikes.)

Getting there: Tlayacapan is not conveniently located. It is reasonably close to the good-sized city of Cuautla and not much farther from Tepoztlán, but prepare to arrive on combis and colectivos that seem to stop everywhere along the way. From Tepoztlán, there is a direct road, but the combis make a major detour to Yautepec, where you will have to change vehicles.

Coming from Mexico City, there are direct coaches to Tepoztlán. From Cuernavaca, you will also go first to Tepoztlán, then Yautepec, and finally arrive in Tlayacapan.

Mitla, Oaxaca

I had visited the ruins of Monte Alban many years earlier, and I did again on this trip. They are magnificent. I was aware that there were also well-known ruins in Mitla, only 55 kilometers (35 miles) to the southeast of the big city, and that it was a *Pueblo Mágico*, so it was beyond doubt that I would pay it a visit. Unfortunately, it was a disappointment.

There is nothing particularly special about the town itself. My hotel was one of the least comfortable of my trip and was home to an incessantly barking dog. The nicest looking restaurant on the main drag could be termed simply adequate. In the morning, I walked through the outskirts of the town to the ruins. They were quite a letdown: small, ill-kept, and with none of the mystery and excitement of many comparable sites. Certainly, they paled next to Monte Alban. I spent a desultory half an hour among the ruins before passing the array of mostly deserted souvenir shops on my way back to the main plaza. At that time, I was more than ready to head back to joyful, colorful Oaxaca.

There are very special rock formations called *Hierve el Agua* (the water is boiling) in the area, so named because these natural travertine cliffs look like cascades of water, but at 18 kilometers from Mitla, the site can hardly be thought of as one of the town's attractions.

Overall rating: 3 (Perhaps a tad higher if you are an archaeology aficionado.)

Getting there: There are frequent departures from the Oaxaca bus terminal.

I mentioned above that the Mexican states of Jalisco and Puebla each boast 12 Magic Towns. While I have been somewhat lackadaisical about visiting the Magic Towns in Jalisco, I have done much better in the state of Puebla, where I have visited ten of the twelve *pueblos*. Actually, I passed through an eleventh, Teziutlán, but could not stay due to having pre-booked a hotel stay in the nearby town of Tlatlauquitepec.

Atlixco, Puebla

One of the primary attractions of this town, only 31 kilometers (20 miles) west of the city of Puebla, is its gorgeous close-up view of "Popo," the second highest volcano and the fourth highest mountain in North America, behind the Pico de Orizaba. Up through the fifties this magnificent summit, alongside its twin sister "Ixta," was routinely visible from the Zocalo in Mexico City. Soon afterward, smog and miasma began to blanket the city, obscuring this breathtaking vista. But there is hope: As Mexico's crusade to clear up its air stumbles along, windy days occasionally give a fleeting view of these titans.

Atlixco has no such pollution problem. But it was partly cloudy during my visit, and even at the park at the top of the hill, Popo did not show his face. But then, miracle of miracles, the clouds parted, and I was transfixed by the summit's majesty.

The ride from the Puebla bus terminal took a frustratingly long time, the majority of which was spent wending its way through the city. My first business was to secure lodging. Spoiled by my recent discount finds (on my 2021 trip), I headed for the main plaza with a mind to find an inexpensive, pleasant place to bed down. I walked into one hotel, and they were asking for 1,950 pesos. Whoa. That was certainly luxury I neither needed nor wanted, and about four times the $25 I had been regularly paying.

Moving on to the tourist office, I asked the man about a basic but comfortable alternative. He directed me to a nearby side street where there were three such establishments. I chose the Hotel San Miguel, which looked a bit tired and funky. I was attracted by the lobby, which was brimming with antiques. The staff were friendly and welcoming, unlike the snobby reception I received at the place on the plaza. The room was 400 pesos and was comfortable, clean, basic, and quiet. The hot water was great, with good pressure. I would guess that this kind of place is in the 500-600 peso range in 2025. The internet was a bit erratic, but in that year, I was accustomed to that. 5G today has mostly fixed any problems.

I strolled around the Centro, which turned out to hold little of special interest. Then I wandered steadily up in the direction of the hilltop chapel. The district became more colorful, with fun mom-and-pop outlets and cozy eateries. I even found a place selling homemade kombucha, one of my weaknesses. I continued to climb stairs and sloped alleyways, passing some old churches and winding around the hill. All I cared about was heading upward. There were no more cars, only scooters. Finally, I reached the base of the steep stairs leading to the summit. There was a parking lot here at the end of the paved road. (That is how the "normal" people arrive – wink, wink.)

Walking up the stairs, I passed quite a few of those motorists, all of them huffing and puffing. I also had a number of brief conversations. People are really wonderful, kind, helpful, and happy to converse with a stranger in these parts.

It was glorious at the top, even with the clouds hiding the view. The old chapel was austere— my favorite kind. Closer to town than the regal volcano, there were vistas of the verdant countryside. After taking in my fill of the beauty, I headed down. Back in the town center I easily found a Chinese buffet, with its main draw for me of plentiful broccoli. I filled my plate with fish, chicken, broccoli, and noodles for 60 pesos and could barely eat it all.

While I ate, a man came in with his three-year-old son, who spoke quite precociously. The man ascertained that I was American. He told me he had relatives in New Jersey and New York and was desperate to practice his English. After weeks of speaking only Spanish, it felt genuinely odd be switching back to my native tongue.

Back at the tourist office, I chatted about my onward route. For some reason, it began due south, in the direction of a town called Izúcar de Matamoros, farther from my next destination of Cuautla/Tlayacapan than I was presently. I asked why, and he responded with a very Mexican shrug. He called the town "azúcar" (sugar), though "izúcar" is Náhuatl for "flint path." Then he laughed and spoke a typical Mexican response: "*Ni modo.*" What can you do?

Grandeur in Atlixco

Atlixco is atmospheric and very pretty. It may not have too many obvious attractions beyond the ordinary, but it is very friendly and, for me, carried that nice aura of magic in its hillside barrio.

Overall rating: 7

Getting there: Slowly but surely from the Puebla bus terminal. If you are heading from Cuernavaca, you will need to take the significant detour that I did. From Mexico City, you will have to crawl through Puebla, then crawl back out again. Yep, a little inconvenient.

Twin Towns: Chignahuapan, Puebla, and Tetela de Ocampo, Puebla

With Chignahuapan only a stone's throw from Zacatlán and Tetela an hour to the east of the former, the three towns could have been included together in this book as a package deal. But Zacatlán is hands-down my favorite *Pueblo Mágico*, and as such I didn't want to conflate it with any others. Part of the problem, though, was that I visited these two towns during the height of the pandemic, which shut down a lot of sites. (Ironically, of the three, Zacatlán was the only one not on my original list.) Information on Tetela de Ocampo is below in this chapter.

Chignahuapan, Puebla

I feel that the website of the National Tourist Office overrates this town. Chignahuapan is surrounded by a number of fine nature attractions but, as I've mentioned before, I don't think outlying areas should be factored in when determining if a town is "magic." This town has a natural *laguna*, which provides visitors with a relaxing, park-like afternoon a short walk away from the Centro. The top-billed sight is the colorful Moorish-style *parroquia* (parish) complex in the main plaza. It could well be the jewel of the town, but when I visited, it was obscured by a lot of tenting and scaffolding. Otherwise, the square was filled with a typical bustling market.

Chignahuapan, like Tlalpujahua (your tongue-twister for the day), has a thriving Christmas tree ornament business. A slim reed upon which to base fame, I would say.
Overall rating: 3

Cholula, Puebla

This *Pueblo Mágico* is pretty much a suburb of the large city of Puebla, which is only 14 kilometers (9 miles) away. I'm sure that many would disagree, but I consider Cholula to be rather a one-trick pony. However, it is certainly an impressive pony. The grounds of the ancient, ruined city, a short walk from the center, are vast, covering 154 hectares or 350 acres, so even large crowds of visitors are spread out enough that you can feel almost alone. Scattered about are excavated pits that reveal various aspects of daily life from the past. The crown jewel is the Great Pyramid of Cholula, the largest monument ever constructed anywhere in the ancient world, at almost twice the size of the Great Pyramid in Egypt. It is not so visually impressive as that world wonder, though, since much of it is now covered by a hill. The south side is excavated and honeycombed with tunnels. The entire complex is topped by the Nuestro Señora de los Remedios sanctuary, built on the then-totally undisturbed hill in the sixteenth century. For those passionate about archaeology, the site can provide a least a full day of study. I enjoyed walking around and soaking up the ambience. Personally, I prefer the more compact sites, such as the ruins of Palenque and Copan, in Honduras. But if you are in Puebla, a colonial city more than worth a visit, it would be silly not to drop over to Cholula.

Apart from this, I found the town fairly pedestrian. The main plaza is wide and handsome, surrounded by colonnades. There are a number of old churches, too. The municipal market was a bit disappointing—it was small and dingy, and much less attractive than many of its counterparts in other towns. All three of the great volcanoes of Mexico are said to be visible from the top of the pyramid, but having visited on a cloudy day, I didn't see any of them.

The best way to get to Cholula is to ride the tourist train, which leaves and returns three times daily on weekdays, and more frequently on weekends. In Puebla it is next to the National Railway Museum, which I found fascinating with its large amount of old rolling stock on display. The stated fare was 60 pesos, but it was running for free at the time of my visit. (After some recent research, I am not sure whether the train is still in service or not.)

In retrospect, I would have been happy to make this *Pueblo Mágico* a daytrip, visiting the ancient city and then returning to Puebla. Except for the very archeologically-minded, I give the town a rating of 6.

Getting there: From Puebla, ride the tourist train if it is available; otherwise, you are stuck with a long, slow, weaving city bus ride.

Huachinango, Puebla

After leaving Pahuatlán, I headed south toward Zacatlán, Tlaxcala, and Puebla. The first place I passed through was the non-descript town of Huachinango (the name means "red snapper"), which was fairly large for a *Pueblo Mágico*, with a population of 80,000. Did I say *Pueblo Mágico*? I can't imagine why it was chosen. The Mexican tourist site calls it an ideal place for nature, mountain biking, boat rides, and hiking, but even they have basically nothing to say about the actual town itself, which is unfortunately completely unremarkable.
Overall rating: 1

Getting there: If you are traversing the region, you will likely pass through Huachinango. Otherwise, don't bother unless you are set up with gear and transportation for adventure sports in the outlying areas.

Tetela de Ocampo, Puebla

This town, isolated way out in the countryside and surrounded by green hills, was the biggest disappointment of my 2021 trip. I was attracted by the name Tetela, which translates to "teat." (Kathy says that men are dogs. Who am I to argue with the *jefa*, "boss lady.") Also, after Pahautlán I was more than ready for a rural refuge from the modern world. In fact, I had planned for two nights in Tetela, but was forced to make it a day trip due to a bad storm front that was moving in. This dire forecast never quite materialized, but I became bored with the town in very little time and was ready to depart anyway. Some of the *pueblos* make good use of government refurbishment funds, but, like in Cuitzeo, I found no signs of any renovations or improvements being done here. In the center, there were a couple of very shabby-looking hotels and one or two equally unappealing restaurants. The town's main claim to fame is some monuments commemorating one of the seemingly countless Mexican wars, which always get muddled up in my brain. And there were a couple of accompanying museums. However, in the dark fall days of 2021, both were closed. I walked around for a couple of hours, ate some Chinese food (not nearly as good as in Atlixco), then grabbed a colectivo back to Chignahuapan.

Overall rating: 2

Getting there: Chignahuapan is easily accessible from both nearby Tlaxcala and Puebla, and only 16 kilometers (10 miles) from Zacatlán.

Tlatlauquitepec, Puebla (Hidden Gem)

And now for something completely different. Not far southwest of Cuetzalán, this mouthful of a town is one of those where you worry about running out of breath before getting the whole name out. Maybe the locals have the same problem. I discovered that most of them just settle for saying "Tlatlauqui."

The name is Náhuatl for "colored hill." Since "tepec" means place of, maybe those final two syllables are redundant anyway.

I am content to include this town in my short list of hidden gems, as it's off the beaten track and not well known even to domestic travelers. Most people who come this way head for the much more eminent Cuetzalán, and I can't blame them. Both towns are at fairly high altitudes, and the weather is usually cool to cold. While I was there, mornings were warm and sunny, but by midday clouds rolled. This encouraged me to get up earlier, but that can be frustrating with breakfast or even coffee hard to find before 8:30.

The main plaza and cathedral are very attractive indeed, and it's all particularly pretty at night, with the church colorfully lit by a moving light show. The ex-convent Santa Maria de la Asunción grandly towers over the town and is rightly its main attraction.

Tlatlauqui—see, I can learn—is a fantastic place for hiking. Thick vegetation is present at every turn, and there are ups and downs, gushing water, and satisfying vistas above the town. Towering above it all is the enormous rock formation of Cerro Cabezón, "the pig-headed hill." (Its shape gave me no hints as to why it is called that.) It seemed a long way by road, but Apple Maps showed a steep but more direct route. Unsurprisingly, Apple was wrong. The app showed a through-street which instead very much dead-ended. No loss, though; every hike was delightful, with villages and churches, country stores, and friendly people to encounter. In the middle of nowhere, I saw a cottage with a sign advertising massages. I looked in the door and found a modern young matron who said her fee was 300 pesos. She had certificates on the wall and was an engaging conversationalist. The seventy-minute massage was both competent and relaxing. I also found a good restaurant with Mexican fusion food in town, very tasty and reasonable, and took many of my meals there. As always, the friendliness and conversation were top-notch.

Some places you just plain like. Friendly and scenic Tlatlauqui is one of them.
Overall rating: 8

Getting there: A little bit if work. Take a Puebla-Cuetzalán bus and get off in Zaragoza, then continue onward by combi. I took the roundabout route originating in Jalapa, bussing to the nearby *Pueblo Mágico* of Teziutlán and then to Tlatlauqui by colectivo.

Xicotepec, Puebla

This town is only 20 kilometers (12 miles) from Huachinango, where I certainly had no interest in spending a night. So, to mix things up, I rode over to Xicotepec instead. It's a nice town. There was a good strenuous hike up to a Christ statue with magnificent views. I've really never met a hill hike I didn't like.

Back in the town, I enjoyed wandering down some alleys into a kind of rock quarry which featured an array of striking street art. A relaxing, laid-back town, but not a lot here.
Overall rating: 4

Getting there: A detour from Huachinango takes you to Xicotepec, but you still have to go through the big town again to get anywhere else.

Coscomatepec, Veracruz

After visiting the wonderful town of Orizaba in the fall of 2022, my plan was to proceed east to the city of Veracruz, one of the only major metropolises of Mexico that I had failed to visit, then head back west to the state capital of Jalapa and its adjacent *Pueblo Mágicos*. But then I was told at the tourist office that there was a country bus that went to Córdoba and then veered up on a side road north, passing through Coscomatepec and then directly through the mountains, terminating in Jalapa. Much shorter and cheaper, with an extra *pueblo* thrown in! Perfect. Of course, I have still not made it to the famous

Veracruz, but I do plan to remedy that during my fall tour of 2025.

For some reason, I had never spent much time in the state of Veracruz before I hit some *pueblos* in 2022. I'm not sure why. The region is green and scenic, and now one of my most favored destinations in eastern Mexico. The only rationale for my previous neglect is that my travel has always been more random and less planned than most people's. I thoroughly enjoyed the three other towns in the state, but Coscomatepec, while interesting, was almost bizarre in terms of its departure from many norms. All the other towns were clean, prosperous, modern, and worthy of being called magical. This orphan feels tired, beat up, and poor. Outside of the architecture around the plaza and cathedral, there was disrepair everywhere. The *tía* (aunty) food nooks were almost uniformly dark and dingy—anything but inviting. Unlike almost any other *Pueblo Mágico*, there was a disconcerting amount of litter, a sure sign of a lack of civic pride. But it turned out that Coscomatepec has a lot to recommend it, too.

Even though it was Day of the Dead, with the markets thronged with visitors, the tourist office was empty. Having walked about looking for a legitimate restaurant but only finding one meager establishment, I had decided to drop into the office to seek some counsel. The girl confirmed that she knew of no other dining establishments. She was clearly bored and talked my ear off, her services otherwise not in demand.

In Orizaba, bad weather had obscured views of its namesake volcano. But in Coscomatepec a couple of days later, the skies were clear, and the grand peak stood out vividly. (One of the town's few industries is hiking and climbing expeditions.) On Sunday, the entire town center, covering many square blocks, was one endless *tianguis* (the indigenous word for market). All the lanes leading down from the plaza were narrow and packed with people, making my progress very slow. Despite the hundreds and hundreds of stands, the variety of goods on offer was unexpectedly small. I always continue to wonder how anyone can make a living operating market stalls in Mexico. Maybe they don't. As I said, Coscomatepec felt as impoverished as anywhere I had seen in my recent travels.

Inside the aviary, the author makes some new friends

Most interesting was the impromptu outdoor restaurant

section that filled a significant part of the plaza, with at least sixty mini-fondas full of people chowing down. At least one sector of the local economy was making money. There were also numerous carts with ice cream, pancakes, and all kinds of assorted treats and beverages. It was festive party time for sure. Everybody was eating. But outside of the small Centro, there was little to see apart from the splendid views of the mountain.

The town's main attraction, as well kept as everything else was neglected, was the Recreation Park—a haven with lawns, streams and fountains, a nice petting zoo, an interesting small museum detailing the town's history and commerce, with some striking old looms on display, and, best of all, a closed-roof aviary. A young college student took my 10-peso admission fee and showed me around, explaining all the different species. She was fulsomely friendly and handed me a stick encrusted with seeds to feed the smaller birds. They spotted me instantly, swooped down, and darted about my extended arm. The petting zoo was fun, too, particularly the miniature horses, which are called *ponis* here.

Despite its general seediness and lack of good cuisine, the location, great views, and Recreation Park are enough for me to up my rating to a 7.

Getting there: Coscomatepec is certainly off the track, but there is a slow bus that plies both ways between Orizaba, Cordoba, and Jalapa.

PART III:
In Closing

Author's Note
I mentioned that I did not write up a few towns that I have not visited in a long time, perhaps decades. Although I don't have a current take on them, those places were beautiful back then and almost certainly are today. Some that come to mind are Comala, Colima; Álamos, Sonora; El Fuerte and Cosalá in Sinaloa; and San Blas, Nayarit. Just for fun, I can think of a couple of places that, while not yet *Pueblos Mágicos*, could also be strong candidates to join in the fun: Catemaco (Veracruz) and Mulegé (Baja California Sur).

Guide to Mexico City
Mexico City is one of the most vibrant, energetic, and exciting cities in the world, and it's also a paradise for foodies. But the city still carries the same intimidating reputation for danger that the whole country of Mexico is burdened with. Don't pay attention to it. Any of the central districts of the city (which contain pretty much anywhere you would want to go) are completely safe in the daytime, including the early evening, when there are crowds of people on the streets. I don't care what kind of nonsense they print in the U.S. State Department advisories.

I am not the perfect person to address this subject, as I am more or less invisible while traveling through the country. It is likely that you will not have that same good fortune and will be easily recognizable as a foreigner. The byword is common sense. Dress down. Leave the expensive watches and jewelry behind. Try to avoid carrying more than petty cash, don't keep valuables and important papers anywhere outside of your clothes (sometimes including your pockets). The city can get crowded, and pickpockets might hang around major tourist attractions. Your chances of any mugging or violent assault are extremely low. If you use taxis (I hardly ever do, as explained earlier), choose official ones, preferably with meters. Your hotel desk will be happy to call one for you. Avoid obviously poor and seedy districts, though the only way you would be likely to wind up in one is by accident. People in Mexico City are not unfriendly. That is rare anywhere in this fabulous country. But they do tend to mind their own business more than their small-town and countryside brethren. Of course this is true anywhere. If somebody calls out to you loudly or actually confronts you (unlikely), use your judgment and check them out carefully before responding. I have been to Mexico City numerous times over five decades and have not once had any serious problems.

There are plenty of foreigners and tourists in Mexico City, but it suffers from the same problem that this book is meant to address, i.e., the modern travel industry and its propensity to encourage herding. The majority of visitors tend to visit the same relatively few places, the ones that are touted and best known. It is a shame to treat this magnificent city in such a manner. There is a staggering number of museums, architectural wonders, parks, plazas, and gorgeous neighborhoods. For standard tourists, most of it dies on the vine. So, relax and take your time. You will never see anything close to all of the city, so don't try. I have been there many times and still find new delights while re-enjoying older ones.

Some of the standards are the Zocalo, the Cathedral, the National Palace, the recently unearthed ruins adjacent to the cathedral, the Palacio of Bellas Artes, the Frida Kahlo house (for which you need a reservation), the floating gardens of

Xochimilco, Teotihuacan, and Chapultepec Park with its two famous museums of history and anthropology. Of course, you want to see all of these, if possible, but there is so much more. You can get the *Lonely Planet* guide to the city, which is chock-full of suggestions. Serious students can read *La Capital: The Biography of Mexico City*, a tome which runs to seven hundred heavy pages.

I am only going to supply a short list of some of my favorites, which do not get anywhere the amount of traffic they merit. The Leon Trotsky House in Coyoacán is fascinating and ignored by the hordes that flock to Frida's place. The Museum of Popular Art near Chinatown is a joy. In Chapultepec, the Museum of Contemporary Art is one of my favorites. Almost all of these are free (and crowded) on Sunday. One of the biggest delights of the city is simply promenading around the many sumptuous central districts. They are jammed full of parks, plazas, sculpture, monuments, and fountains, along with innumerable fine dining opportunities. You can spend countless carefree hours in any and all of them, such as San Angel, Coyoacán, Condesa, Roma, and Polanco. And you should.

My number one suggestion lies off the beaten path. The Merced Market is likely the largest of its kind anywhere in the world. It is difficult to give a fitting description of the enormity of this place, which goes on forever and where you can spend hours viewing the unusual and fascinating. The flower section alone is as least as big as a large supermarket. There is virtually everything here. In the middle of it all stands a picturesque old chapel in a small open plaza, which is a nice quiet spot to rest your feet. On the busy street just outside the main entrances, there is a profusion of mouth-watering street food. In late 2024, I breakfasted on a plate of five mini-tacos for 15 pesos, or about 75 cents.

Merced even has its own Metro stop, on Line 1 between the Zocalo and Airport. You'll walk out the turnstile and find yourself right in the center of the action. Merced is a unique experience. When you leave the market, I suggest that you walk back to the Zocalo, which is less than a mile away. The walk passes through a thriving commercial district, all Mexican, with not a foreigner in sight. Half an hour traversing this area will teach you more about authentic Mexican life than months lolling around in a place like Puerto Vallarta.

I could go on and on, but you can fashion your own itinerary. Just consider this a nudge.

Mexico City Transportation

I have spent a lifetime avoiding tours. They are expensive, restrictive, and put a wall between you and the locals and their culture. I would hope that most of you who have made your way this far through this book are on the same page.

Mexico City is enormous and can be a challenge to get around. Taxis are not at all cheap. But mainly they are very slow, and traffic is a horror. The bus system goes everywhere, but learning to use it is a task that I would never want to take on. And it goes without saying that it is also very slow. In the center of the city, as well as the fashionable districts I named, you should walk as much as possible. And there is so much to see on the way.

There is also the Metro. The guidebooks say to avoid it. I consider this to be madness. The system is an astounding achievement and will get you almost anywhere in the metropolitan area as fast as is possible. There can be a lot of walking involved, as the junctions between the nine lines often involve several subterranean blocks. Many of these walkways have worthwhile exhibitions that you can stop and take in. The way to tackle the Metro is to use that old friend common sense and to have a bit of foreknowledge, which I am happy to supply you with. Number one, once again, is to carry all money and papers inside your clothes. I recommend riding only with a daypack, though I regularly go to the airport and four major bus terminals carrying my mid-sized backpack. When it is crowded, carry your daypack in front of your chest. Simple.

There is plenty of good news, too. If you are over 60, you are a senior citizen in Mexico. The Metro system is free for all Seniors, including non-citizens. Enter the station and find the turnstiles. There will be a guard at the far right one. Say, "*Tercera edad, Senior*," and they will let you in. Usually, they see you and just wave you through. Not only does this save money, but also time and hassle—you won't have to deal with machines in Spanish, figuring out how to correctly insert your ticket, et cetera. And more good news: Every train has a car up front exclusively for women and children. Don't hesitate to split up and meet under the closest exit sign to the front when you get off.

It is best to avoid the two rush hours, which can be horribly crowded. I also tend to avoid getting on the train on the stops along Line 1 in the Centro, depending on how crowded it is. If there are mobs pushing to get on, that is when you can get pickpocketed. Of course, you aren't carrying anything important that they can get to, are you? Getting off is less problematic and you are much less likely to be targeted. One strategy, if you have plenty of time, is to devise routes that link some of the outer lines. It may take longer going a circuitous way about, but it is much less crowded. I have been using the Metro forever and love it. Follow my lead and you should be just fine.

Mexico's Hidden Colonial Cities

This is the same old story. Herding. Everybody keeps going to the same places while neglecting others. I am definitely not trying to discourage people from going to these well-known places. They are great. They are famous for good reason. Please go and visit them. But please consider branching out and visiting some of the numerous other cities, even if you have never heard of them.

Here is a list of the most popular Mexican cities, places where you will expect to see significant numbers of foreign visitors: Oaxaca, Mexico City, Puebla, Guadalajara, Guanajuato.

Here are a few others which are well-known, but not nearly as touristed: Querétaro, Morelia, Cuernavaca, Merida.

And finally, a few of my favorites which, like the country as a whole, are sadly overlooked and under-appreciated. This is a book about *Pueblos Mágicos*, so I am not going to spend a lot of energy writing about the excellent attributes of these venues. Once you have heard of them (you're welcome), that's what the internet is for. There is so much to see and do, and what might amaze you is finding that you might have it all to yourself. Envelope please! And the nominees for best Hidden Gems are Zacatecas (often considered to be the loveliest city in Mexico), San Luis Potosí, Durango, Jalapa (Xalapa), and Tlaxcala.

If these cities were in Europe, they would all be thronged with tourists. But in Mexico, all you hear is the sound of crickets. And that is a shame.

A Few Suggested Itineraries

In the populous central region of Mexico, many of the *Pueblos Mágicos* are in clusters, making it possible to see several with minimal travel time. If you want to get your feet wet, some of these suggestions are a way to ease yourself in, and I hope to stoke your appetite for future travels.

Take a bus from Mexico City to Pachuca and visit three of the best *pueblos*, all reachable by combi: Huasca de Ocampo, Mineral del Monte and Mineral del Chico. If you are feeling ambitious, you can continue from Huasca through the city of Tulacingo to the isolated village of Pahuatlán in Puebla. Be sure to go for the Sunday market.

Base in Cuernavaca with easy access to Tepoztlán, Tlayacapan, and Malinalco.

Base in Puebla, so close to Cholula and Atlixco and the

adjacent state capital of Tlaxcala. A little bit farther is my favorite *Pueblo Mágico*, Zacatlán de las Manzanas.

For more adventure and to experience traditional indigenous culture, travel a few hours north of Puebla to Cuetzalán with its famous market and Tlatlauquitepec. Another *pueblo*, Teziutlán, is quite close to Tlatlauqui.

Base in Querétaro and Tequisquiapan, Cadereyta. and Bernal. A side trip from Tequisquiapan gets you to Tecozautla and Huichapan in neighboring Hidalgo. North of Querétaro is close access to San Miguel de Allende and Dolores Hildalgo.

Base in Morelia for an easy bus ride to Pátzcuaro and Tzintzuntzan and the island of Janitzio. Not far north of Morelia you can cross over into the state of Guanajuato and see Yuriria (also Salvatierra) The return trip passes through Cuitzeo del Porvenir.

And for Those Who Like It Nice…

I am not even close to an upscale traveler, as you have all heard over and over by now. But I know that some of my readers would enjoy a touch of the luxury that little interests me. Many Mexicans ply the *Pueblos Mágicos* circuit filming YouTube videos. Possibly the most prolific is the inimitable Alejandra Toledano. This well-off girl (a category known in Mexican slang as "*una torta de lana*" or a "wool sandwich") hosts the YouTube series "Costo X Destino" ("Cost Times Destination"), and she enjoys everything classy. She will lead you straight to that boutique lodging and fine dining that I haven't. I like her videos for her other suggestions on attractions and her breezy and entertaining speaking style - in Spanish, but does it matter it is easy enough to follow. Even if you don't understand what she says, she will still connect with you.

Part of the reason Alejandra's videos are so popular is predictable: She is gorgeous and voluptuous, and she has a full wardrobe of scanty attire that she knows how to use to its full advantage. I particularly love her restaurant scenes. She homes right in on a fancy place and always orders something traditional that looks absolutely delectable. After showing off her plate to the camera, she takes a bite and loudly exclaims "Mmmmm!" Every single time. It just cracks me up.

On that note, I wish you all *buen viaje*! Have a great trip!

Afterword

In 1972 I began slow traveling, which turned out to become a lifetime passion. At that time, there were three major limitations. Two of them were communications and information. A third, on a very personal level, was a definite paucity of funds.

My main mode of contact back then consisted of Aerograms. I wrote a raft of them to my mother and a few to some friends. If I knew that I would be grounded someplace for a while, I arranged to get some return correspondence via General Delivery or, as the case might be, Poste Restante or *Lista de Correos*. Mexico was harder than other countries because the postal system was (and still remains) rather erratic and sluggish.

Telephones were mostly out of the question. International service was unreliable, difficult to hear, and very expensive. As a last resort there were telegrams. Remember those? It was sad to see some scraggly guy who had run out of money spending his days sitting on the steps of a telegraph office, waiting for his ship to come in. Speaking of money, everyone carried travelers' checks, often suffering extended frustrating waits when cashing them in the bureaucratic morass of a foreign bank. Now I am in and out of an ATM with money in hand in a minute.

More difficult was the almost nonexistent amount of travel information available. At best, I knew what country I wanted to visit. Beyond that it was all happenstance. In Europe I could read about London, Paris, and Rome. But I had almost no interest in those destinations. As I do today, I wanted to be out in the country wandering small towns and exploring beautiful nature. Things were much cheaper and there was generally no problem in sleeping rough, which I did more often than not throughout the seventies. There is something intrinsically peaceful about sleeping under the stars - assuming it isn't raining.

When I started wintering in Mexico, visiting new places was even more difficult. There was simply no information at all. My tribe lived by word of mouth. There existed a regular gringo trail that ran down the Pacific Coast to places like Mazatlán, Yelapa, Tenacatita, Melaque, Zihuatanejo, and Puerto Escondido. Sometimes we ventured inland, but it was mostly limited to Oaxaca and San Cristóbal de las Casas before heading down to the wonderlands of Panajachel on Lake Atitlán and Chichicastenango in Guatemala. Who knew about all the beautiful small towns that now comprise the *Pueblo Mágico* program? Nobody.

Much later I discovered books by famous writers like D. H. Lawrence and Aldous Huxley about their Mexican journeys. But no one really knew about those works back then, or even if one did, where to find them. Carl Franz's brilliant and delightful *The People's Guide to Mexico* was published in 1972, though once again I didn't hear about it until much later. It was the consummate guidebook on travel in Mexico. In fact, it is still useful, if somewhat dated, today. But it was a how-to, not a where-to-visit, book.

Everything has changed today. Communications are no longer difficult—they are inescapable. It seems that if someone doesn't hear from you in two or three days, they start worrying. And the modes of interaction that we enjoy feel like magic. Instead of committing words to paper and bringing them to a specified building for handling, I am tapping my finger on a screen and everything moves seemingly at the speed of light, with no effort on my part. I just got off of Facetime with my daughter. We can talk and see each other anytime we want. And most remarkably, it doesn't cost a thing. Even today, after many years of this, it can be difficult for us "old folks" to grasp that this is reality.

As for information, we are awash in it. We can get on our devices and plan our trips anywhere in the world down to the smallest detail. I don't like it very much, personally. Almost all the spontaneity, the mystery, the romance, and the adventure have been washed away. In return we receive security and surety. To this old curmudgeon, that is not an equal exchange.

But somewhere along the line, Mexico has been left out. Tourists are still flocking to beautiful resorts on the Pacific Coast, with the addition of their cousins on the Yucatán Peninsula. Only a handful venture into the interior, and Oaxaca still tops that list. Looking on websites, groups, and videos, almost all feature the same limited roster of destinations. Even as an ultra-experienced Mexican traveler, I only discovered the *Pueblos Mágicos* fairly recently, and I was surprised that I had never heard of the great majority of them. Looking through the ones I have covered in this book, most continue to fit into that category of being generally unknown, and they will likely continue to be so for the foreseeable future.

The *Pueblos Mágicos* represent a wonderful opportunity. They offer the adventurous and open-minded traveler a gateway into an authenticity that no longer exists in much of the well-trodden world. Of course, the towns are subject to the same forces of modernity as anywhere else. After all, "the times they are a-changin." But these towns are also an almost untapped repository of culture, tradition, and history, as well as being utterly off the beaten tourist track. They all feature something special. And for the most part, you still have the chance to enjoy them outside the straitjacket of conventional tourism—these are real places with real people, and you can have them nearly all to yourself.

And so, I am offering you this modest guide in the hope that I can help and encourage you to share in my pleasures.

Acknowledgements

AFTER WRITING THREE novels and sending out hundreds of queries for many years, the number of responses I ever received (all rejections naturally) could be counted on my fingers. It seemed apparent that the vast majority of my efforts were being rejected after only, or perhaps even without, a glance. With so much work overflowing inboxes, whether good, bad, or middling, an unknown writer without connections has but an infinitesimal chance of gaining an audience. So, I am happy to offer total appreciation to my publisher Julie Connor for taking a chance on this unknown writer so long waiting in the wings.

Resigned to the fact that no agent would represent my work, I finally self-published my books on Amazon. Besides my own numerous re-readings, the only professional assistance I sought was for formatting and cover design. I wish to thank Ava Fails for her generous support and free advice throughout that process.

After writing *Pueblos Mágicos*, I foolishly thought that my work was finished. Working with my editor Luke Walker has opened my eyes to complexities that I didn't even know existed. He has been more than generous, patient, and supportive in revealing the mysteries of publishing to me. He has also encouraged me to make the book more personal and to add anecdotes which I hope will make it a more pleasant reading experience. This advice was a welcome boost to my creative energy. All this would not have happened without his care.

A shout out to my friend Teri Keating who expressed so much delight after reading my first novel *Full Moon on the Ganga*. Following years of discouragement, believing that my work would never be published, I temporarily gave up writing another. Teri persisted in urging me to continue, if only because she wanted to read more of my stories. Even if nobody else wanted to read them, she did. So, thanks, Teri.

Usually, acknowledgements speak to those who have helped with research, fact-checking, expert commentary, etc. I really have nobody like that. Writing about the *Pueblos Mágicos* grew from my incessant wanderlust and the enthusiasm to share my love for Mexico. So, I would be remiss not to mention all the generous help and freely offered information from all the kind and friendly Mexican people I have encountered along the way, the real authors of this book.

Glossary

Abuela - Grandmother. It is rumored that there are no *abuelas* in Mexico, only *abuelitas* ("little grandmothers"). Mexicans love to use the diminutive *ito/ita* in their speech, and they do so almost indiscriminately.

Aguardiente - Unlike mildly alcoholic *pulque,* this is the real country distilled "firewater." Handle with care.

Ahuhuete - A Mexican cypress tree.

Atole - A hot and sweet beverage made from cornmeal, often sold from street carts in the early mornings, when it can be challenging to find anything else available. Very popular in the cooler mountain regions, it is often supplemented with homemade tamales.

Balneario - A spa or bathing place with warm or hot water.

Barranca - Can mean a broad canyon or a narrow river gorge.

Bocas/bocaditos/botañas - What are called *tapas* in Spain are usually called *bocas* ("mouthfuls"), or *bocaditos* ("little mouthfuls"), or *botañas* ("snacks") in Mexico. These savory treats are mainly found in bars and cantinas, where they are served up gratis to encourage patrons to stay and buy more alcohol. In my younger days, I enjoyed bars with cheap beer and tasty *botañas* where, for the price of one bottle, I could make an inexpensive meal out of the *botañas*—until they threw me out.

Bus de paso - *De paso* buses don't originate in your present location but do stop for passengers on their way through.

They do not show in a normal computer search. If you don't find anything online, do not despair. Just check at the bus station for a *de paso* route. There generally is one.

Bus directo - A long-distance bus which begins at your point of origin and continues all the way to your destination with few or no stops along the way.

Campo/campesino - A *campo* is a field, or the general term for the countryside. A *campesino* is a peasant, essentially meaning "one who works in the fields."

Casa de huéspedes - A guesthouse. These small, family-run lodgings are an inexpensive and authentic option for travelers who want to go a little native. They are not often advertised on booking sites.

Cascada/cataratas/salto - Various terms for waterfalls

Cenote - A natural pit or sinkhole filled with groundwater. These pools are popular attractions, particularly in the hot climate of the Yucatán peninsula.

Centro - The central district of a town or city, often also called the *Centro Historico* ("Historic Center"). In any given city, it is generally the area of most interest to travelers.

Cerveza - Beer (of course); often the first word learned by many travelers. *Agua,* water, comes in a distant second place.

Chichimeca – The name given to various indigenous nomadic and semi-nomadic tribes living north of Mexico City.

Cocina - Literally *kitchen,* the word is often used in the names of restaurants, as in *Cocina de Ana. Comedor*, dining room, occurs in the same fashion.

Colectivo (or combi) - The most modest form of public transportation in Mexico, both inter- and intra-city, these white vans are cheap and convenient. Shared taxis are a similar way to get around, but they usually cost a few pesos more.

Cueva - Cave.

Día de Muertos - The Day of the Dead is the most colorful holiday on the Mexican calendar and is celebrated on November 1, the day after the Anglo holiday of Halloween. Celebrations can continue for an entire week.

Efectivo – Cash.

Elote - Corn on the cob, frequently sold on the street in the evening, slathered with mayo, cheese, salt, and hot cayenne pepper.

Fonda - A breakfast or lunch counter mainly found in a municipal market, the *fonda* is where local people come to enjoy cheap, nutritious, and typical meals. *Fondas* close with the markets. In the evening, there are similar establishments called *cenadurías*, from the word *cena* (supper).

Gordita - Literally "a little fat one," these plump pockets of dough are stuffed with a cornucopia of ingredients. They serve as a quick, cheap, and filling snack anytime in the afternoon or evening. They are similar to what are commonly called *burritos* north of the border.

Gringo - A controversial term whose origin is lost in history. Visitors from the USA like to claim that Mexicans use it to describe all foreigners, whereas other nationalities prefer to believe that it applies only to Americans. Since most Mexicans have no idea where you may have parachuted in from, the former group has a better argument. A similar and possibly more derogatory term is *gabacho*, which, to Mexicans, does mean someone specifically from the USA. When asked my nationality in a conversation, I enjoy using *gabacho* with a wink to show that I know the score.

Grutas - Grottos or caves.

Hongo - Fungus or mushroom. Edible mushrooms are

usually called *champiñones*. Hongo is meant to refer to "magic mushrooms" more often than not.

Indígena - Indigenous or native. The term *Indio* (Indian) is considered to be derogatory and should be avoided.

Jardín - Garden. Plazas with a lot of trees and vegetation are often called *jardínes*.

Jugo verde - Green juice. A virtuous drink made from orange juice and whatever greens the vendor has on hand. An excellent and economical source of vitamins and minerals.

Laguna - Lagoon. Small lakes are often called *lagunas* or *lagunitas*.

Malecón - A boardwalk, seawall, or esplanade. Often a wonderful choice for a pleasant walk, particularly in the cool of the evening, when Mexicans love to congregate.

Maquiladora - A foreign-run company inside of Mexico where cars, appliances, and other machinery are assembled, mainly for export back into the United States. These factories have energized the economies of border areas since the NAFTA treaty and have drawn hundreds of thousands of workers attracted by average wages twice that of the rest of the country.

Mestizo - Mestizos, or mixed-race people, constitute 55% of the country's population. Amerindians or indigenous people make up about 30%. I use the word "indígena" to refer to indigenous people. The rest of the population are *Peninsulares* (those whose heritage is from the Iberian Peninsula), plus a small number of Afro-Mexicans.

Michelada - A popular chilled drink made from beer, lime juice, and a hot and spicy ingredient. A *michelada* is a great choice if you are crunching down little whitefish from Lake Pátzcuaro or crickets from the highlands of Hidalgo or Oaxaca.

Náhuatl - The language of the Aztecs. Many place names in Mexico are derived from Nahuatl.

Nicknames - If you want to appear to be "in the know," toss off one of these nicknames for residents of certain cities and surprise your hosts.

> *Chilango*: Mexico City residents are often considered to be haughty or snobbish by the rest of the country. Say it with a smile, and the recipient is unlikely to take offense.
>
> *Jarocho* ("horseman"): A resident of Veracruz.
>
> *Pata Salada* ("salty foot"): A resident of Mazatlán.
>
> *Poblano*: A mild green pepper from the state of Puebla, and the nickname for a resident of that capital.
>
> *Regio*: A resident of Monterrey.
>
> *Tapatio*: A resident of Guadalajara.

Nova - Old-fashioned leaded gasoline that is no longer in use. Often used as a punchline in a joke because "*No va*" means "It will not go."

Palapa - An open-sided structure with a thatched roof.

Parroquia - Parish.

Pico - A mountain peak or a bird's beak.

Pocho - A reference to parts of border-state Mexico and to Mexicans who have been Americanized.

Puente - Bridge.

Pulque - A slightly alcoholic drink, made from the fermented sap of the agave, which comes in various fruity flavors. Definitely an acquired taste.

Purépecha - An indigenous tribe in the state of Michoacán.

Rincón – Corner.

Tarahumaras – An indigenous tribe famous for its long-distance running.

Tarjeta - A card, usually a credit card.

Teleférico - A cable car or funicular.

Tepec - A suffix meaning "the place of."

Tequila - A national alcoholic beverage made from the maguey (blue agave) plant. Also, a Magic Town in the state of Jalisco.

Tercera edad - Literally "the third age," in Mexico it refers to Seniors. Use this at movies, bus stations, museums, or anywhere you might hope for a discount. The Mexico City Metro is free to all Seniors over 60 years of age.

Tía - Aunt or Auntie, often an affectionate name for any older woman.

Topes/vibradores - Speed bumps. Contrary to popular images of banditos or cartels, *topes* are the number one danger to be found in the Mexican countryside. They are particularly hazardous when they appear with no warning signs, which is unfortunately quite common. *Vibradores* are minor league *topes* that will rattle your teeth if you fail to slow down. Before parking in a city, watch out for signs that read "*Se ponche llantas*" ("We puncture tires") in front of exit garages and driveways. As for me, I ride the bus.

Torta – In most of the Spanish-speaking world, "torta" means "cake," but for Mexicans any sort of sandwich is called a "torta."

Tortillería - A tortilla factory. Watching these conveyor belt contraptions roll out hundreds of the culture's mainstay staple food is fascinating.

"Turistas" - Though the literal meaning is "tourists," this refers to diarrhea or having the runs.

Zocalo - What is called the "*plaza mayor*" (main square) in the rest of the Spanish-speaking world is the *zocalo* in Mexico. It is generally bordered by a cathedral and a municipal palace.

Photograph and Map Credits

The front cover photos include three stock photos (the food, skull, and church photos) that our cover designer, Xavier Comas of CoverKitchen, located.

The other three photos on the front cover (the boat, Viva Mexico, and market photos) were taken by the author.

The *Pueblos Mágicos* image on the cover is courtesy of the Secretariat of Tourism of the Government of Mexico.

The back cover photo of the author was taken by robis (sic) Lakewood Camera in Lakewood, WA.

All of the maps of Mexico were prepared by Daniele De Vecchi.

All of the photographs in the book except those that include the author were taken by the author.

All of the photographs in the book that include the author were taken by generous passers-by using the author's camera.

Index

Note: Below, "México" is used for the state of México, whereas "Mexico City" is used for the city.

A
Agua Azul 104
Aguascalientes 10, 63, 108, 114, 119, 145, 146, 149, 186, 188
Ajijic, Jalisco 6, 20, 166, 189, 193, 194, 195, 196
Álamos, Sonora 249
American Dirt 22, 23
Angangueo, Michoacán 42, 211, 225, 226, 227, 228
Angkor Wat 1, 98
Aquismón, San Luis Potosí 189, 204, 205, 206
Areko Lake 175
Atacama Desert 183
Atlán 214, 215
Atlixco, Puebla 233, 237, 239, 240, 243, 254
Avándaro 157

B
Balneario El Geiser 213, 215, 219
Barranca del Cobre, Chihuahua 167, 172
Barranca de los Jilgueros 117
Batopilas, Chihuahua 167, 172, 173, 174, 175
Beach, The 23, 27, 183
Beatles, The 94
Bernal 17, 119, 121, 122, 123, 200, 201, 255
Bernal, Querétaro 119, 121
Breitenbush Hot Springs 219

C
Cadereyta de Montes, Querétaro 123, 189, 200
Calvillo, Aguascalientes 119, 145, 146, 148, 149
Cancún 3, 5, 16, 20, 27, 54, 84, 90
Candela 145

Carrington 79, 80
Catemaco 65, 249
Celaya 193
Cercado 178
Chalma 151, 152, 154
Chapultepec Park 251
Chiang Mai 84
Chichén Itzá 6
Chichicastenango 258
Chignahuapan, Puebla 118, 233, 240, 241, 243
Cholula, Puebla 233, 241, 242, 254
Ciudad Valles 203, 204, 206
Coatepec, Veracruz 63, 87, 88, 89, 90, 92
Comala, Colima 249
Córdoba 68, 71, 74, 245
Cosalá 18, 249
Coscomatepec, Veracruz 68, 69, 233, 245, 246, 247, 248
Costo X Destino YouTube Series 219, 255
Creel, Chihuahua 167, 172, 173, 175, 176, 221
Cuautla 235, 239
Cuernavaca 145, 149, 154, 161, 236, 240, 254
Cuetzalán, Puebla 61, 63, 104, 105, 106, 107, 108, 140, 243, 244, 245, 255
Cuitzeo del Porvenir, Michoacá 211, 228, 255
uitzeo del Porvenir, Michoacán 211, 228

D
Dance of the Little Old Men 165
Dolores Hidalgo 213
Durango 32, 175, 254

E
Eagle Pass 141, 145
Eagles, The 170, 171
El Fuerte 176, 249
El Oro de Hidalgo, México 211, 221
El Rosario, Sinaloa 167, 180, 181

F
Fresnillo 25

G
Gdańsk, Poland 88
Gold Star, The 174, 283

Grand Canyon 172
Great Pyramid of Cholula 241
Grutas de la Estrella 222
Guadalajara 3, 8, 10, 17, 20, 32, 34, 118, 149, 155, 166, 185, 187, 188, 193, 194, 195, 196, 197, 198, 199, 254, 267
Guanajuato 189, 191, 192, 193, 213, 229, 254, 255
Guardian of the Monarchs, The 22
Guaymas 182

H
Hierve el Agua 236
Honey 135
Huachinango, Puebla 115, 118, 233, 242, 245
Huasca de Ocampo, Hidalgo 63, 80, 87, 126, 132, 134, 254
Huasteca (region) 204
Huatulco 3, 5, 16
Huautla de Jiménez, Oaxaca 35, 63, 92, 95, 106
Huichapan, Hidalgo 211, 213, 214, 215, 217, 219, 255
Huxley 258

I
Isla de Janitzio, Michoacán 119, 164
Isla Mujeres 6, 169
Ixtapa 3, 16
Ixtapan de la Sal, México 211, 222, 223
Ixtlán de Juárez 124, 126
Izúcar de Matamoros 239

J
Jalpan de Serra, Querétaro 189, 202
James 74, 76, 79, 204
Jerez de García Salinas, Zacatecas 167, 184
Juárez 124, 126

K
Khao San Road 23

L
La Bufa 173
La Capital: The Biography of Mexico City 251
Lake Atitlán 258
Lake Chapala 3, 194, 195
La Paz 170, 171
La Peña 157

Las Pozas 76, 79
Lawrence. 258
Leon Trotsky House 251
Life in a Mexican Village 158
Lola Beltran Museum 181
Loreto 6, 170
Los Arcos de Saucillo 214
Los Cabos 3, 170, 171
Los Mochis 172, 176
Lourdes 151

M
Machu Picchu 1, 98
Magdalena de Kino, Sonora 167, 182, 184
Malinalco, México 61, 119, 149, 150, 151, 153, 154, 158, 254
Mazamitla, Jalisco,17, 189, 197
Mazatlán 7, 8, 9, 27, 32, 34, 50, 52, 54, 67, 69, 127, 131, 141, 143, 145, 155, 180, 182, 183, 186, 193, 258, 267, 283
Melaque 258
Merced Market 251
Metro 32, 134, 200, 251, 252, 253, 268
Mexcaltitán, Nayarit 63, 65, 66, 67, 68, 113, 181
Mexican Revolution 174
Mitla, Oaxaca 233, 236
Monclova 141, 145
Monterrey 17, 141, 145, 178, 180, 267
Morelia 42, 166, 193, 225, 228, 229, 231, 254, 255
Mulegé 249
Museum of Contemporary Art 251
Museum of Popular Art 251

N
National Railway Museum 242
Night of the Iguana, The 16
Nochistlán, Zacatecas 145, 167, 185, 186, 187, 188

O
Old Man and the Sea, The 85
Orizaba, Veracruz 63, 68, 69, 71, 72, 73, 74, 88, 92, 237, 245, 246, 248

P
Pachuca, Hidalgo 80, 87, 126, 127, 132, 133, 134, 141, 213, 219, 220, 254

Pahuatlán, Puebla 42, 50, 118, 119, 134, 135, 138, 140, 146, 147, 242, 254
Pai 171
Palenque, Chiapas 6, 61, 63, 97, 98, 99, 102, 103, 104, 241
Panajachel 258
Parque Ecológico Los Sabinos 214
Parras, Coahuila 167, 177
Pátzcuaro, Michoacán 50, 61, 119, 164, 165, 166, 229, 255, 266
Perote 35, 88
Piedras Negras 141, 145
Pigadia 129
Pinos, San Luis Potosí 189, 207, 209
Poza Azul, Coahuila 119, 142, 143, 144
Puebla 10, 20, 25, 34, 35, 36, 63, 68, 74, 104, 105, 108, 114, 117, 118, 119, 134, 141, 155, 193, 233, 237, 240, 241, 242, 243, 245, 254, 255, 267
Puente Colgante Miguel Hidalgo y Costilla 138
Puerto Escondido 8, 258
Puerto Vallarta 3, 16, 27, 34, 84, 194, 252

R
Rain of Gold 174
Real de Asientos, Aguascalientes 63, 108, 110
Rolling Stones 94

S
Sabina 94, 95, 96
Saltillo 177
Salvatierra, Guanajuato 189, 191, 192, 193, 231, 255
San Blas, Nayarit 6, 67, 249
San Carlos 182, 183
San Cristóbal de las Casas 6, 258
San José de Gracia 108
San José del Cabo 170
San Juan del Rio 123, 201
San Miguel de Allende 3, 6, 20, 60, 166, 255
Santiago Ixcuintla 9, 17, 67, 167, 178, 179, 180, 282, 285, 286
Santiago, Nuevo León 167, 178
Sayulita 6, 169
Sex and the City 22
Spanish Flu 209

T

Tacámbaro, Michoacán 211, 229
Tamazunchale 206, 220
Tapalpa 17
Taxco 6, 60, 154, 169, 223
Teacapán 181
Tecozautla, Hidalgo 211, 213, 215, 217, 219, 255
Tehuacán, Puebla 36, 97
Tenacatita 258
Teotihuacán 6
Tepic 34, 67, 68, 182
Tepotzotlán, México 211, 223, 224, 225
Tepozteco Pyramid 159
Tequila 6, 268
Tequisquiapan 17, 123, 189, 201, 203, 219, 255
Tequisquiapan, Querétaro 189, 203
Tetela de Ocampo, Puebla 233, 240, 243
Tezuitlán 35
Tijuana 3, 19, 22, 32
Tikal 98
Tlalpujahua, Michoacán 50, 197, 211, 221, 225, 229, 230, 231, 241
Tlaquepaque, Jalisco 61, 189, 198, 199, 200
Tlatlauquitepec, Puebla 34, 35, 50, 108, 233, 237, 243, 255
Tlaxcala 10, 117, 118, 242, 243, 254, 255
Tlayacapan, Morelos 233, 235, 236, 239, 254
Todos Santos, Baja California Sur 6, 167, 170, 171
Tolantongo Waterfall 220
Toledano 219, 255
Toluca 154, 158, 223
Torremolinos, Spain 91
Tulancingo 134, 141
Tulum 6, 60, 169
Tzintzuntzan, Michoacán 50, 119, 161, 255

U

Urique Canyon 173

V

Valle de Bravo 17, 61, 154, 155, 156, 158
Villa 21
Villahermosa 104

W
Wall of the Dead 196
Weeds 21, 22
Wolf Lake 175

X
Xico 63, 87, 90, 91, 92
Xicotepec, Puebla 233, 245
Xico, Veracruz 63, 91
Xilitla, San Luis Potosí 63, 74, 75, 76, 77, 79, 80, 94, 202, 203, 204, 205, 206, 220
Xolotla 138, 141
Xoxoctic Botanical Gardens 107

Y
Yautepec 236
Yelapa 258
Yeso Dunes 142
Yohualichan 107

Z
Zacatecas 10, 20, 25, 49, 108, 114, 127, 149, 167, 184, 185, 186, 207, 254
Zacatlán 63, 114, 115, 116, 117, 118, 240, 242, 243, 255
Zihuatanejo 6, 16, 60, 258
Zimapán, Hidalgo 211, 214, 220
Zitácuaro 43, 225, 226, 228

About the Author

Chuck Burton was born in Manhattan in April 1950. Both sides of the family had fled persecution and violence in Russia and Germany before emigrating to the United States. Fourteen months later, his parents, tired of the rat race of the Big Apple, quit their jobs, gave up their rent-controlled apartment, and bought their first car, a 1951 Chevy. To the horror of both of their extended families, they drove west, destination unknown.

Several months later, they settled in the sunny Mediterranean climate of the San Francisco Peninsula. Life in the fifties and sixties in California was only about looking forward. In the home where Chuck lived with his two younger brothers, stories about past tragedies were seldom (if ever) voiced. Chuck was raised in a conventional, affluent, and entirely secular family, where education and skilled speech were considered the highest of cultural values. If he had come of age five or ten years earlier, he would have almost certainly been on a career track to become a lawyer or similar professional; instead, all such expectations were swept away in the chaos of the late sixties. Chuck's four years at UC Santa Cruz, the archetypical "hippie" school, unmoored him from his upbringing and shredded his connection to its traditional values.

Right after graduation in 1971, Chuck happened to be selected to be one of the guards in the infamous Stanford Prison Experiment. Those six explosive days have reverberated throughout his entire life and contributed to his strong sense of estrangement from the American Dream.

Lacking ambition and any life direction, Chuck saved money by washing dishes, then strapped on a backpack and ventured off into the world seeking adventure. After his first nine months of travel, spent hitchhiking in Europe and then picking citrus at an Israeli kibbutz, he returned to California and found a job as a mailman. He kept that job for fifteen months (the one and only time he has ever worked for more than a few months a year in his life). He saved enough money from that job to continue his chosen lifestyle as a nearly penniless, itinerant traveler, and made that stake last for three years, supplemented by occasionally returns to the Bay Area, where he took temporary jobs and made money from his skill as a championship-level tournament bridge player.

In 1979, he married Barbara, another dreamer, and five years his senior. Their friends all laughed at them; "You can't get married. Neither of you wants to work," everyone said. Chuck and Barbara celebrated their partnership by taking a six-month trip from San Francisco to Santiago, Chile, and then to Quito, Ecuador, riding buses too numerous to count (often repurposed American Bluebird school transport). Chickens and piles of produce rode right along with the human passengers. In 1985, the couple returned to South America to adopt their daughter, Marisol, a seven-month-old baby, from a Colombian orphanage.

By that time, Chuck had learned how to do taxes, a career that he worked at for eleven weeks a year until he retired in 2014. He continued to make money on the side as a professional bridge player, and the family survived by living a life of Voluntary Simplicity. He has always valued time off and freedom over a materialistic lifestyle.

In 1999, Chuck suddenly became the single parent of a teenage daughter, which put a crimp in his passion for travel. In the fall of 2003, champing at the bit, he dropped Marisol off at a college dormitory. Dusting off an old backpack, he was in India three days later. Since then, the only obstacles slowing down his wanderlust were the COVID years. With few travel restrictions in Mexico, unlike most of the planet, Chuck seized upon the pandemic period to solidify his expertise regarding all things Mexican, spending many months riding buses around the Mexican mountains with his backpack, visiting the *Pueblos Mágicos* (Magic Towns), the subject of this book.

In 2001, Chuck got together with his loving partner, Kathy. They bought a condominium on the beach in Mazatlán, Mexico, in 2017. Each year, Kathy spends six months there before fleeing the heat, humidity, and mosquitoes by returning to her home in the Pacific Northwest. Chuck spends the four warmest months with her in this green and mild region before continuing his *Pueblos Mágicos* travels, finally returning to Mazatlán in time to greet Kathy upon her arrival.

Chuck is a passionate reader, writer, tennis and disc golf player, hiker, and beachcomber. Blessedly still slim and fleet of foot at 75, his nickname on the tennis court is *El Conejo* (The Rabbit).

Over the years, Chuck has contributed many articles to community newspapers and bridge publications. Since 2018, he has been the senior moderator and regular poster on a Facebook group that was once called *Earth Vagabond* but is currently named *Budget Slow Travel in Retirement.*

Chuck has written three adventure novels that, while loosely based on the experiences of a lifetime of wandering, feature fictional characters and plots. Invariably, his protagonists are young, coming-of-age women, a result of decades spent hanging out with fearless female travelers and raising a strong, independent daughter. His novels *Full Moon on the Ganga*, *The Gold Star*, and *The China Girl* are available as ebooks on Amazon.com.

You can keep up with Chuck via his author's website www.chuckburton.com.

About Bayou City Press

Founded in 2019, Bayou City Press, located in Houston, Texas, has four areas of concentration: travel, history, international affairs, and Houston.

Bayou City Press launched its website in May 2019, showcasing columns penned by Houston authors about foreign travel and Houston. In October 2019, Bayou City Press threw open the doors of its new offices for the official launch of the company.

The first book published by Bayou City Press, *Savoring the Camino de Santiago: It's the Pilgrimage, Not the Hike*, appeared in late 2019. Written by Julie Gianelloni Connor, the book is a mixture of travel information and travel memoir about journeying down the French route of the Camino de Santiago in Spain.

While hit hard by the 2020 COVID pandemic, Bayou City Press continued operations, publishing a children's book on adoption: *The Baby with Three Families, Two Countries, and One Promise: An International Adoption Story*. Telling a fictional story about an adoption, the book explains the adoption process in a way that children can understand and gives parents a way to discuss adoption with their children as they read this story to them.

For a third publication, Bayou City Press launched another travel hybrid in late 2022. Written by Houston author Carrie Carter, the book takes a traveling author and her cat to Japan to visit a series of towns and sites. *Whiskers Abroad: Ashi and Audrey's Adventures in Japan* is a beautifully illustrated mixture of fact and fiction, with lots to laugh about along the way.

The Nine Lives of Tito d'Amelia, our fourth book, by Italian author Ettore Farrattini Pojani, continued the Bayou City Press tradition of publishing hybrid books, books that cannot neatly be categorized into a genre or even be listed as wholly fiction or non-fiction. Moreover, this is the first translated book Bayou City Press published. Winner of seven awards in Europe, this unique and fascinating narrative about a town, a family, and a cat delights readers who want to learn more about a town in Italy that is older than Rome and a family that has survived through numerous turbulent historical periods.

With this, our fifth book, Bayou City Press returns to its roots. *Pueblos Mágicos* is a travel book of the best kind, one that introduces readers to a country and its culture, history, and people. Like our original title (*Savoring the Camino de Santiago*), Chuck Burton's *Pueblos Mágicos* revels in the art, architecture, and hidden cultural gems of Mexico to give unique insight into the soul of a country and its people.

Bayou City Press maintains its focus on travel, history, international affairs, and anything Houston-related, but we invite book-length submissions on any topic for consideration. Submission guidelines are available on the website at BayouCityPress.com. Submit letters of inquiry to the following address:

Bayou City Press
10303 Scofield Lane
Houston, TX 77096

www.ingramcontent.com/pod-product-compliance
Lightning Source LLC
Chambersburg PA
CBHW061754070526
44586CB00023B/2607